ATTENTION DEFICIT DISORDER

Attention Deficit Disorder

Edited by Lewis M. Bloomingdale

*DIAGNOSTIC, COGNITIVE, AND THERAPEUTIC
UNDERSTANDING*

Attention Deficit Disorder

DIAGNOSTIC, COGNITIVE, AND THERAPEUTIC UNDERSTANDING

Edited by
Lewis M. Bloomingdale, M.D.
Associate Professor of Clinical Psychiatry
New York Medical College
Valhalla, New York

SP

SP MEDICAL & SCIENTIFIC BOOKS
a division of Spectrum Publications, Inc.
New York

SPECTRUM PUBLICATIONS, INC.
175-20 Wexford Terrace
Jamaica, NY 11432

Library of Congress Cataloging in Publication Data
Main entry under title:

Attention deficit disorder: diagnostic, cognitive, and therapeutic
understanding.

   Bibliography: p.
   Includes index.
   1. Minimal brain dysfunction in children.
I. Bloomingdale, Lewis M. (DNLM: 1. Hyperkinetic
syndrome. W1 CH644M v.6 / WS 340 A883]
RJ496.B7A87   1984   618.92'8589   83-14995
ISBN 0-89335-193-8

Printed in the United States of America

Contributors

Leopold Bellak, M.D., Ph.D. ● Clinical Professor of Psychiatry, Albert Einstein College of Medicine, Bronx, New York; Clinical Professor of Psychology, Postdoctoral Program in Psychotherapy, New York University, New York, New York

Raymond Berte-Depuydt, Ph.D. ● Professor of Psychology, Center for Research in Psychodiagnosis, Faculty of Psychology and Educational Services, Catholic University of Louvain, Brussels, Belgium

Lewis M. Bloomingdale, M.D. ● Associate Professor of Clinical Psychiatry, New York Medical College, Valhalla, New York

André Bouckaert, M.D. ● Professor of Epidemiology, Epidemiological Service, Public Health School, Faculty of Medicine, Catholic University of Louvain, Brussels, Belgium

Dennis P. Cantwell, M.D. ● Joseph-Campbell Professor of Child Psychiatry, and Director of Residency Training and Child Psychiatry, University of California at Los Angeles, Neuropsychiatric Institute, Los Angeles, California

C. Keith Conners, Ph.D. ● Professor of Psychiatry and Behavioral Sciences, George Washington University School of Medicine, Washington, D.C.: Director of Research, Department of Psychiatry, Children's Hospital, National Medical Center, Washington, D.C.

Robert J. Corboz, M.D. ● Professor of Child Psychiatry, and Director, Psychiatric Clinic for Children and Adolescents, University of Zurich, Zurich, Switzerland

Michael Cuenod, M.D. ● Professor of Neurology, and Director, Brain Research Institute, University of Zurich, Zurich, Switzerland

Robert K. Davies, M.D. • Lecturer in Psychiatry, Yale University, New Haven, Connecticut; Medical Director, Fair Oaks Hospital, Summit, New Jersey

Nicole de Leval, Ph.D. • Fellow in Psychology, Research Service, Psycho-Medico-Social Center, Public Health School, Catholic University of Louvain, Brussels, Belgium

Virginia I. Douglas, Ph.D. • Professor and Chairman, Department of Psychology, McGill University; Senior Psychologist, Montreal Children's Hospital, Montreal, Canada

Philippe P. Evrard, M.D. • Professor of Neuropediatrics and Neuroanatomy, and Associate Director of the Neuropediatric Center, Department of Pediatric Neurology and Neurosurgery, Catholic University of Louvain, Brussels, Belgium

Barry D. Garfinkel, M.D. • Associate Professor and Director, Division of Child and Adolescent Psychiatry, University of Minnesota Medical School, Minneapolis, Minnesota

Mark S. Gold, M.D. • Lecturer and Psychiatric Consultant, Yale University, New Haven, Connecticut; Director of Research and Training, Fair Oaks Hospital, Summit, New Jersey

Hans R. Huessy, M.D. • Professor of Psychiatry, Department of Child, Adolescent, Family, and Community Psychiatry, University of Vermont School of Medicine, Burlington, Vermont

Marcel Kinsbourne, M.D. • Lecturer and Clinical Associate in Neurology, Harvard Medical School, Boston, Massachusetts; Adjunct Professor, Department of Psychology, Brandeis University, Waltham, Massachusetts; Director, Behavioral Neurology Department, The Eunice Kennedy Shriver Center for Mental Retardation, Waltham, Massachusetts

Hallgrim Kløve, Ph.D. • Professor of Clinical Neuropsychology, and Dean, Faculty of Psychology, University of Bergen, Bergen, Norway

André Noel, M.D. • Professor of Preventive Medicine, Public Health School, Catholic University of Louvain, Brussels, Belgium

Irvin Schonfeld, Ph.D. • Research Associate, College of Physicians and Surgeons, Columbia University, New York, New York; Psychiatric Institute, New York, New York

David Shaffer, M.D. • Director, Division of Child Psychiatry; Professor of Clinical Psychiatry and Pediatrics, College of Physicians and Surgeons, Columbia University, New York, New York

Bennett A. Shaywitz, M.D. • Associate Professor of Pediatrics and Neurology, Department of Pediatrics, Yale University School of Medicine, New Haven, Connecticut

Mary V. Solanto, Ph.D. • Department of Psychiatry, Albert Einstein School of Medicine, Bronx, New York

Robert L. Sprague, Ph.D. • Professor of Psychology, University of Illinois at Urbana-Champaign, Champaign, Illinois; Director, Institute of Child Behavior and Development, University of Illinois at Urbana-Champaign, Champaign, Illinois

Paul H. Wender, M.D. • Professor of Psychiatry, College of Medicine, University of Utah, Salt Lake City, Utah

John S. Werry, M.D. • Professor of Psychiatry, School of Medicine, University of Auckland, Auckland, New Zealand

Guy Willems, M.D. • Assistant Professor of Neuropediatrics, and Director of Special Education, Neuropediatric Department, Catholic University of Louvain, Brussels, Belgium

Preface

The question of whether or not there exists a "syndrome" Minimal Brain Dysfunction ["Attention Deficit Disorder," listed in DSM-III as 314.0, With Hyperactivity; 314.00, Without Hyperactivity; and 314.80, Residual Type (American Psychiatric Association, 1980)] has been well reviewed by Ross and Ross (1976). They concluded that MBD does not meet the criteria for a syndrome as defined by English and English (1958), Eysenck (1960), and Thomas (1973). Wender (1978), comparing MBD/ADD with rheumatic fever and schizophrenia, established different criteria and concluded that MBD/ADD is a syndrome.

More recently, populations for research studies of hyperactivity, frequently associated with ADD, have been established by using a specific cutting score on one of the variations of the ubiquitous Conners' Teacher Rating Scale for hyperactivity (Conners, 1979). This method of population selection has significantly raised the level of sample comparability in research on ADD.

While the Conners' Teacher Rating Scale does provide us with an operational classification of hyperactivity in children (Trites, 1979), unfortunately it depends on the subjective evaluation of teachers. We have found teachers' evaluations to be not so reliable as to support the elegant statistical analyses that have been forthcoming on normative values of the several forms of the Conners' Teacher Rating Scale. The data of Trites on over 14,000 children in Ottawa with the 39-question Conners' Teacher Rating Scale are most impressive. He found the percentage of 1,154 children independently rated above the 1.5 cut-off score by two teachers were in high agreement for conduct problems, inattentive passivity, and hyperactivity, but not for tension-anxiety. There was poor reliability between teachers and trained raters.

While a comparison of the percentage above the chosen cut-off point is crucial for validating prevalence studies, it is regrettable that Trites did not publish his data to give the reliability of scores on the same children by independent teachers (Trites, 1979). Furthermore, this operational definition of a population excludes a population of children with ADD *without* hyperactivity, unless a teacher scale for learning dysfunction, sometimes appearing with ADD, is used as well* (see Myklebust, 1973, and Bloomingdale and Bloomingdale, 1978).

---

*My remarks on the CTRS have only to do with sample selection. Its value as a research tool has been well demonstrated.

Hyperactivity, or hyperkinesis, is discussed in several of the chapters of this volume. Of course, "hyperactivity" simply means exceeding the median on a distribution curve of "activity," (Conners, 1979), and it is "purposeless hyperactivity" in which we are interested.

Recent research in the nuerosciences, particularly by Cools and his associates (1981) at the University of Nijmegen in the Netherlands, has strongly suggested the possibility that selective behavior is also an issue with which we should concern ourselves. For example, the Continuous Performance Test (CPT), while considered primarily a test for vigilance and/or selective attention requires selective behavior (usually pressing a button) for the complete evaluation of subject's performance. Cools' (1980) work on the neostriatal dopaminergic activity in the sequencing and selecting behavior strategies is, I think, worth bringing to the attention of those interested in MBD/ADD, although his findings on the cognitive function of the neostriatum have not been replicated (Kellett, 1978).

We would like to suggest that the following criteria be developed for the description of a syndrome for ADD, as proposed by Kellett (1978):

1. It isolates a group of mental symptoms which appear together sufficiently consistently to suggest that they are produced by the same common physiological dysfunction. [Dr. Cantwell has pointed out that the same syndrome may have different etiologies, e.g., depression. −LMB]
2. By so defining the syndrome, it becomes possible to study the nature of the dysfunction and to find treatments which restore the function to normal. [Or, at least, rationally, to ameliorate the dysfunction. −LMB]
3. It provides a knowledge of the natural history of the condition against which the treatments can be assessed and through which effective counseling [can be] given.

To achieve the goal of meeting these criteria for ADD may or may not be possible in the future. It is in the interest of approaching the delineation of such a description of ADD that we have focussed this volume.

LEWIS M. BLOOMINGDALE, M.D.

REFERENCES

American Psychiatric Association. *Diagnostic and statistical manual of mental disorders* (third edition). Washington, D.C., 1980, pp. 41–50.
Bloomingdale, L. M., and Bloomingdale, E. C. *World-wide survey of minimal brain dysfunction*, Section 6. Scarsdale, Privately distributed, 1978.

Conners, C. K. Discussion of "Prevalence of hyperactivity in Ottawa." In R. L. Trites (Ed.), *Hyperactivity in children*. Baltimore: University Park Press, 1979, pp. 7, 57.

Cools, A. R. Role of the neostriatal dopaminergic activity in sequencing and selecting behavioural strategies: facilitation of process involved in selecting the best strategy in a stressful situation. *Behav. Brain Research*, 1980, 1:361–378.

Cools, A., van den Bercken, J., Horstink, M., van Spaendonck, K., and Berger, H. The basal ganglia and the programming of behavior. *TINS*, May 1981, 4:124.

English, H. B., and English A. C. *A Comprehensive dictionary of psychological and psychoanalytical terms*. New York: Longmans, Green, 1958, p. 540.

Eysenck, H. J. (Ed.) *Behavior therapy and the neuroses*. New York: Pergamon, 1960, p. 11.

Kellett, J. Commentary: Diagnosis of schizophrenia. *TINS*, Sept. 1978, pp. 68–69.

Myklebust, H. R. Identification and diagnosis of children with learning disabilities: An interdisciplinary study of criteria. In S. Walzer and P. H. Wolff (Eds.), *Minimal cerebral dysfunction in children*. New York: Grune & Stratton, 1973, pp. 55–77.

Ross, D. M., and Ross, S. A. *Hyperactivity: research theory and action*. New York, John Wiley and Sons, 1976, pp. 8–12.

Thomas, C. L. (Ed.) *Taber's cyclopedic medical dictionary*. Philadelphia: Davis, 1973.

Trites, R. L. Prevalence of hyperactivity in Ottawa, Canada. In R. L. Trites (Ed.), *Hyperactivity in children*. Baltimore: University Park Press, 1979, p. 50.

Wender, P. H. Minimal brain dysfunction: an overview. In M. A. Lipton, A. DiMascio, and K. F. Killam (Eds.), *Psychopharmacology*. New York: Raven Press, 1978, pp. 1429–1435.

Acknowledgment

The participants, moderator and invited guests of the First High Point Hospital Symposium on ADD, held October 31, 1981, wish to acknowledge their gratitude to the Gralnick Foundation, High Point Hospital, Port Chester, New York, whose sponsorship made the symposium and these Proceedings possible.

Contents

APPENDICES

Introduction

The concept of minimal brain dysfunction in children, the history of which has been reviewed in detail elsewhere (Werry, 1979), is at least four decades old. In that period, it has undergone a number of mutations, but the genotype remains much as one of its originators, Strauss, stated it in 1947; that is, a disorder of the brain occurring before birth or early in postnatal life that does not manifest itself in traditional neurological ways but in abnormalities of behavior, emotion, cognition, and minor or equivocal neurological signs (Strauss and Lehtinen, 1947).

Ignorance, then, of much of brain function, especially in the "silent" (now called *intrinsic*) areas; the popularity of Lashley's and Hebb's notion of mass action of the brain and of gestalt psychology; and the clearly abnormal nature of the original children studied (institutionalized retardates) led to the adoption of the term *minimal brain damage*. As study moved from institutions for the retarded to child psychiatric populations in the 1960s, the term was softened into the etiological description of *minimal brain dysfunction* and into the behavioral syndrome of *hyperkinesis*, or *hyperactivity* (Clements and Peters, 1962). This was necessitated because such studies began to throw doubt on Strauss's view that there was an easily demonstrable, or even necessary, connection between the syndrome and acquired brain damage (see Werry, 1979).

The concept swept North American child psychiatry in the 1960s and 1970s, but academic English child psychiatry and developmental medicine have always maintained a skeptical position, buttressed later by the research findings of Rutter and his colleagues (Rutter, 1976) that there was no specific brain behavior syndrome, only an increase in the likelihood of all kinds of psychiatric disorders as a result of brain damage. Nevertheless, research, clinical interest, and supposedly specific treatment (primarily stimulant pharmacotherapy and various forms of cognitive and motor therapies) continued unabated and spread across much of the Western world, even to the remote Antipodes!

The voices of criticism, especially against pharmacotherapy, also gained momentum in the late 1970s, with accusations of social, clinical, and academic irresponsibility (see Sprague, 1978). By 1980, the concept had changed its name once more from *hyperactivity* to *Attention Deficit Disorder* (ADD), officially sanctified in the DSM III, but the assumption of and search for the brain etiologies remained. These have ranged from (not necessarily exclusively) an heritable disorder, temperament, biological variation, anoxia, trauma, infection, toxicity, and metabolic deficiency.

To date, no one etiology has demonstrated either its necessity or sufficiency, and there are those who wonder if the whole idea, whatever its guise or appellation, is in fact only a chimera or a synonym for *Conduct Disorder* (Quay, 1979; Sandberg, Wieselberg, and Shaffer, 1980; Shaffer, McNamara, and Pincus, 1974).

As noted, the original idea was rooted in vague, holistic notions of brain function and was quantitative rather than qualitative. Such a notion is probably no longer tenable, and Wender's now classical monograph (1971) was an attempt to localize what had hitherto been only a homeless waif, roaming the brain like a nomad.

Developments in neuropharmacology, neurotransmitter physiology, depth electrodes, radioimmune assays, noninvasive tomographic organ imaging techniques, and power spectral analyses of the EEG have all greatly advanced our knowledge of the so-called silent areas, and, as a result, they have also greatly increased the sophistication of research and theorizing about ADD, or Minimal Brain Dysfunction (MBD), as this book shows.

The brain has at least two types of systems: the nonspecific modulators and the specific functional systems.

The nonspecific modulators "tune" the brain in whole or in part. The general noradrenergic projections are of this nature, as can be seen by their diffuse polysynaptic cortical connections, their varicosities leaking neurotransmitter into the extracellular fluid, and by the relatively long duration of their postsynaptic action (around 500 msec), all arising from less than 2,000 neurons in the locus ceruleus (see Green and Costain, 1981). In theory, damage or dysfunction in one such system could result in Attention Deficit Disorder and, secondary to this, hyperactivity, though it would not explain easily the specific (e.g., cognitive, neurological) rather than general effects.

Some of the specific functional systems, such as the sensory and motor systems, are relatively well understood, but the more complicated ones are much less so; yet their relevance to problems of attention activity, motivation, and excitability is compelling. It will suffice to describe one of these, the septohippocampal system. The brilliant work of J. A. Gray at Cambridge, outlined in his recent monograph (1982), suggests that this system is rather like a burglar alarm in which most of the energy is spent in keeping the standing waves generated and monitored for expected reflections. Any mismatch results in: (1) a sudden cessation of ongoing activity; (2) fixation of attention at the perceived source of the mismatch, like a herd of cows watching a man approaching; (3) triggering of the alerting or fight/flight or investigation systems; (4) triggering of the emotional system with anxiety/fear or, if less intense, curiosity resulting.

It takes little imagination to see that a deficit in this system, however caused, could result in a form of Attention Deficit Disorder that was originally described by Wender (1971). Yet the septohippocampal system is only one of a number of possible loci of the "lesion" in ADD. This may be one reason why research findings are so much in conflict.

Gray's work also makes clear that nature did not design the brain systems to suit a pharmacologist! All of the major neurotransmitters are involved in the septohippocampal system, and most of them are also involved in other systems as well. The dream of a simple, specific pharmacotherapy, free of side effects, to modulate Attention Deficit Disorder thus seems unlikely, unless it can be shown that neurotransmitter receptors in this system are in some way unique from each other and those in other systems.

Where does all this leave Minimal Brain Dysfunction and/or Attention Deficit Disorder? Whatever the purported misuse of stimulant drugs in American children, the simplistic reductionism of the diagnosis and treatment as clinically applied, and the possibility, even, that the idea may be wrong, as currently held, from an heuristic point of view, the concept has been one of the most effective stimulants to research in the history of child psychiatry. The current volume illustrates this well. Can we afford to let it disappear? Surely not, until a better idea comes to take its place!

John S. Werry, M.D.
Auckland, New Zealand
August, 1983

REFERENCES

Clements, S., and Peters, J. Minimal brain dysfunction in the schoolage child. *Archives of General Psychiatry*, 1962, 6:185–197.

Gray, J. A. *The neuropsychology of anxiety: an enquiry into the functions of the septohippocampal system.* New York: Oxford University Press, 1982.

Green, A. R., and Costain, D. W. *Pharmacology and biochemistry of psychiatric disorders.* New York: Wiley, 1981.

Quay, H. C. Classification. In H. C. Quay and J. S. Werry (Eds.), *Psychopathological disorders of childhood* (2nd ed.) New York: Wiley, 1979.

Rutter, M. Research report: Institute of Psychiatry, Department of Child and Adolescent Psychiatry. *Psychological Medicine*, 1976, 6:505–516.

Sandberg, S. T., Wieselberg, M., and Shaffer, D. Hyperkinetic and conduct problem children in a primary school population: some epidemiological considerations. *Journal of Child Psychology and Psychiatry*, 1980, 21:293–312.

Shaffer, D., McNamara, N., and Pincus, V. H. Controlled observations on patterns of activity, attention and impulsivity in brain-damaged and psychiatrically disturbed boys. *Psychological Medicine,* 1974, 4:4–18.

Sprague, R. L. Legal and ethical issues and principles of clinical trials. In J. S. Werry (Ed.), *Pediatric psychopharmacology: the use of behavior modifying drugs in children.* New York: Brunner/ Mazel, 1978.

Strauss, A., and Lehtinen, L. *Psychopathology and education of the brain-injured child.* New York: Grune and Stratton, 1947.

Wender, P. *Minimal brain dysfunction in children.* New York: Wiley, 1971.

Werry, J. S. Organic factors. In H. C. Quay and J. S. Werry (Eds.), Psychopathological disorders in childhood. (2nd ed.) New York: Wiley, 1979.

ATTENTION DEFICIT DISORDER

1

Remarks on the Epidemiology of MBD/ADD

HANS R. HUESSY

With research into the etiology of MBD/ADD, there are several points to keep in mind when we design our studies. For example, in our original epidemiologic study of the prevalence of MBD behavior among a group of 500 second-graders, we found the behaviors associated with the syndrome distributed along a normal curve of distribution. By most current standards, somewhere between 2%–5% of boys are diagnosed as suffering from this disorder. Our data indicate that 20% of all boys are at risk for the long-term consequences of these behaviors. In other fields of medicine facing similar problems, the diagnostic cut-off point is determined by follow-up study. All those who are at risk, even though they do not seem to need treatment at the moment, are included in the diagnosis.

We also found that the lower end of the curve of distribution is an even more powerful predictor of good outcome than the high scores are predictors of poor outcome. This is important for your control groups. You have to be sure of where they are on that curve. Are they average kids or are they unusually good kids? It will make a big difference in your outcome studies. I believe our diagnosis, at the moment, is too tight. We need to classify our cases along at least two dimensions: (1) the temperamental traits present, including short attention span, hyperactivity, emotional overreaction, impulsivity, learning disability, trouble in groups, insomnia, lying and stealing; and (2) environmental factors, which would include at least whether these children are living in a

1

well-structured environment or a poorly-structured environment, whether they have a parent with similar problems or not, the amount of large muscle activity they engage in regularly, and the general resourcefulness and stability of the family. We then should monitor these cases in regard to treatment and outcome and see whether certain constellations do better with certain treatments. DSM-III on Attention Deficit Disorder forces us to make qualitative judgments on the basis of very quantitative measures. Some of these quantitative measures are influenced by the group in which the subject is observed. Dr. Tom Achenbach, of our department, has developed a behavioral profile that picks up a large group of children with high scores on a hyperactive and impulsive dimension, who can be separated into subgroups on the basis of other characteristics. Therefore, we would propose that we classify our patients in regard to each of the symptoms mentioned at the beginning, as listed in the tables, with the hope that this would help us separate out different groupings.

Our work further indicates that for research purposes, boys and girls should be handled separately. The natural history, documented in our work, also indicates that we have to be careful as to what ages we include. There are children identified as "hyper" at age 7 who spontaneously stopped being so identified by age 11 or 12, and there are other children who are not identified as suffering from ADD in the early years but are so identified at around age 11 or 12. For this reason, having research groups that span the ages from 8 to 12, which is commonly done, produces complications, in that one is mixing two different groups.

Our subjects should also be classified by the age of onset. In the earlier literature, there are frequent distinctions made between onset at birth, onset when learning to walk, or onset at first participation in groups, i.e., nursery school or first grade. This may have to be taken into account in creating our subgroups. Our work further indicates that being identified as having a high score twice makes for a clearly bad prognosis; whereas, having a high score only once in your life doesn't necessarily make much difference. For example, we have data on our children in second grade, fourth grade, and fifth grade. If there was a high score for hyperkinetic behavior only once, that didn't make much difference in the prognosis. If they were identified twice, that had a very negative impact on the prognosis. Data on these children are tabulated in Tables 1-3.

As to the psychopharmacologic treatment of these patients, I no longer use Ritalin because it is so short-acting and the children really are on a yo-yo, going in and out of control all day long.* Taking together the experiences

---

*This statement is based on short-acting Ritalin, before the matrix, sustained-release Ritalin became available in 1982—Editor.

Table 1. General Characteristics of Normal and Hyperkinetic Children, Classified by the Huessy Scale[a]

Group	Grade identified	Number	Percent boys	Mean IQ	Percent repeating one or more grades	Percent school dropouts
1	Never	216	45	105.4	3	9
2	2	20	60	97.7	30	24
3	4	13	62	98.0	8	0
4	2,4	13	62	86.0	38	33
5	5	20	75	96.3	10	28
6	2,5	12	75	84.9	33	18
7	4,5	13	92	97.0	23	46
8	2,4,5	11	82	91.8	50	20
Normal (1,2,3,5)	Never or once	269	50	104.9	6	11
Hyper (4,6,7,8)	At least twice	49	76	91.1	31	30
0–20 Percentile	Hyperactivity scale	123	42	116.7	0	0
Number of subjects for analysis		318	318	196	318	318

[a]All differences between normal and hyper significant at $p < 0.01$.

Table 2.   Behavioral and Achievement Outcomes for Normal and Hyperkinetic Children in 9th and 12th Grades[a]

Group	Grade identified	Number	Percent with poor social adjustment		Percent remedial English		Percent advanced English		Grade-point average	
			Grade 9	Grade 12	Grade 9	Grade 12	Grade 9	Grade 12	Grade 9	Grade 12
1	Never	216	7	8	11	5	19	17	2.61	2.68
2	2	20	10	37	11	8	0	0	2.12	1.61
3	4	13	23	17	8	0	0	0	2.01	2.00
4	2,4	13	27	36	25	25	0	0	1.79	2.03
5	5	20	63	29	11	8	0	8	2.02	1.70
6	2,5	12	25	50	36	8	0	0	2.30	1.90
7	4,5	13	27	27	27	22	0	0	1.50	1.90
8	2,4,5	11	50	56	40	12	0	0	1.38	1.42
Normal (1,2,3,5)	Never or once	269	12	12	11	5	13	15	2.50	2.50
Hyper (4,6,7,8)	At least twice	49	27	43	33	16	0	0	1.76	1.84
Percentile (hyperactivity score)	0–20	123	0	0	8	0	46	33	3.05	2.58
Number of subjects for analysis		318	307	287	302	258	302	258	305	258

[a] All differerences between normal and hyperkinetic children significant at $p < 0.01$.

Table 3. Selected Interview Data

Variable	Normal (pct)	Hyperactive (pct)	Significance
Completed high school	88	59	**
Education beyond high school	40	18	**
College preparatory curriculum	36	4	**
Reading problems in school	22	55	**
Suspended from high school	23	49	**
Employed as laborer (if employed)	36	62	**
Has had 4 or more more full time jobs	25	50	**
Characterizes self as "happy"	71	53	*
Characterizes self as "always out"	23	40	*
Considers self "daring"	14	27	*
Considers self "not accident prone"	74	51	**
Has had broken bones	61	78	*
Has been injured in fight	14	35	**
Rejected for military enlistment	8	18	*
Recent police trouble	14	37	**
Ever arrested	10	31	**
Ever received traffic ticket	41	60	**
Has had driver's license suspended	20	36	*
Smokes marijuana at least once/day	10	29	**
Satisfied with life	78	65	*

*p < 0.05
**p < 0.01

with anxiety states, phobias, and certain kinds of insomnia, all responding very rapidly to small doses of tricyclics, makes me believe that these conditions are leftover symptoms from childhood ADD. Despite what Paul Wender says, many of us feel that the tricyclics work well. I have many patients who have been on them for years and I feel it works very well. Tricyclics are not interchangeable. If imipramine does not work, one should try amitriptyline. It is fascinating to speculate about the cause of the loss of effectiveness of imipramine in about one-fifth of the patients after three to six weeks (the very time it takes for these medications to have their antidepressant effect).

I think we must also develop a clear differentiation between depressive illness and poor self-image. Poor self-image is almost a hallmark of the ADD child, but the child is still affectively responsive. The same is true about the hyperkinetic adult who may come in with a suicide attempt but, if you do something really nice for him (or her), can be affectively responsive, which is not true of the typical endogenous depressive.

The Conners' questionnaire, which is now used by almost everyone, is weak in picking up the dimension of educational handicap. Our own questionnaire,

Score on Conners Rating Scale

Score on Huessy Questionnaire

35 children (10%)

21 children (6%)

Cutoff level defined for Huessy

18 children
(5%)

277 children
(79%)

← Cutoff level
defined for Conners

57	4		3	2		1	1		3	1			1	1
55.5	1	1			1	1			1	1				2
54	3	1		1		1			1	1		1		
52.51	1	2	4	3		2			1			1		
51		2	1		5	1								
49.54	2		1	3					1		1			
48.3	3		1	1		2								
46.54	1	2	2	1		1								
45.1	1	2	1	3		1								
43.56	3		2	2				1						
42.1				1										
40.53	1		1											
39	1	2		1				1						
37.53	4	1	2	1	1									
36.2	2													
34.55	2	2												
33	1													
31.53	1		1				1							
30.1			1											
28.51														
27.3	1				1									
25.52														

Figure 1. Scattergram of scores on 34 item Conners Rating Scale and 90 item Huessy Questionnaire. Numbers designate number of children at (x,y), where x is score on Huessy Questionnaire and y is score on Conners Rating Scale (r = 0.7558). Thirty-five children had scores above both cutoff levels, while 277 had scores below both cutoff levels, while 277 had scores below both cutoffs; 21 had scores above Huessy cutoff only, while 18 had scores above Conners cutoff only. N = 351.

Table 4.   Scores on Huessy Retrospective Hyperactivity Questionnaire.
Alcoholics Compared to 21-Year-Old Subjects
Previously Evaluated in 5th Grade

	Hyperactivity score[a]		
	Low[b]	High[b]	Alcoholics
N (population of sample)	57	25	50
Total Score = 0	27 (47.4%)	0 (0%)	5 (10%)
Total Score = 1–5	27 (47.4%)	14 (56%)	23 (46%)
Total Score = 6–20	3 (5.3%)	11 (44%)	22 (44%)

(A high score is indicative of childhood hyperkinetic behaviors.)

[a] Assessed by Huessy Retrospective Hyperactivity Questionnaire.
[b] As assessed by the Huessy Questionnaire administered in fifth grade to a total population
followed from second grade to age twenty-one.

used in our study, does better in this regard. Figure 1 shows a scattergram when both of these questionnaires were used on the same school population of 350 students. Our questionnaire picked up an additional group because of educational problems that Keith Conners' does not, and Keith has been aware of that. The positive correlation between the two, even so, is still 0.76.

As to the question of genetics, large populations are needed to study this. Our experience indicates ADD problems are overrepresented amongst adopted children (we believe because impulsive young adults are more likely to produce children for adoption) and we now have some families with four generations of documented ADD. We also are trying to study alcoholics to see whether they have a higher rate of histories of childhood MBD/ADD. Our exploratory data, as seen in Table 4, show that the rate is definitely higher. Close to 50% of identified older alcoholics had a definite childhood history of MBD behaviors. In a standard population, the rate should be around 20%. We think children with histories of MBD are overrepresented among delinquents and among adult criminals.

Years ago, Herbert Birch speculated that one of the most important deficits in the development of MBD children was their inability to respond to conditioning (Birch and Demb, 1959). Since most social learning does occur through conditioning, this would be a pervasive handicap. In experimental work on hyperkinetic rats at the University of Vermont, we have also found this deficit in learning through conditioning. They do not accommodate. We haven't tried, yet, to see if they will accommodate on amphetamine. Biochemically, in our rats, we find what somebody else mentioned before, a deficiency of dopamine and an excess of NE, but not in the basal ganglia, rather in the frontal-mesolimbic system. Minute doses of amphetamine placed in the nucleus accumbens produced immediate behavioral control. Some of our difficulties in pharmacological treatment may be due to the fact that we only address one of these biochemical abnormalities and perhaps we could increase our success by dual treatment.

I would like to suggest to you that if you have available an institution for the retarded, it is an excellent place to try out the therapeutic effects of pharmacological treatment. We now have, in our state institution for the retarded, 11% of the children on small doses of tricyclics and the nonmedical staff, who were very opposed to medication, now are enthusiastic about it and even ask, "Couldn't we put this child on medication to improve his performance?" It doesn't give them a new brain, but they are easier to manage, they are more stable, perform better, and you don't have to sedate them with Thorazine or Mellaril.

Many studies are done in institutional settings, the child being placed in an institution temporarily to do certain studies. Remember these children, when placed in a new setting, particularly an institutional setting, often show no problem behavior for as long as 3 to 6 weeks. Many a child gets sent to a hospital for an evaluation and does beautifully and a report is written implying that the family and the school/teacher must be just awful because there is nothing wrong with this child. Then, the last week before the child goes back to court, his true colors start showing up but it is too late to write a new report and so that report still goes out. If you are doing a study in which you place children in an institutional setting, you may eliminate the very behaviors you are studying. Since these children frequently do very much better in an institutional setting, does their chemistry change with the setting? This is another research challenge.

REFERENCES

Achenbach, T. M. The Child Behavior Profile, I. Boys aged 6–11. *J. Consult. Clin. Psychol.* 1978, *46*:478–488.

Achenbach, T. M. and Edelbrock, C. S. The Child Behavior Profile, II. Boys aged 12–16 and girls aged 6–11 and 12–16. *J. Consult. Clin. Psychol.* 1979, *47*:223–233.

Birch, H. G., Demb, H. The formation and extinction of conditioned reflexes in "brain-damaged" and mongoloid children. *J. Nerv. and Ment. Dis.*, 1959, *129*:162–170.

2

Biological Correlates of ADD

ROBERT J. CORBOZ AND MICHAEL CUENOD

EDITOR'S COMMENTS

This chapter is of considerable interest because it gives American experts on ADD an opportunity to compare a specific subgroup of ADD patients with a more extensive group of patients selected by the looser, symptomatic description of the syndrome published in DSM-III. This is emphasized in the discussion.

Dr. Corboz is one of the foremost experts on the Psycho-Organic Syndrome (POS), which includes the rigorous criteria he describes for prenatal, perinatal, or immediately postnatal incidents to children with early infantile POS. Careful anamnesis in a group of patients studied by Kløve and Hole (1979) found a list of "risk factors" for POS. The criteria Kløve and Hole used to define this group of ADD children was that they exhibited hyperactive behavior associated with low autonomic reactivity, which normalized after the administration of methylphenidate (MPD):

Risk Factors for POS with Highest Incidence (N = 62)

	N	Pct
Vaginal bleeding	7	11
Precipitous delivery	15	24
Protracted delivery	14	19
Cyanosis at delivery	14	19
Neonatal feeding problem	14	19
Fever above 40°C	7	11
Convulsive episodes	6	11
O_2 at delivery (hypoxia)	6	10

From Kløve and Hole (1979).

It will be noted the incidence of risk factors exceeds 100%; obviously, some children had more than one of these abnormal factors. Kløve (personal communication) estimated that approximately 60% of his group of patients had some form of "risk factor," which would, presumably, compare with the criteria described by Dr. Corboz for POS.

One may conclude from Dr. Corboz's careful research on the very large series of POS patients reported that this subgroup of ADD patients (which Kløve's data suggest to be over one-half of hyperkinetic children) are adventitious, in comparison to the hereditary factors that have been described for ADD in a number of papers by American experts. This suggests that future criteria need to differentiate ADD children with POS from those who may be considered "idiopathic."

*   *   *

INTRODUCTION

This monograph deals with a still controversial field of child and adolescent psychiatry. The ADD syndrome has received numerous names, according to L. and E. Bloomingdale (1980). This linguistic fact indicates that it is not easy at all to define the concept of ADD. We essentially run the risk that the definition is understood and handled differently from country to country and from hospital to hospital. In Switzerland, particularly in the German-speaking part of the country, we consciously stayed with the definition "infantile psycho-organic syndrome" (POS).

This not only reflects our being conscious of tradition (the definition psycho-organic syndrome goes back to E. Bleuler), but also demonstrates that, in this clinical picture, we include all those psychopathologic symptoms that, as far as we know, go along with a chronic disturbance of cerebral function. In this chapter we consequently consider the terms ADD, MBD, and infantile POS as synonyms, unless otherwise indicated.

In Zurich, research concerning infantile POS started with the examination of clinical pictures of which the organic origin was unquestioned. To be mentioned are the studies about the effects of brain injury after fractures of the skull (Lutz, 1949) and those about the psychiatric effects of brain tumors (Walther Buel, 1951; Corboz, 1958). In other publications, attention has been paid to the consequences of brain injuries in early childhood (e.g., Lempp, 1970; Annell, 1953). Comparing the results of the studies, it was found that the symptomatology of infantile POS differs depending on the time of its origin. For instance, hyperkinesis and specific learning disabilities are nearly always connected with an origin of infantile POS in early childhood. Hyperkinesis is very seldom a lasting symptom and can hardly ever be observed after

---

We thank M. Corboz, M. D., and D. Gibbons, M. D., for the revision of the English translation.

a brain tumor or a brain injury. Specific learning disabilities—e.g., dysphasia—that belong to the syndrome of early childhood cerebral damage, are only exceptionally found in lesions of the central nervous system acquired later, i.e., at school-age (Corboz, 1962). Initially, infantile POS had, therefore, a clearly defined clinical picture, that could be attributed to definite causes. The development of POS could be examined, whereby certain regularities appeared. Therefore, a prognosis was, and is, still possible.

The situation changed with the discovery of infantile POS of early childhood, which is usually acquired prenatally or perinatally or in the first year of life and for which the psychopathologic symptoms often appear only after a latency of several years. The responsible damage can often not be proven with necessary certainity, either in the prenatal or in the perinatal period of development (see Figure 1). Today we do not yet have enough knowledge of the possibilities of fetal damage, whereby physical, as well as mental, factors are taken into consideration. The fetal thalamus must probably be, in the fourth month of development, so far developed that it can be influenced by neurotransmitters that circulate in the blood of the mother. The expressions that are used in today's prenatal and perinatal medicine, as for example, "birth and child at risk," are much too uncertain (Shaffer, 1978). Future prenatal and perinatal medicine will have to help to prove cerebral damage with the necessary reliability. Only when this is possible will common studies of neonatologists, neuropsychologists, and child psychiatrists enable us to connect the syndrome of late childhood with damage of early childhood.

In the course of the last decade, knowledge about ADD has quickly spread, in medical as well as in nonmedical circles. Undoubtedly the diagnosis of infantile POS was made too often. Almost every learning and behavior disorder was labeled *psycho-organic*, obviously unacceptable if one adheres with any rigor to established criteria.

Therapeutic success in the treatment of the hyperkinetic syndrome, first with amphetamines, later with methylphenidate and pemoline, raised the hypothesis that a pharmacological definition of the MBD syndrome should be possible, especially since the hypothesis of the disturbance of catecholamine metabolism (Wender, 1971) gained recognition. However, not all hyperkinetic children, only about 70% of them, reacted positively to treatment with psychostimulants. This neurochemical hypothesis, with its pharmacological correlation, is valuable only for a portion of POS children.

In the meantime, studies dealt with relatives of the families of ADD children. Certain authors (e.g., Silver, 1979; Morrison and Stewart, 1974; Cantwell, 1975) have demonstrated that relatives of ADD children, particularly their fathers, showed an accumulation of psychic symptoms, especially of psychopathy, sociopathy, hysterical personalities, and alcoholism. Longitudinal studies found that infantile POS does not improve in all cases, that symptoms can

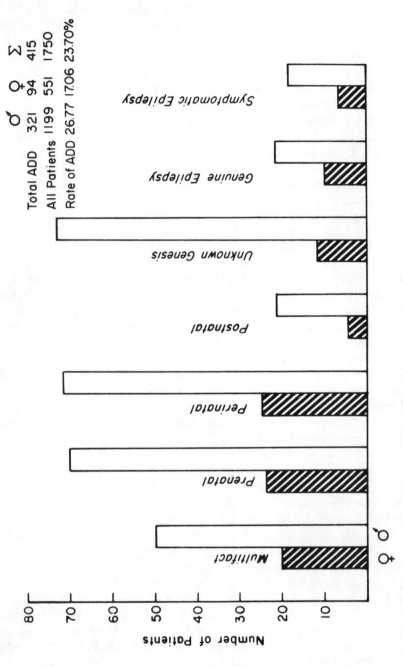

Figure 1. ADD in the child psychiatric clinic of Zurich.

persist and successfully be treated in adults (Bellak, 1979). The hypothesis was obvious that there are at least some fundamental disturbances that are passed on in a hereditary way from generation to generation.

NEUROPHYSIOLOGICAL, NEUROCHEMICAL AND NEUROPSYCHOLOGICAL ASPECTS OF ADD

Both authors of this chapter, who are engaged in different research fields, tried independently and together to evaluate the importance of today's knowledge in the neurophysiological and neurochemical field for the comprehension of ADD. Even though studies in both research fields converge on a common path, definite conclusions still have not been reached. However, certain observations can be made that are important for the understanding of ADD and maybe even for direction of future research. The fact is that the clinical coding of information in the central nervous system relates to large numbers of substances (see, e.g., Blum, 1979). An isolated disturbance of catecholamine, e.g., in disordered storage or too rapid depletion of the dopamine and norepinephrine reservoir, may indeed influence the entire synaptic activity in the brain, even though the dopaminergic neurons only make up a very small part of all neurons. Considering the large number of neurotransmitters, it is rather unlikely that, in infantile POS, only catecholamine metabolism is affected. It may well be assumed that the balance of several transmitter systems is disturbed. The vegetative disturbances especially, particularly sleep disorders, lead us to assume that serotonin metabolism could contribute, also.* Recent investigations at the Brain Research Institute of Zurich have shown that in Alzheimer's Disease, the activity of cholineacetyltransferase, the acetylcholine-synthesizing enzyme, is markedly reduced in all layers of the human hippocampus and frontal cortex while it seems to be increased in the cingulate gyrus (Henke and Lang, 1981).

Disturbances of catecholamine metabolism may explain some facts, particularly with respect to disorders of vigilance. First, there may be mentioned the impairment of continuous attention. L. and E. Bloomingdale (1978) have developed a clinical method with their SIC test, to demonstrate such a disturbance quickly and simply. Difficulties in continuous attention probably go along with general learning problems, as, for the person who has attention problems, the flow of information is full of gaps and can only be processed incompletely. However, the origin of specific learning disabilities, or even the primary disturbances of affectivity, such as lability, excitability, impulsiveness, or deficient emotional control, cannot currently be explained directly by the disturbance of a transmitter system.

*Cf. with Kløve's discussion, this volume, pp. 60–62.

Neurochemists and neuropathologists suggest that clinicians should pay more attention to the extrapyramidal part of the nervous system than has been done up to now. Sydenham's chorea and Huntington's chorea, which only rarely start in infancy, go along with pronounced changes of the subcortical nuclei, especially the caudate nucleus. The latter could be of outstanding importance for the planning, harmonization, and execution of movements. It is possibly highly relevant for associated cognitive and emotional functions. Clinical experience with psychomotor therapy speak for such a hypothesis (Borner, 1978; Borner and Corboz, 1978). It turned out that psychomotor therapy is not only able to improve disturbed movements but is also able considerably to improve perception of the body and its movements. The same applies to the concomitant emotions, as improvement of the motor and sensory functions regularly occur with better cognitive achievements, which, again, are related to improvement of mood and increased ego strength. We are aware that, in this regard, cerebral functions are exceptionally complicated. A too simple explanation would, therefore, be inadequate.

At the end of this section, we would like to consider how the biochemical foundations of ADD could be explored in the future. Particularly, Shaywitz, Shaywitz, and Cohen (1978) have clearly and fully informed us about the latest situation of knowledge. The same is true for Zigmond and Stricker (1977). Chemical analysis of the cerebrospinal fluid would probably be most interesting, because it could reflect directly anomalies of metabolism in the central nervous system. However, such research is difficult because it is not easy to get cerebrospinal fluid of children for comparative purposes. Examinations made in this regard (e.g., Shetty and Chase, 1976) resulted in finding a reduction of homovanillic acid after amphetamine administration and point out the central role of the catecholaminergic system. But those results are not undisputed, particularly because, after the application of probenecid loading, it was not possible to find a difference between ADD patients and a control group.

Analysis of blood and urine were even less successful. The content of serotonin was measured in thrombocytes, on the basis of an analogy between metabolism in the thrombocytes and in the central nervous system. No correlations could be proved. The same holds true for the determination of catecholamine metabolites in urine. Wender and collaborators (1971) measured the urinary concentration of homovanillic acid in children with ADD and did not find a difference from the levels in a healthy control group. This finding is not surprising, as the concentration of different substances, namely, of metabolites of neurotransmitters in the urine, can only approximate the situation in the central nervous system.

Finally, regarding animal research, attempts have been made for several years to produce a clinical picture of ADD in rats equivalent to the one of human beings. It was, indeed, possible to damage newborn animals in such a way that, in their development, hyperkinesis and also disturbances of cognitive functions were produced. But the reaction to psychostimulants, namely, to amphetamines, was so disappointing that today it is questionable if, with animal research, a real model for ADD can be produced that could facilitate a deeper understanding of the pathogenesis of the syndrome.

CLINICAL EXAMINATIONS

From the clinical point of view, there are different possibilities for obtaining better information about the nature of ADD and answers to today's controversial questions. The investigations about which we are going to report now were made on our service. Some of them are not finished yet, therefore, they will have to be considered provisional. But they are of interest as they give some insight into some of the main points of clinical research. They deal with longitudinal studies, with studies of families, with a statistical examination of ADD children with pathological parents, and, finally, with studies of twins and adopted children.

Follow-Up Studies

Clinical experience points out that numerous children with ADD show a substantial remission in puberty and adolescence. There are some studies on this subject, such as the ones of Shaffer (1978) and Roesler, et al. (1979).

Previous studies were not entirely convincing. We are not sure if there is a conformity between the initial diagnosis and that of our patients. Therefore we decided to undertake our own investigations. One of them was undertaken by Sieber (1981). By comparing psycho-organic with psychoreactive disturbed children after an interval of 6 years, it was found that children with POS were less successful in their final examination at school than were children with psychoreactive disturbances. A significant number of them still showed attention deficit disorders and disorders of visual-motor function.

Further research was undertaken by Lehmann and Gundelfinger (in preparation) with a follow-up study of 20 men and 20 women tested at the age of 20, for whom a diagnosis of ADD was established at the age of 10. The symptomatology can be taken from Table 1. First of all, it must be emphasized that at the age of 10 all these boys and girls revealed attention deficit disorders. This symptom is the only one that was found in nearly all tested persons (92.5%). Other symptoms appeared less frequently, such as increased fatigability and disorders of visual-motor function, while hyperkinesis was manifested only in half of the cases.

Table 1. Symptomatology of ADD (N = 40, Age 10)

	Males (n=20)	Females (n=20)	Total	Pct
1. *Biologic field*				
1.1. easy fatigability	17	10	27	67.5
1.2. hyperactivity	12	8	20	50
1.3. motor retardation	4	5	9	22.5
2. *Cognitive field*				
2.1. attention deficit	20	17	37	92.5
2.2. distractibility	17	9	26	65
2.3. perseveration	15	7	22	55
2.4. discrimination weakness	4	–	4	10
3. *Emotional field*				
3.1. emotional lability	17	5	22	55
3.2. excitability	17	3	20	50
3.3. lack of fear	1	–	1	2.5
4. *Additional reactive disturbances*				
4.1. overdemanding	18	6	24	60

From Lehmann and Gundelfinger (in preparation).

Regarding the results of follow-up at the age of 20, I am now able to report only on the men. Lehmann and Gundel finger reported that 30% of the test cases (6) were cured, 50% (10) showed relatively insignificant residual symptoms in the emotional or cognitive field, which did not seriously interfere with their social integration. In at least 20% (4), there persisted typical symptoms, such as: concentration deficit, increased fatigability, bradyphrenia, emotional lability, and irritability, which severely interfered with their social and, particularly, their professional integration. In the meantime most of the girls have had a checkup: the results do not show essential differences from the males.

All patients who showed progressive cerebral disease were excluded from this investigation. The only exception among the initial case reports was the presence of neurotic disorders. It was of special interest to ascertain that psycho-organic and neurotic symptoms regress in parallel. However, there were improvements in the psycho-organic field. More details about the findings of this study will be reported, together with the evaluation of the results in further cases, in another paper.

Table 2. Psychiatric Illness through Generations

	Males	Females	Total
Patients (N = 69)			
Parents 1945–1973	9	18	27
Children 1969–1981	18	11	29
Total	27	29	56
Brothers and sisters of parents			13
All patients			69

From Rufini-Gachnang (in preparation).

Family Studies

The Department of Child and Adolescent Psychiatry has now been in existence for 60 years in Zurich. This fact makes it possible to pursue investigations over generations. For the International Congress for Child and Adolescent Psychiatry in Dublin [1982], we collected and compared case reports of 25 families, in which the parents had been examined as psychiatric patients in their childhood. This is, so far, an investigation without selection, as we include all children whose parents had been examined and treated in their childhood as well. A total of 69 case reports were studied thoroughly by Rufini-Gachnang (in preparation); the distribution is shown in Table 2. Counting all the people considered in genealogical tables in this study, one gets a total number of about 600 cases. It became evident that certain patterns of disease were transmitted from generation to generation. This applies, for instance, to neurotic disorders, syndromes of educational and/or emotional deprivation and, to a certain degree, to eccentric personalities. On the other hand, possible heredity of ADD could be discussed only in one of the 25 families (see Figure 2). Yet, in this case, several arguments speak against a heredity of the POS, because there was a prenatal lesion in the child born in 1975, and his own father, born 1950, showed a serious oligophrenia with ADD. Thus, both showed other clinical reasons for ADD besides heredity. While this very careful and extensive study has detected heredity in many connections, it could not find any signs for heredity in ADD.

Statistical Study

By electronic data processing in our clinic, we made a statistical survey of the personalities and educational attitudes of the parents of our patients. Thereby, we were able to correlate the disorders of the children with the personalities

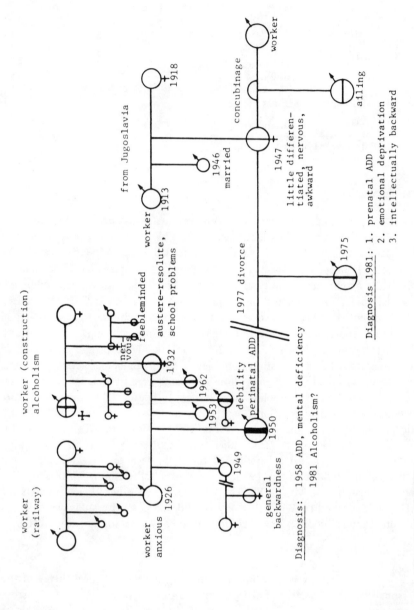

Figure 2. "Heredity" of ADD.

Table 3. Overview 1979-1980 of Children's Disorders
and Parents' Personalities

Children's groups		N
Sample 1:	ADD children (inf. POS) (ICD 9: 310, 314, 348.4)	306
Sample 2:	Children with emotional and personality disorders (EPD) (ICD 9: 309, 312, 313)	238
Sample 3:	Children with neurotic disturbances (NEU) (ICD 9: 300)	680
	TOTAL	1224

From Corboz and Scheidegger (in preparation).

and the educational attitudes of their parents (Table 3). This we have done with ADD children (Sample 1) and also with two control groups. One of the control groups (Sample 2) consists of children with emotional disorders and disorders in the development of the personality and social adaptation (EPD). The third group consists of neurotic children (NEU). A total number of 1,224 cases was evaluated in the years 1979 and 1980 (Corboz and Scheidegger, in preparation).* Table 4 gives the age range and the average age, as well as the first standard deviation. The average age of neurotic patients is 2 years older than that of both of the other groups, because neurotic patients often come for child psychiatric consultation in later childhood. This distribution is illustrated in Figure 3. The boys are, as expected, over represented; the girls, on the contrary, were underrepresented (see Table 5). Among only children, ADD and neurotic disorders appeared infrequently; emotional disorders and sociopathies (EPD), were manifested relatively more often. This investigation was done in order to find out if, as parents of ADD children, psychopathic and sociopathic personalities and alcoholics are more prevalent than are other parents. From a computerized comparison of all relevant results, we report only the ones that are significant for the answering of this specific question.

Table 6 summarizes the disorders of the fathers of ADD children, EPD children, and NEU children, and the educational attitude of the fathers. Neurotic

---

*We would like to thank again Mr. Paul Scheidegger, lic. phil., head-assistant at the Psychiatric Clinic, University of Zurich, for the processing of the information and the statistical survey.

Table 4.   Age of Patients in Each Group

	N	Age range	Average age	S.D.
Sample 1: ADD	306	3–19	8.585	±2.994
Sample 2: EPD	238	1–16	8.718	±3.630
Sample 3: NEU	680	3–19	10.716	±3.184

From Corboz and Scheidegger (in preparation).

disorders in the fathers of ADD children were infrequent. The fathers of ADD children were also found to have a less authoritarian educational attitude than the other fathers. It is characteristic of fathers of neurotic children that they are, to a significant degree, authoritarian compared with fathers of the other groups. Alcoholism was found with average frequency in the fathers of the ADD group, while it was considerably more frequent in the fathers of the second group (EPD children) and considerably less frequent in the fathers of the third group (neurotic children, NEU group).

The mothers show similar findings (Table 7). Mothers of ADD children reveal considerably less frequent neurotic disorders compared with mothers of neurotic children. They tend, only to an average extent, to show overprotection and spoil their children less than one would expect. Mothers of ADD children are also rarely educationally overdemanding. Accordingly, one could say, all together, that parents of ADD children represent a positive selection. They reveal fewer neurotic disorders, including hysteria; the fathers tend, only

Table 5.   Comparison of the Samples and Calculation of Significance

Group	Boys	Girls	Only children	Children with siblings
ADD	234 (+)	72 (−)	49 (−)	257 (+)
EPD	144 (−)	94 (+)	74 (+)	164 (−)
NEU	447 (−)	233 (+)	114 (−)	566 (+)
	$\chi^2 = 17.467$ DF = 2 p > 0.001		$\chi^2 = 26.111$ DF = 2 p > 0.001	

From Corboz and Scheidegger (in preparation). (+) = more than statistically expected. (−) = fewer than statistically expected.

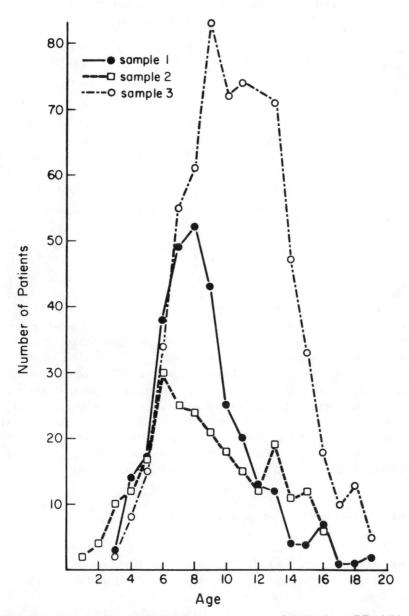

Figure 3. Distribution of age in the three samples. Sample 1 = ADD children; sample 2 = EPD children (children with emotional and personality disorders); sample 3 = NEU children (neurotic children). From Corboz and Scheidegger (in preparation).

Table 6. Fathers, Compared for Presence of Neurotic Disturbances, Alcoholism, and Authoritarian Attitudes

Children's group	Neurotic disturbances		Alcoholism		Authoritarian attitudes	
	Absent	Present	Absent	Present	Absent	Present
ADD	285	21 (−)	299	7	291	15 (−)
EPD	213	25	221	17 (+)	219	19
NEU	574	106 (+)	665	15 (−)	596	84 (+)
	$\chi^2 = 15.768$ $DF = 2$ $p < 0.001$		$\chi^2 = 14.998$ $DF = 2$ $p < 0.001$		$\chi^2 = 14.381$ $DF = 2$ $p < 0.001$	

From Corboz and Scheidegger (in preparation). (+) = more than statistically expected. (−) = fewer than statistically expected.

to an average extent, to alcoholism; they are less frequently authoritarian-minded in their educational attitude than one would suppose. The mothers are neither overprotecting nor spoiling, nor overdemanding above average. The results, which cannot be questioned because of the large number of cases and of the comparisons with other groups, are in disagreement with the hypothesis that the POS is predominantly hereditary.

This result can also be confirmed by comparison of the outputs of three clinics in Berlin, Mannheim, and Zurich (Corboz, et al., in press). For the year 1979, 2,525 recently examined patients were compared, supported by ICD 9 (Rutter, et al., 1975) in combination with MAS (Schmidt and Remschmidt, 1977). Thereby, it became apparent that patients with classification 314.0-314.9 seldom showed irregularities in the psychosocial field. The normality of parents of POS children established in Zurich is, obviously, also relevant for Germany.

Studies of Twins and Adopted Children

In a comparison of 68 twins, Schaub established that 40% of these cases revealed ADD (Schaub, 1980; Schaub and Corboz, 1981). Its cause correlates neither with the birthweight nor with the order of birth. The most important factor seems to be the prenatal phase.

Finally Bircher compared 80 adopted children with 80 nonadopted children (Bircher, 1981; Herzka, et al., 1981). Both of the groups were ranked and compared according to age, sex, and number of brothers and/or sisters. The number of ADD patients was equal in both of the groups. This supports

Table 7. Mothers, Compared for Presence of Neurotic Disturbances, and Attitudes of Overprotectiveness, Spoiling, and Educationally Overdemanding

Children's group	Neurotic disturbances		Overprotectiveness		Spoiling		Educationally overdemanding	
	Absent	Present	Absent	Present	Absent	Present	Absent	Present
ADD	262	44 (−)	264	42	291	15 (−)	144	162
EPD	187	51	219	19 (−)	218	20	102	136 (+)
NEU	481	199 (+)	585	95 (+)	594	86 (+)	362	318 (−)
	$\chi^2 = 26.709$ DF = 2 p < 0.01		$\chi^2 = 6.036$ DF = 2 p < 0.05		$\chi^2 = 14.939$ DF = 2 p < 0.001		$\chi^2 = 8.711$ DF = 2 p < 0.02	

From Corboz and Scheidegger (in preparation). (+) = more than statistically expected. (−) = fewer than statistically expected.

the thesis that ADD does not appear more frequently in children who grow up with their own parents than in adopted children.

CONCLUSIONS

The concept of infantile POS or ADD was originally associated with a cerebral lesion or, at least, with a cerebral dysfunction. Soon it became evident that the pattern of disease showed differences according to the time at which damage affected the brain. It therefore became possible to differentiate between early infantile POS and POS that occurred later on. Within about two decades, this syndrome achieved great popularity. Child psychiatrists could finally enlarge the perspective that had made the influence of the surroundings, especially the educational attitude of parents, overly responsible for all disorders of childhood. This was not only of scientific but also of practical importance, as the diagnosis of ADD leads, in many cases, to a relief of feelings of guilt in the parents. Besides, it appeared more and more clearly that psychostimulants represented, in many cases, an effective way of treatment that facilitated and supported the use of other methods, such as psychotherapy and educational methods. The reaction to psychostimulants led to the adoption of a pathogenic hypothesis—namely, a disorder of catecholamine metabolism.

Our knowledge of ADD is still by no means adequate. Critics are justified in rejecting as unsatisfactory the delineation of the terms ADD/POS. For many years, it was not possible to say ânything reliable about the prognosis of ADD patients. Investigators are presently concerned with the latter problem, and we can anticipate that follow-up studies into adulthood will shed light on this issue.

Furthermore, sometimes ADD shows development to normal psychic functioning. Every clinician knows children who are improving thus and it is moot to call them "healthy" or still psycho-organically disturbed. Lastly, ADD appears very often with consequences of educational failures, as well as within a neurosis or a syndrome of educational deprivation. Especially in such mixed patterns, an exact definition of psycho-organic disorder is often very difficult. We warn against a too general extension; otherwise, the investigation of etiology and pathogenesis will be impeded.

Regarding the diagnosis of POS/ADD, we finally recommend that the following criteria should be present:

1. Appropriate cause, such as prenatal and/or perinatal lesion, postnatal incident such as trauma, encephalitis, tumor, or hemorrhage.

2. In the case of early childhood origin, transitional signs in infancy and childhood, wherein, at the beginning, biologic manifestations dominate the field and specific psychopathologic symptoms gradually appear later.
3. Neurologic findings, such as asymmetry of reflexes, pathologic reflexes, motor disorders, secondary left-handedness, speech disability, pathologic fatigability, weather-sensitivity, etc.
4. Signs in the cognitive field, particularly: disorders of attention or perception, difficulty with word retrieval, bradyphrenia, perseveration, or imprecision.
5. Affective disorders: lability, irritability, deficits in impulse control or emotional control (the later related often to a retardation in emotional maturation).

If one utilizes all these criteria and there exist specific signs in at least 4 out of 5 items, ADD/POS will be defined sufficiently. Thereby, a basis for later practical and scientific work with this syndrome is established.

ADD, known by this and many other names, runs the risk of being discounted. First, this is connected with the difficulty in distinguishing mild forms of ADD from the norm. Further, ADD very often appears in combination with other disturbances, particularly with neuroses and with deprivation syndromes. In these cases, it often presents outstanding difficulties in the correct understanding of the etiologic circumstances and clear separation of the pathogenetic links. Primarily because of these two reasons, ADD, as a syndrome, has been rejected by certain authors. The efficient treatment of hyperkinetic children with psychostimulants has led to a pathogenetic theory that involves disturbance of catecholamine metabolism as responsible for ADD. Today, it is still questionable if this hypothesis alone is sufficient for the explanation of ADD, or if additional neurotransmitters are involved. Probably a disturbance of the balance of different neurotransmitters has to be considered. This is a large field for future research. Newer studies, which started from loose criteria in the definition of MBD/ADD, attempt to prove the presence of a polygenetic syndrome, similar to schizophrenia. Our research, using strict criteria for ADD/POS, which was undertaken with the collaboration of clinics in Germany, does not support such a conclusion. A genetic cause in some illnesses, as in the chromosomal anomalies in Klinefelter's and Turner's syndromes, has been demonstrated. Our conclusions are that the etiology of POS/ADD does not appear to involve such a genetic factor, nor that parental/environmental influences contribute to the primary pathology (although they may affect the course) but that prenatal, perinatal or postnatal brain lesions or effects on the embryonic or infantile neurochemistry account for the predominant pathogenesis of the syndrome.

DISCUSSIONS

Leopold Bellak

Dr. Corboz's contribution reviews briefly some of the earlier studies of psycho-organic syndrome. For specific reasons, I would like to add to those whom he mentions. Goldstein and Gelb, who studied brain-injured soldiers after the First World War, noticed not only attention deficits, but disturbances in gestalt perception, aside from impulse disorders, etc. This has been observed, of course, anywhere from the postencephalitic disorders and impulsivity in children to the famous Harvard steel-bar man who, after he got a large steel bar through the brain, only complained of headaches and occasional temper outbursts.

Another person we might want to mention as having been a great neurologist and psychiatrist was Paul Schilder, who, neurologically, introduced the idea of the body schema, which was then translated psychiatrically into the self-image and indirectly related to his wife's, Lorretta Bender's, development of the Bender-Gestalt test.

It is my feeling that focusing too much on attentional deficit reduces psychiatry once more to neurology. It is entirely unnecessary to throw out one field in order to pay enough attention to the other field. In these disturbances, there are many more factors involved than attention deficit problems. This reductionism is in part due, of course, to the oversimplifications of DSM-III, which simply describes things that are easily measurable rather than matters that have clinical importance.

The next important point that Dr. Corboz makes is that only 70% of the hyperactive children responded to amphetaminelike drugs. I can report the same for adult psychotics with MBD/ADD, who are my special interest. This would certainly support the notion that there is more than one neurotransmitter involved. On the other hand, there is some support for the dopamine hypothesis in MBD/ADD, or whatever term we might settle on, by virtue of the fact that a patient with schizophreniform psychosis and MBD who receives phenothiazine, in my experience, invariably becomes worse because of the further depletion of dopamine. I think that this is a kind of therapeutic test of the diagnosis. It may lend itself to an examination of some subgroups.

Furthermore, Dr. Corboz and his collaborator Dr. Cuenod make the important differentiation between early and later onset of the psychoorganic syndrome.

Now let me turn to his major original contribution, his follow-up study, which shows that 20% of the adult males still had significant aspects of ADD. This is quite consistent with American findings, though, by and large, the prevalence of ADD in adults in several studies is a bit higher than that.

The main thrust of the research presented is really in the family studies. The sampling of 1,224 people involved is most impressive and not to be taken lightly. Again, however, it runs counter to the American studies. In my own clinical experience with about 40 marked cases, I would say that not only is there abundant evidence in siblings and in parents that they also suffer in various aspects, in different degrees, from some symptoms of ADD, but I make the categorical statement that, in severe cases of ADD, I found heavy involvement every time in both parents and in the parents' families. Now, maybe different things occur in different populations. We will have to look and see why there should be such differences, if the differences that we have seen here do indeed hold up. One small item is indeed puzzling: all other things being equal, I would expect the mothers and fathers of children with POS to fall on the bell curve and to be average. Why are they of a particularly highly functioning level?

I can certainly agree, again, with the multifactorial aspects, as Corboz mentioned, with multitransmitters.

Dennis P. Cantwell

The six-stage model that I present is a slight modification of the five-stage model that was proposed by Eli Robins and Sam Guze (1970) many years ago for validation of psychiatric syndromes. Patients come in the door because they've got a clinical syndrome, one type or more. The model states that if we limit ourselves to descriptions of psychiatric syndromes based on phenomenology, the likelihood is that there are multiple etiological factors that probably lead to the same clinical syndrome. If the factors are looked for in other areas—physical areas, neurological areas, laboratory studies, natural history studies, treatment studies, family studies, etc.—then you might come up with some meaningful subgroups that would allow you to go back and modify any other areas in the model.

Here are two examples that I think have been rather successful. If we start with adults, with a clinical picture of depression, and we make a very simple distinction (as George Winokur did many years ago) between those who have had no pre-existing psychiatric disorder of any type (*primary depression*) and those who come in with an episode of depression but who have had a preceding episode of some other type of psychiatric disorder, most commonly alcoholism, antisocial personality, etc. (*secondary depression*), we then have a primary group and secondary group. If you take that primary group and secondary group and look at, for example, natural history, you find that the primary depressives have a different untreated natural history than those who come in with a secondary depression. If you do family studies, you likewise find that there are different family patterns of psychiatric illness in the family study. So, it is not surprising that if you start off with a different clinical description, you are going to get different family patterns of psychiatric illness. But you can use those family patterns of psychiatric illness to go back and further look at other areas. For example, if you go back to the clinical descriptions and take only those who have a primary affective disturbance, no pre-existing type of psychopathology, they fall into two groups as well: those who are bipolar, that is, they have pre-existing episodes (or later episodes) of mania as well as depression; a second group has only pre-existing (or succeeding episodes) of depression, a unipolar depression group. Again, if you go to the family study area, you find different family patterns of psychiatric illness, which you wouldn't find if you lumped bipolars and unipolars together. If you then look further at the unipolar group and divide them up on the basis of family studies, you find out there are those that are called *sporadic*; that is, they seem to have no family history of any type of psychopathology in their first-degree relatives. A second group, which George Winokur calls *familial pure*, have first-degree family members with only depression. A third group he calls *depression spectrum disorder*, in which a fair number of the family members do have depression but also a fair number have the "St. Louis Holy Trinity of alcoholism, sociopathy, and hysteria." It's very interesting; if you go down to the laboratory area of the model and take those three groups of unipolar depressives, who differ on family patterns of psychiatric illness, you find that they differ in their response to the Dexamethasone Suppression Test. So the bottom line is that when you start off with a group of patients and you use a different clinical description than other people do, it is not surprising you are going to get different findings in the other areas.

Let me give you one other example. It's a well-known clinical fact that if you take all children who walk in the door with *Leo Kanner autism*, they are overrepresented in the upper social classes. It doesn't mean that autism doesn't occur in lower social classes; it is overrepresented in upper classes. However, if you go to the physical or neurological area of the model and you select out those children who look like Kanner's autistic children behaviorally but they have definite evidence of brain damage, and you compare the brain-damage versus the non-brain-damage group, you find out that the upper social class bias no longer occurs in those who have definite evidence of brain damage, even though the clinical picture is exactly the same. So again, you are going to get family differences depending on how you select out your population.

In the area of biological correlates of ADD, if we start off with a clinical description of ADD and use the entire group of ADD (let's limit it to males because I think there are a variety of individuals who feel that males and females may be different and certainly we don't know as much about females), you do find out that there have been studies in just about all these areas. Some of them are contradictory and some of them tend to hang together. For example, in the physical and neurological area, there is a substantial amount of evidence that in ADD children, a subgroup does have an excess of minor physical anomalies seen in Downs' Syndrome and in other forms of retardation. A common one is the Simian crease. If you crease your palm and the line goes straight across, that is a Simian crease. What is quite interesting with the minor physical anomaly group is that they are not specific for the ADD syndrome. They have been described, not only with retarded children; they tend to be, maybe, overrepresented in different clinical pictures. So if you look for a subgroup of ADD children who do, in fact, have minor physical anomalies, you will find them, but there is nothing specific about that and, certainly, it can't be used as a biological validating factor for the presence of a specific syndrome.

In discussing prenatal and perinatal risk factors, I think if you read Sameroff and Chandler's (1975) review of several years ago, which they entitled "Reproductive Risk and the Continuum of Caretaking Casualty," they showed that most of the prenatal and perinatal insults, except for the very severe, tend to wash out over time, when we see these children at age 18 as opposed to age 4 or 5. Also, there seems to be an interactive effect between psychosocial factors and some of the more minor perinatal and prenatal insults that lead to more deviant outcomes, although not necessarily to the ADD syndrome, as the Kaui study shows (Werner and Smith, 1977). In fact, it was not one of the most common outcomes at all.

Regarding natural history, Jim Satterfield and I, for the last ten years have been following a group of ADD boys that we saw initially when they were age 8 and 9. We followed up 121 of our ADD population and 109 of our normal controls with a mean age of 17. We looked at the official arrest records of Los Angeles County and we classified the offenses into nonserious offenses and serious offenses. The serious offenses included robbery, burglary, grand larceny, and assault with a deadly weapon. We compared our ADD and control groups at age 17. We divided them up into lower social class, middle social class, and upper social class. We found an arrest rate of at least once by age 17 for a serious offense in the three social class groups in the ADD population to be 58%, 36%, and 52%. For the same three social class groups in the control group, it was 11%, 9%, and 2%. If you go to multiple, meaning at least more than one arrest for serious offense, it is: the ADD group, low, middle, and high social class, 45%, 25%, and 28%; normal controls, 6%, 0, and 0. If you look at institutionalization for delinquent behavior by age 17, it is 25% of the ADD group as opposed to 1 of the 109 control children. If you look at ADD boys and their brothers who were not ADD (ADD boys being 17.6 years at follow-up, mean age, and the brothers 18.4 years) the percent of the ADD youths arrested at least once for a serious offense was 46% as opposed to 14% for their brothers, controlling somewhat for genetic factors and for environmental rearing factors. Percentage of ADD youths with a record of multiple arrest was 27% as opposed to 5%, and for institutionalization it was 27% versus zero, for their non-ADD brothers. So I think that the correlation between ADD and late adolescent or early adult antisocial behavior is quite strong, especially when you look at brothers, who are not ADD, growing up in the same environmental and genetic background. Satterfield has some very interesting psychophysiologic data, which were done initially in both groups and were done in follow-up in both groups. The childhood evoked potential measures and two low-frequency bands in the power spectral analysis of the resting EEG were examined in two ADD subgroups: the group who were multiple offenders and the group who were nonoffenders. All of the evoked potential amplitudes were larger in the multiple-offender groups, with the N2 amplitude being the most strongly significant. The amount of power in the two bands of the EEG was lower in the multiple-offender group, but only the theta difference was significantly different. At follow-up, 12 of the multiple-offender group returned for evaluation and there was a group difference between the multiple offender and nonoffender also at follow-up. The ADD subjects who later became delinquent had larger evoked potentials as children but they had smaller evoked potential as adolescents than children who did not become delinquent from the same group. This suggests an age effect that correlates with the clinical picture at the time of follow-up and corroborates something shown previously in the ADD population suggesting high arousal for younger and lower arousal for older groups. To get back to this kind of a model, the clinical picture that you start off with is very important and how you subdivide it is greatly important, in terms of what kind of findings you will get in other areas: biological, genetic, natural history, or what have you. The subgroups determined on the basis of biologic studies or treatment studies, say, responders versus nonresponders, or offenders versus nonoffenders, may correlate with some of the other areas and then allow you to go back to your clinical description earlier, if the records are kept nicely, to identify possible different subgroups on the basis of clinical description.

General Discussion

Dr. Huessy: It is difficult to know how to look at patient populations unless one knows exactly the pattern, in a community, of how patients get to the various resources of help. Many of the differences in our studies are due to the fact that the populations we deal with not only differ, but differ in different ways. In certain communities, ADD children get to the child psychiatrist; in other communities, they get to the pediatrician; in other communities, they get to the child neurologist; in some communities, they get to nobody. A clinic population in one place is very seldom comparable to a clinic population someplace else. I think the group that Dr. Corboz most clearly described is one we have literature on: children who suffer an insult to the nervous system at or around the time of birth who tend to have, in general, a good outcome. The outcome is heavily influenced by socioeconomic status and is not so good in families that also suffer from poverty or other problems.

C. Keith Conners: Since there is obviously a high rate of delinquency in Dr. Cantwell's studies, I would guess that the measures that were used to select these children included not what we would consider a pure ADD group but a group with a lot of aggressive behavior. So, when you begin to follow-up these children and look at the natural history, you see that one group diverges into a delinquent path and the other group does not. I think this reemphasizes that the selection procedure or your clinical description is all-important in what you end up with. Fortunately, if you do follow-up study, you can go back and look. You can then identify a subtype, which shows that your original classification was, in fact, somewhat in error. I think it is extremely important that we have some way of separating out those who have very distinctive clinical features from the group we are calling ADD, hyperactive, or what have you. Again, work has clearly shown now that the long-term prognosis for ADD with aggression is very different and much poorer than for those without aggression. I think this suggests that we are either dealing with a multiform group or a group in which there are different weightings of interacting factors; it may be very difficult to tell in a young child whether his psychopathology represents the kind of aggressive, uninhibited, impulsive pattern that later leads to delinquency, and whether that same overt behavior really reflects a different underlying neurodisorder.

Dr. Cantwell: When we go back to the original data, we find a large number of children who have ADD symptomatology, but that doesn't protect them from having other symptoms. Acting-out aggressive behavior has to be one of the more common ones and Jan Loney's data (1979) really do show that that seems to be a high predictor variable. My feelings about the family studies are probably the same thing. If you can study the "pure" ADD group, with no evidence of what in DSM-III is called *conduct disorder*, you are going to find an increase in ADD-like disorders in family members, but it will be less than that which you find in the ADD plus conduct disorder groups. That is part of the rationale for the rather extensive subgrouping that was done in DSM-III: ADD with and without hyperactivity; residual state plus four possible types of conduct disorder; plus the category of *oppositional disorder* for the kids who kicked their parents in the shins and said: "You . . . , I ain't gonna do this," as opposed to the kid who is seriously antisocial.

The DSM-III criteria are structured so that a child must be a "bad-acting" kid to be judged as having a conduct disorder. I think it important at our stage of knowledge to separate out what might be a mild conduct disorder, oppositional disorder, and the ADD group at face value and to look and see if the follow-up is, in fact, different. I think it is, for the pure ADD versus the conduct disorder with or without ADD. If these disorders are lumped all together into *mixed disturbances of misery and conduct*, the result is a hodge-podge. It is much easier to lump things that were initially split than it is to split things that were initially lumped. So if you begin with an area of ignorance, you start off by being splitters. If ADD with or without hyperactivity have no differences later on when people begin to study this, then there is no reason to have both types. But if you don't have them to start off with, if you lump them all together—biologically, genetically, outcome-wise, treatment-wise—then you are going to come up with conflicting results from different centers because they are all different children.

Dr. Corboz: I agree with the importance of the disturbances in the field of the gestalt. Symptoms in motoric functions are very, very often found and very important and persist in a high percentage until the age of 20. It is my opinion that the factor of selection is very important; my patients are pure POS patients who have never shown a mixed clinical picture with an educational or emotional lack, but who only have ADD. If there is no separation, if you take mixed cases with ADD as the consequences of emotional and education problems, you will have awful results.

Dr. Bellack: Obviously, a child or a person who has concrete thinking available, has severe cognitive defects and problems in impulse control and will show many difficulties in daily adjustment. Equally obviously, a child with a disturbance in the body schema, and eventually in the self-image, will be particularly prone to symbiotic disturbances and all other kinds of psychiatric conditions, including the borderline, as a result of the neurological deficit due to neurological problems. And, naturally, a child who's given to lack of impulse control will run into social difficulties that will affect his entire social interaction in later life. That seems to me to be getting lost in the excessive concern with attention deficit.

REFERENCES

Annell, A. L. *Pertussis in infancy as a cause of behavior disorders in children.* Uppsala, Sweden: Almqist and Wiksell, 1953.

Bellak, L. *Psychiatric aspects of minimal brain dysfunction in adults.* New York: Grune and Stratton, 1979.

Bircher A. Das adoptionssyndrom. Eine Vergleichsstudie von 80 Adoptivkindern mit 80 Nichtadoptivkindern. Med. Diss., U. of Zurich, 1981.

Bloomingdale, L. and E. World-wide survey of minimal brain dysfunction. Manuscript, 1978.

Bloomingdale, L. and E. MBD: a new screening test and theoretical considerations. *Psychiat. J. of the Univ. of Ottawa/Rev. de psychiatrie de l'Univ. d'Ottawa*, 1980, 5:295-306.

Blum, F. E. Chemical integrative processes in the central nervous system. In F. O. Schmitt and F. G. Worden (Eds.), *The neurosciences*. Fourth Study Program, Cambridge, Mass., and London: The MIT Press, 1979, pp. 51-58.

Borner K. Die Bedeutung der psychomotorischen Therapie. Eine katamnestische Untersuchung von psychoorganische gestörten Kindern. Med. Diss. U. of Zurich, 1978.

Borner, K. and Corboz, R. J. Katamnestische Erhebung nach psychomotorischer Therapie. *Acta Paedopsychiatr.*, 1978, 44:53-56.

Cantwell, D. P. Genetic studies of hyperactive children. In R. Fiere, D. Rosenthal, and H. Brill (Eds.), *Genetic research in psychiatry*. Baltimore: Johns Hopkins University Press, 1975, pp. 273-280.

Corboz, R. J. Die Psychiatrie der Hirntumoren bei Kindern und Jugendlichen. Vienna: Springer, 1958.

Corboz, R. J. Zur Pathologie der Hirnschussverletzungen im Kindesalter. *Wiener Z. für Nervenheilkunde und deren Grenzgebiete*, 1962, 19:123-134.

Corboz, R. J., et al. Gemeinsamkeiten und Differenzen der Inanspruchahme-populationen dreier Kliniken: Artefakt oder Ralität? *Zeitschrift für Kinder- und Jugendpsychiatrie*. In press.

Corboz, R. J., and Schaub, C. Behavior disturbances fostered by the twin situation. European Symposium of Human Genetics, Zurich, March 26-28, 1981. In W. Schmid and J. Nielsen (Eds.), *Human behavior and genetics*, Amsterdam: Elsevier/North Holland Biomedical Press, 1981, pp. 225-230.

Corboz R. J., and Scheidegger, P. Die Eltern von neurotisch und psychoorganisch gestörten Kindern—Eine vergleichende Studie. In preparation.

Henke, H., and Lang, W. Cholinergic parameters in Alzheimer's disease: Topographical distribution of choline acetyltransferase activity in hippocampus, frontal cortex and gyrus cinguli, 1981. Submitted for publication.

Herzka, H. S., et al. Psychopathology and mental health in adopted children. In W. Schmid and J. Nielsen (Eds.), *Human behavior and genetics*. Amsterdam: Elsevier/North Holland Biomedical Press, 1981, pp. 221-224.

Huessy, H. R., et al. 8-10 year follow-up of 84 children treated for behavioral disorder in rural Vermont. *Acta Paedopsychiatr.*, 1974, 40:230-235.

Kløve, H. and Hole, K. The hyperkinetic syndrome: criteria for diagnosis. In R. L. Trites (ed.), *Hyperactivity in children*. Baltimore: University Park Press, 1979, p. 131.

Lehmann, S., and Gundelfinger, R. Langzeitverlauf der Symptomatik bei leicht hirngeschädigten Kindern. Nachkontrolle, 10 Jahre nach erfolgter Diagnosestellung. Psychiatrische Universitäts-Poliklinik für Kinder und Jugendliche. In preparation.

Lempp, R. *Frühkindliche Hirnschädigung und Neurose*. (2nd ed.). Bern-Stuttgart-Wien (Vienna): Hans Huber, 1970.

Loney, J., et al. The hyperkinetic child grows up: predictors of symptoms, delinquency, and achievement at follow-up. Presented at the Annual Meeting of the American Association for the Advancement of Science, January 7, 1979.

Lutz, J. Psychische Symptome und Rekonvaleszenz nach Contusio cerebri. *Z. Kinderpsychiatr.*, 1949, *16*:97–109.

Morrison, J. R., and Stewart, M. A. Bilateral inheritance as evidence for polygenicity in the hyperactive child syndrome. *Journal of Nervous and Mental Disease*, 1974, *158*:226–228.

Remschmidt, H., and Schmidt, M. Multiaxiales Klassifikationsschema für psychiatrische Erkrankungen im Kindes- und Jugendalter. Bern, Switzerland: Verlag Hans Huber, 1977.

Robins, E., and Guze, S. Establishment of diagnostic validity and psychiatric illness: its application to schizophrenia. *Am. J. Psychiatry*, 1970, *126*: 983–987.

Roesler, H. D., et al. Katamnestische Untersuchungen an normalintelligenten Enzephalopathen im Kindes- und Erwachsenenalter. Leipzig, (GDR), S. Hirzel Verlag, 1979, *25*:18–24.

Rufini-Gachnang C. Die Eltern Waren es Gestern—ihre Kinder sind es Heute: Patienten des Kinderpsychiatrischen Dienstes. Psychiatrische Universitäts-Poliklinik für Kinder und Jugendliche, U. of Zurich, Med. Diss. In preparation.

Rutter, M., et al. *A multi-axial classification of child psychiatric disorders.* Geneva: World Health Organization, 1975.

Rutter, M., Graham, P., and Yule, W. *A neuropsychiatric study in childhood.* Philadelphia: J. B. Lippincott, 1970.

Sameroff, A. J. and Chandler, M. J. Reproductive risk and the continnum of caretaking casualty. In F. D. Horoqitz, M. Hetherington, S. Scarr-Salapatek, and G. Siegel (Eds.), *Review of child development research* (vol. 4). Chicago: University of Chicago, 1975, pp. 187–244.

Schaub, C. Zwillinge in der Kinderpsychiatrie. Med. Diss., U. of Zurich, 1980.

Shaffer, D. Longitudinal research and the minimal brain damage syndrome. *Adv. Biol. Psychiat.*, (Basel, Karger), 1978, *1*:18–34.

Shaywitz, S., Shaywitz, B. E., and Cohen, D. The biochemical basis of minimal brain dysfunction. *The Journal of Pediatrics*, 1978, *92*:179–187.

Shetty, T., and Chase, T. N. Central monoamines and hyperkinesis of childhood. *Neurology*, 1976, *26*:1000.

Sieber, M. Das leicht hirngeschädigte und das psychoreaktiv gestörte Kind. (2nd ed.) Bern, Switzerland: Verlag Hans Huber, 1981.

Silver, L. B. The minimal brain dysfunction syndrome. *Bas. Handbook Child Psychiatry*, 1979, *2*:416–439.

Walther-Büel, H. *Die Psychiatrie der Hirngeschwülste und die Cerebralen Grundlagen Psychischer Vorgänge*. Vienna: Springer, 1951.

Wender, P. H. *Minimal brain dysfunction in children*. New York: John Wiley, 1971.

Wender, P. H., et al. Urinary monoamine metabolites in children with minimal brain dysfunction. *Am. Journal Psychiatry*, 1971, *127*:1411.

Werner, M. E. and Smith, R. S. *Kaui's children come of age*. Honolulu: University of Hawaii, 1977.

Winokur, G. The Division of Depressive Illness into Depression Spectrum Disease and Pure Depressive Disease. *Int. Pharmacopsychiatry*, 1974, *9*:5–13.

Zigmond, M. J. and Stricker, E. M. Behavioral and neurochemical effects of central catecholamine depletion: a possible model for "subclinical" brain damage. In *Animal models in psychiatry and neurology*. Oxford: Pergamon Press, 1977, pp. 415–429.

3

Some Possible Neurological Substrates in Attention Deficit Disorder

LEWIS M. BLOOMINGDALE, ROBERT K. DAVIES, AND MARK S. GOLD

EDITOR'S COMMENTS

In working clinically with parents of ADD children, one often encounters strong parental resistance to a trial of psychostimulants. Patients with ADD who respond to stimulants will improve with increasing doses of psychostimulants to an optimum point, beyond which they experience the same subjective sense of tension and anxiety as non-ADD individuals. They do not develop tolerance, as do addictive patients. Since this type of dose-response is similar to that of hormonal treatment of endocrine deficiencies, it is pragmatically useful in clinical work to discuss ADD as a deficiency disease, like diabetes or hypothyroidism.

Of course, we do not know the target groups of cells, as we do with the endocrine glands, to substantiate such an analogy. It was with this interesting dose-response of ADD patients to psychostimulants that the authors undertook their investigation. Their paper is tentative. Their aim is to suggest the possible useful convergence of neuroscientific investigation of psychopharmacology and neuroanatomical neurophysiology with the clinical experiments that have, thus far, formed the basis of our knowledge of ADD.

*   *   *

Although it is unclear whether Attention Deficit Disorder (ADD) is a behavioral entity, or group of entities, whether it is due to structural or infrastructural impairments, or to biochemical abnormalities, or to faulty learning, it is of value to discuss neurological substrates. Complicating an already muddy picture is that attention is composed of, or related to, several processes and components: arousal (alertness), selection (focusing), vigilance (sustained attention), and motivation (effort), each of which may have its own neurological and biochemical aspects.

An early description of "organic drivenness" was made by Kahn (Kahn and Cohen, 1934), who likened it to the postencephalitic hyperactivity and distractibility noted in children recovered from von Economo's disease. In this prescient article, Eugene Kahn also noted that: "We surmised that quite a few individuals who are now labeled psychopathic personalities may really have organic drivenness." In addition, one of his cases was a 29-year-old and none had had encephalitis. Kahn postulated that the neuropathology of this disorder was located in the brain stem. Subsequently, the entity became known as

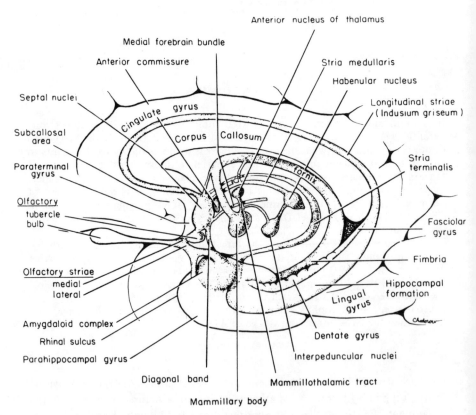

Figure 1. Semischematic drawing of rhinencephalic structural relationships as seen in medial view of the right hemisphere. Both deep and superficial structures are indicated. (Modified from a drawing by Krieg.) From M. B. Carpenter, *Human neuroanatomy*, (8th ed). Baltimore: Williams and Wilkins, 1982.

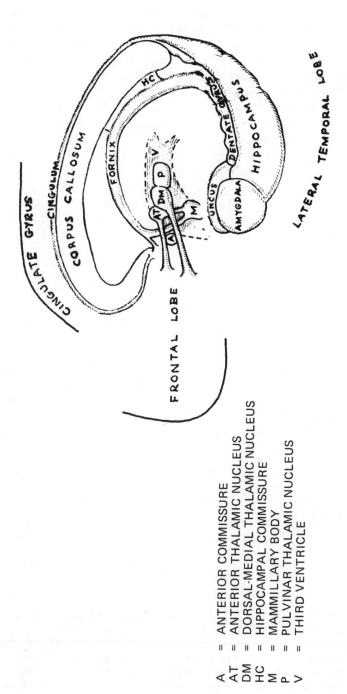

A   = ANTERIOR COMMISSURE
AT = ANTERIOR THALAMIC NUCLEUS
DM = DORSAL-MEDIAL THALAMIC NUCLEUS
HC = HIPPOCAMPAL COMMISSURE
M   = MAMMILLARY BODY
P   = PULVINAR THALAMIC NUCLEUS
V   = THIRD VENTRICLE

Figure 2. A schematic diagram of the limbic system. From R. G. Ojemann, Correlations between specific human brain lesions and memory changes, *Neurosciences Research Program Bulletin*, 1966, 4:1–70, p. 20.

"minimal cerebral dysfunction," so that the pendulum swung rostrally from the base of the brain to the apex, indeed, even to primarily a frontal lobe dysfunction (Stamm and Kreder, 1979). A table showing brain sites of dysfunction in hyperactivity by various authors appears in Ferguson and Pappas (1979).

We suggest the consideration of the hippocampus is essential in the neuroanatomical and neurophysiological aspects of the brain that are important to the study of ADD. As described by Nauta and Feirtag (1979), the hippocampus is part of the telencephalon, which includes, besides the hippocampus, the striatum and other basal ganglia proximal to the periventricular gray (wherein is found the locus ceruleus). These comprise the older parts of the forebrain that, in man, are enfolded within the newer portion of the forebrain, the neocortex. Figure 1 shows a sketch of the hippocampus in a medial view of the brain. Figure 2 is a schematic diagram of the limbic system, and Figure 3 shows septo-hippocampal connections.

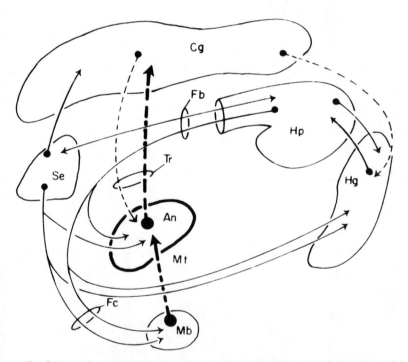

Figure 3. Principal septal and hippocampal connections are shown by solid lines. Broken lines represent some main secondary connections. An, Anterior nuclei (n); Cg, cingulate gyrus; Fb, fornix body; Fc, fornix column; Hg, hippocampal gyrus; Hp, hippocampus; Mb, mammillary body; Mt, mammillothalamic tract; Se, septum; Tr, thalamic radiations. From Powell, E. M. and Hines, G.: Septohippocampal Interface. In Isaacson, R. L. and Pribram, K. H. (eds.). The Hippocampus, Volume 1. New York: Plenum Press, 1975, 54.

A more specific connection between ADD patients and the hippocampus was suggested by the classical work of Milner and her colleagues (Scoville and Milner, 1957), with their description of a patient whose bilateral excision of the hippocampus grossly impaired the faculty of long-term memory. Many ADD patients are reported to show a dysfunction of retention of learning, suggesting impaired hippocampal function. In addition, patients with lesions in this area show poor goal-directedness, distractibility, irrelevant associations, and memory impairments (Luria, 1973). Vigilance was not specifically tested in posthippocampectomized patients, but may be inferred to have been defective from the observation that ". . . they forgot the instant attention was diverted to a new topic" (Scoville and Milner, 1957).

SELECTIVE ATTENTION: THE HIPPOCAMPUS AS COMPARATOR

If attention involves the "directivity and selectivity of mental processes" (Luria, 1973), then the hippocampus becomes important because this structure compares incoming stimuli to already stored memory traces and assesses the novelty of new stimuli. This enables the organism to respond to novel stimuli and to extinguish responses to habituated ones. The conclusions of Vinogradova (1975) are noteworthy in this regard.

Vinogradova and her colleagues demonstrated, quite convincingly, that the limbic system could be regarded as a complex hierarchy, wherein each of the architectonically different links exhibit a specific subfunction. The units form a system of two connected circuits. The main limbic circuit, called the *informational circuit*, receives, processes, and preserves coded information from widely different sensory sources. This circuit was regarded as serially connected integrators of the incoming signals, each having an individual critical threshold, determined by the number of repeated stimuli.

Vinogradova called the second circuit, the hippocampo-reticular circuit, the *Regulatory Circuit*. The circuit is linked to an additional "emotional" system (amygdala-hypothalamus), by which neural and viscerohormonal influences, related to emotional states, may augment and prolong the excitation developing in the regulatory circuit.

The most important link of the system is the hippocampal nucleus CA_3, which Vinogradova believes evaluates the degree of novelty of a stimulus. This is attained when the signal coming through the reticuloseptal input does not find its counterpart in the cortical input. In the event of such "mismatches," the neurons in CA_3 react, while in the event of coincidence of two input signals, the neurons return to a steady-state background level of activity. When a novel stimulus is received, the majority of the CA_3 neurons are inhibited and only the minority are activated. The result is a *decrease* of general hippocampal output to the reticular formation. Since the hippocampus exerts a tonic, inhibitory influence on the activating cells of the reticular formation (probably indirectly through nonspecific, inhibitory structures), the *decrease* of hippocampal output should lead to *increase* in the activity of the ascending reticular formation, causing a general increase in the level of brain activity (arousal). With repeated presentations of the stimulus, there is increased partial "recognition," leading to the gradual decrease of the general arousal reaction until its disappearance. (At that time, there is no longer need for a high level of reticular formation activation as the novel signal has been processed and the fixation of the corresponding trace completed.)

Vinogradova's work received general acceptance at a recent Ciba Symposium on septo-hippocampal function as a comparator, according to Gray (1982), who expanded the theory of septo-hippocampus function as a comparator extensively. His diagrams of the general function of such a comparator and of Vinogradova's concept are illustrated in Figures 4a and 4b.

Gray hypothesized that a general comparator must have access to information about both current sensory events (the world) and expected (predicted) events. To function successfully, such a system needs to exercise control, i.e., to form a plan or motor program. According to Gray's theory, the septo-hippocampal system is responsible for both the generation of predictions and the comparison between these and actual events.* Gray assumes further that "the septo-hippocampal system does not normally exercise control over behaviour when a series of expectations is confirmed by actual events (except when these include punishment); that it normally does take control when expectations are disconfirmed ('mismatch'); and ... the theta rhythm quantizes the operation of the comparator in time." He believes the septo-hippocampal comparator has two modes of operation: "just checking" (not controlling behavior) and "control" mode (directly controlling behavior). Thus, a hippocampal rat or one without the septal area (and thus, without theta rhythm) runs just as efficiently as an intact animal, in expectable circumstances. Gray supposes that the hippocampus is not controlling such behavior, it is "just checking."

Following various deductions from clinical experiments, Gray arrives at the conclusion that the subicular area may function as a comparator, providing the introduction of emotional input through the anteroventral thalamus and providing planning via the cingulate cortex (that has afferent and efferent pathways to the frontal cortex). This provides the planning component selecting the behavior that the "comparator" controls. Gray's diagram of the subicular connections is shown in Figure 4c.

The reader is referred to Gray (1982) for his extensive, detailed analysis of the septo-hippocampal system as comparator. Briefly, he points out:

---

*See chapters by Douglas, Kinsbourne, and Sprague, in this volume, re: strategies in children with ADD.

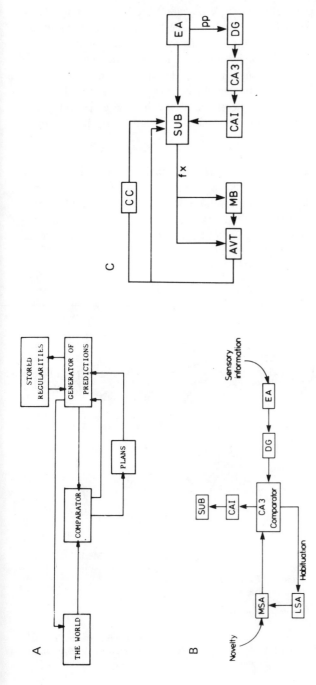

Figure 4. (a) The kinds of information processing required for the successful functioning of the hypothetical comparator. From J. A. Gray, *The neuropsychology of anxiety: An enquiry into the functions of the septo-hippocampal system.* New York: Oxford University Press, 1982. (b) Vinogradova's CA₃ comparator of novelty. DG, dentate gyrus; EA, entorhinal area; LSA, lateral septal area; MSA, medial septal area; SUB, subicular area. From J. A. Gray, *The neuropsychology of anxiety: An enquiry into the functions of the septo-hippocampal system.* New York: Oxford University Press, 1982. (c) Connections of the subicular area which might allow it to function as a comparator. AVT, anteroventral thalamus; CC, cingulate cortex; DG, dentate gyrus; MB, mammillary bodies; SUB, subicular complex; fx, fornix; pp, perforant path; EA, entorhinal area. From J. A. Gray, *The neuropsychology of anxiety: An enquiry into the functions of the septo-hippocampal system.* New York: Oxford University Press, 1982.

From the present point of view, . . . Vinogradova's CA_3 comparator serves an auxiliary role, passing novel stimuli along for the particular attention of the subicular comparator and filtering out familiar stimuli. But the latter action can be overcome by other influences if the familiar stimuli are important. However, though familiar, important stimuli and novel ones are both passed on for further action, the type of action they provoke is different. . . . (When) there is a mismatch between expected and actual events (then) the septo-hippocampal system assumes direct control over behaviour.

Gray further infers, citing numerous experiments, that behavior controlled by punishment or nonreward is disrupted by (large) septal and hippocampal lesions. A dysfunction of the septo-hippocampal system would, then, account for the fact that ADD patients responded to positive reinforcement but not to (predicted) aversive operant conditioning in Kinsbourne's experiment (this volume). (Cf. also Douglas, this volume.)

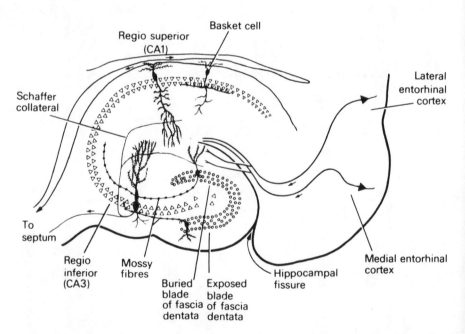

Figure 5. Diagram of the architecture of the hippocampus. Reproduced with permission from J. O'Keefe and L. Nadel, *The hippocampus as a cognitive map.* London, Oxford University Press, 1978, p. 108.

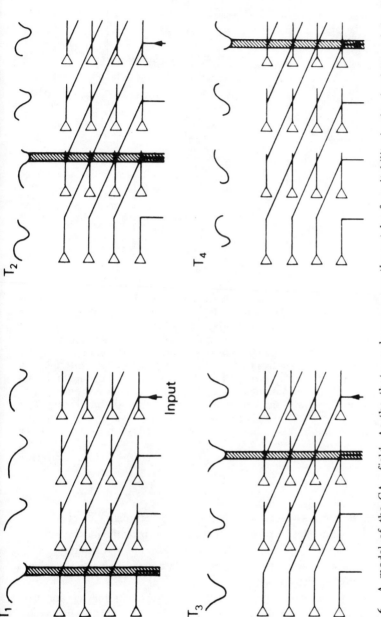

Figure 6. A model of the CA$_1$ field. As the theta cycle progresses the patch of excitability in the dendrites of the CA$_1$ pyramids changes from the most distal part (T$_1$) through middle parts (T$_2$ and T$_3$) to the most proximal sections (T$_4$). The same input entering the CA$_1$ field (far right) will excite a different cell depending on the timing of its arrival relative to the theta cycle. At T$_1$, it excites the topmost cell in A, T$_2$ the second cell from the top in B, etc. Reproduced with permission from J. O'Keefe, and L. Nadel, *The hippocampus as a cognitive map.* Oxford: Oxford University Press, 1978, p. 228.

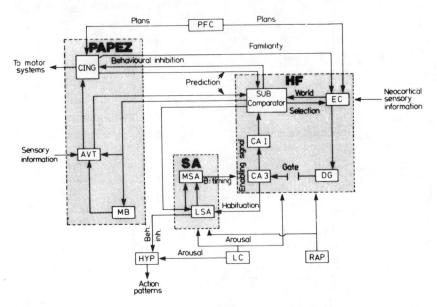

Figure 7. A summary of the theory developed in this book. The three major building blocks are shown in heavy print: HF, the hippocampal formation, made up of the entorhinal cortex, EC, the dentate gyrus, DG, CA_3, CA_1, and the sub-icular area, SUB; SA, the septal area, containing the medial and lateral septal areas, MSA and LSA; and the Papez circuit, which receives projections from and returns them to the subicular area via the mammillary bodies, MB, anteroventral thalamus, AVT, and cingulate cortex, CING. Other structures shown are the hypothalamus, HYP, the locus coeruleus, LC, the raphe nuclei, RAP, and the prefrontal cortex, PFC. Arrows show direction of projection; the projection from SUB to LSA lacks anatomical confirmation. Words in lower case show postulated functions; beh. inh., behavioural inhibition. (For further explanation, see text.) From J. A. Gray, *The neuropsychology of anxiety: An enquiry into the functions of the septo-hippocampal system.* New York: Oxford University Press, 1982.

Gray furthermore explored what he terms the "enigmatic" theta rhythm. He concludes that this plays a role in timing and quantizing the passive information around the septo-hippocampal system. His assumption is supported by evidence that the hippocampal neurons fire preferentially in particular phases of the locally recorded theta wave.

O'Keefe and Nadel (1978), for instance, suggest that the septum plays the role of a synchronizing device that rhythmically modulates the excitability of the CA_3 dendritic system and creates the conditions necessary for the "comparison" interaction only of those signals that come in certain

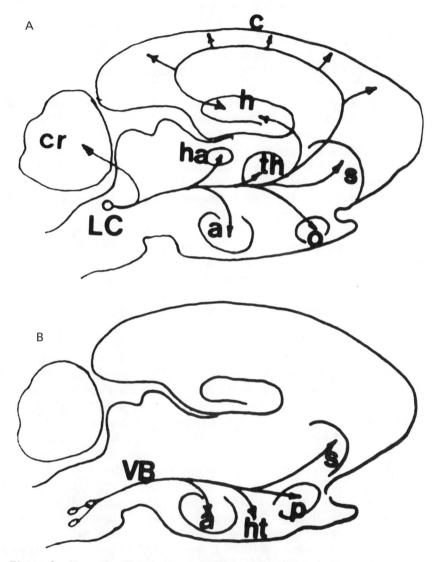

Figure 8. The ascending projection of noradrenergic nuclei in the brain. (a) Dorsal and (b) ventral bundles. LC = locus coeruleus, VB = ventral bundle, c = cerebral cortex, cr = cerebellum, h = hippocampus, ha = habenula, ht = hypothalamus, p = pryiform cortex, o = anterior olfactory nucleus, s = septum, the = anterior thalamic nucleus, a = amygdala. Reproduced with permission from W. Kostowski, Noradrenergic interactions among central neurotransmitters. In W. B. Essman (ed.), *Neurotransmitters, receptors and drug action*. New York: Spectrum Publications, 1980, p. 49.

microintervals of time. Signals from the cortical input via the perforant path may not be able to act on the CA_3 pyramidal neurons if they are not in phase with the medial septal neuronal bursts (theta rhythm). O'Keefe and Nadel believe that this may occur via the matrix formed by the basket cell axons (thick, vertical lines in Figure 5) and the Schaffer collaterals (thin, horizontal lines) as shown in Figures 5 and 6 (O'Keefe and Nadel, 1978).

Duffy, Denkla, et al. (1980) and Hanley and Sklar (1976) have found significant differences between dyslexic and normal children in 3–7 Hz (theta) rhythms using topographic mapping of brain electrical activity (BEAM). Since there is a considerable covariance of dyslexia and ADD, it would certainly be of interest to examine a cohort of ADD children with the noninvasive BEAM to determine whether there is a similar abnormal theta rhythm.

Gray concludes his extensive analysis with a diagram summarizing a theory developed in his book, which is reproduced in our Figure 7.

Very recently, further confirmation of the role of the hippocampus in selective attention (in the rat) was demonstrated by Deadwyler, West, and Robinson (1981). Even more recently, Fuster and Jervey (1981) have shown the inferotemporal cortex to be involved in selective attention to differently colored visual stimuli.

Numerous variations of the Continuous Performance Test (CPT) have been the standard measuring device for improvement of ADD with psychopharmacological agents. The measure is based on "mismatch" errors, either of omission or commission or both (Mason, 1979). The CPT is so well-known that it need not be described. The juxtaposition of letters to be matched may be considered as cortical input from the neocortex to the loops described by Vinogradova as expanded by Gray. It appears to us that this congruence of neuroanatomical and neurophysiological systems, with the data on which so much of our empirical knowledge of ADD is based, deserves further study.

If the hippocampus is related to selective attention, then the destruction of some major afferent to the hippocampus should interfere with selective attention.

Mason and Iversen (1975) used 6-hydroxydopamine (6-OHDA) to destroy the dorsal bundle. The resultant change in learning behavior has been called by Mason (1979) the "dorsal bundle extinction effect (DBEE)." The most promising theory regarding the DBEE is that it interferes with selective attention. Mason states that the NA (NE) projection to the hippocampus may "inform that area that memories are not to be laid down about the irrelevant stimulus; inform the cortex not to continue processing the information contained in that stimulus, inhibit the cerebellum from using that stimulus to lay down motor learning . . ." (Mason, 1979, p. 83). The nuclei involved in the tracts of the dorsal and ventral bundles, respectively, are shown in Figures 8a and 8b, from Kostowski (1980).

Mason (1980) believes that the DBEE (resulting from norepinephrine depletion in the rat) causes impairment of selective attention. Mason also discusses "perseveration of inappropriate behavior (resistance to extinction)." It should be pointed out that Mason's views have not been universally accepted.

VIGILANCE

Vigilance may, for the purpose of this discussion, be operationally defined as the period in which (selective) attention is maintained prior to extinction (exhaustion). We should point out that psychologists have defined vigilance as "that behavior required to detect infrequently occurring signals over a prolonged period of time (20 to 45 minutes) when those signals are embedded in a background of other regularly occurring events."

It has taken ten years for the concepts of those pioneers, Clements and Peters, in the study of ADD by Dykman, Ackerman, Clements and Peters (1971), to come to fruition in the APA's DSM-III (American Psychiatric Association, 1980). Virginia Douglas deserves recognition for her discussion, a

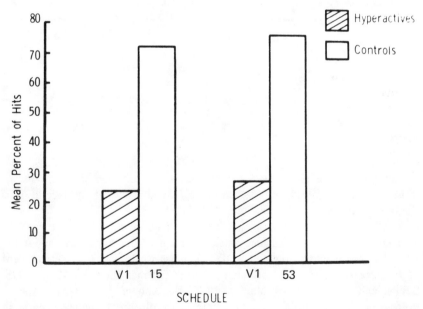

Figure 9. Mean percentage of hits by the hyperactive and control children under each schedule of signal presentation. Reproduced with permission from J. O. Goldberg and M. M. Konstantareas, Vigilance in hyperactive and normal children on a self-paced operant task. *J. Child Psychol. Psychiat.* 1981, 22:59.

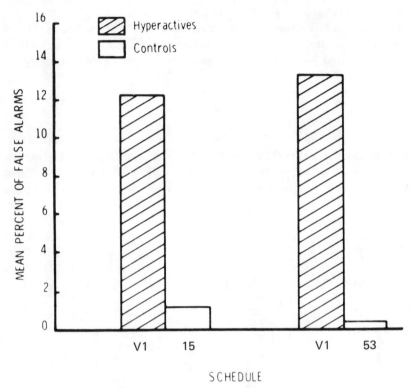

Figure 10. Mean percentage of false alarms by the hyperactive and control children under each schedule of signal presentation. Reproduced with permission from J. O. Goldberg and M. M. Konstantareas, Vigilance in hyperactive and normal children on a self-paced operant task. *J. Child Psychol. Psychiat.*, 1981, *22*:59.

decade ago, of the significance of vigilance in the disorder (Sykes, Douglas, Weiss, and Minde, 1971). An extensive analysis and review of vigilance in ADD children appears in Douglas and Peters (1979).

Bloomingdale and Bloomingdale (1980) have pointed out that the CPT is essentially a test for vigilance and that much of our knowledge about the effect of psychoactive drugs on ADD really has to do with the measurement of vigilance (Conners and Rothschild, 1968; Gittleman-Klein and Klein, 1976; Looker and Conners, 1970; Mairlot, 1977; Nooteboom, 1967; Owen, Adams, Forrest, Stolz, and Fisher, 1971). There is an obvious congruence between Vinogradova's (1975) and Gray's (1982) concepts regarding the function of the comparators and the hippocampal detection of "mismatches."

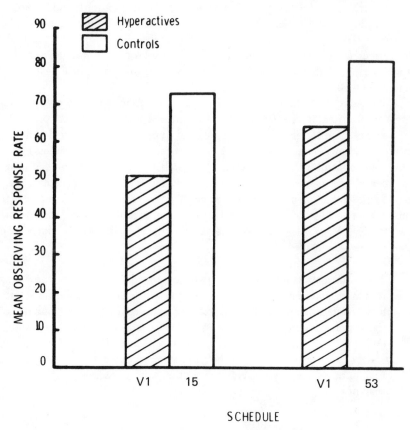

Figure 11. Mean observing response rates (responses per minute) for hyper-active and control children under each schedule of signal presentation. Reproduced with permission from J. O. Goldberg and M. M. Konstantareas, Vigilance in hyperactive and normal children on a self-paced operant task. *J. Child Psychol. Psychiat.*, 1981, *22*:60.

Our findings on the sudden interruption of continuity suggest that the maintenance of attention does not show a gradual decline on the Bender designs with repeated circles or dots but, rather, a discontinuity. Although these findings have not been confirmed, they are suggestive of possible depletion of neurotransmitter storage in some neurons of ADD children (we suggest in some nucleus or nuclei of the septo-hippocampal system). Since d-amphetamine and methylphenidate are both dopamine agonists, although acting on different storage pools, cytoplasmic dopamine or vesicular, respectively, according to

Brown (*Attention Deficit Disorder*, volume 2, in preparation), and pemoline is also a dopamine agonist effective in treating ADD children, it may be that dopamine (DA) is implicated. (However, as described below, neurons are probably affected by the system interaction of various neurotransmitters and it should be noted that the various nuclei in the septo-hippocampal system are stimulated by different neurotransmitters.)

A recent study of vigilance in hyperactive and normal children by Goldberg and Konstantareas (1981), using Holland's self-paced modification of the CPT, shows the difference between groups of hyperactive and normal children, as illustrated in Figures 9, 10 and 11. The range and the mean between hyperactive and control subjects were closely matched regarding chronological age and mental age as measured by both the Peabody Picture Vocabulary Test and the Columbus Mental Maturity Scale. The two schedules in figures 9, 10, and 11 refer to high density, VI 15 (15-second interval for signal delivery) and low density, VI 53 (53-second interval for signal delivery). Goldberg and Konstantareas concluded:

> This task distinguishes between two components of vigilance, observing responses and signal detection responses which are further divided into hits and false alarms. All subjects were exposed to the same number of signal presentations under a low (VI 53) (53 seconds interval) and a high (VI 15) (15 seconds interval) density schedule. Hyperactive children emitted a lower percentage of hits and a greater percentage of false alarms than normals. Hyperactive children showed slower observing response rates than normals.

HYPERKINESIS

As noted in the Bloomingdales' previous article (1980), adult patients describe the subjective feelings associated with hyperkinesis in a manner that we have found, clinically, to be indistinguishable from akathisia, a known side effect of neuroleptics that block dopamine receptors. It is noteworthy that children who have sociopsychological hyperactivity do not have sleep impairment because of motor activity. However, patients with ADD and akathisia both complain of sleep disturbance due to motoric neuronal discharge.* Another

---

*Cf. Kinsbourne's discussion, this volume. We disagree. Akathisia is usually associated with fasciculation of the tongue. Also, trunk and arm movements, though less common than the legs, are described by some patients. Cf. Munetz and Cornes 1982, re: the association of akathisia and tardive dyskinesia, with emphasis on the dopamine receptors—Ed.

neuropathological condition attributed to dopamine deficiency (in the corpus striatum) is Syndenham's chorea (Bannister, 1973), in which it has been noted: "Onset is usually insidious, the first complaint being that the child is clumsy and drops things . . . the child is described as restless, fidgety or unable to keep still" (Bannister, 1973). This is, of course, similar to the clumsiness and restlessness we see in ADD children and the "choreatiform syndrome" described by Prechtl and his group in Groningen, (Prechtl and Stemmer, 1959), which seems to us indistinguishable from ADD. Unfortunately, to the best of our knowledge, the precise neuropathology of akathisia has not been fully explored.

However, Van Putten (1975) believes that akathisia is subjective and that mild akathisia is not infrequently experienced as vague feelings of apprehension, irritability, impatience, or general unease *without* muscular movement. If this is true, akathisia may be related to a dopamine deficiency in the limbic system, as well as possibly the striatum. O'Keefe and Nadel (1978) have reviewed hyperactivity in hippocampectomized rats.

NEUROTRANSMITTERS

Any understanding of the biochemical substrate(s) for ADD is hampered by the lack of certainty as to the limits of the syndrome, as well as by the lack of clarity as to whether there is one or several ADDs, each of which might have its own unique neurophysiology. Since Wender's (1971) early advancement of a monoamine hypothesis, there have been numerous contributions, most of them concluding that a disturbance in the activity of dopamine (DA) is related to the pathophysiology of ADD.

Catecholamine metabolite studies, although limited in scope, point to possible alterations in monoamine metabolism (especially dopamine). Shaywitz (Shaywitz, Cohen, and Bowers, 1977) showed a decrease of the major DA metabolite, homovanillic acid, in the cerebrospinal fluid of a small group of ADD children. Studies of norepinephrine (NE) metabolism have been less conclusive. Although Wender (1971) found no difference between urinary 3-methoxy-4-hydroxyphenylethylene glycol (MHPG) levels in hyperkinetic and normal children, Shekim (Shekim, Dekirmenjian, and Chapel, 1979) found decreased levels and Khan and Dekirmenjian (1981) found increased urinary excretion of the metabolite. The discrepancies may be explained by sampling and other methodological differences.

Most recently Irwin (Irwin, Beludink, McClosker and Freedman, 1981) has demonstrated hyperserotonemia in children with ADD, thus implicating yet a third neurotransmitter system. Although serotonergic mechanisms have been related to arousal and motor activity, the significance of the finding is uncertain. Coleman (Coleman, Steinberg, Tippett, Bhagavan, et al., 1979) has shown the clinical importance of serotonin, relating 5-hydroxytryptamine levels following pyrodixine administration to the improvement of hyperkinetic symptoms.*

Shaywitz (Shaywitz, Klopper, Yager, and Gordon, 1976; Shaywitz, Yager, and Klopper, 1976; and Pearson, Teicher, Shaywitz, Cohen, et al., 1980) has described an interesting animal model for ADD. In a series of experiments, rat pups were administered 6-hydroxydopamine, thus producing a profound depletion of brain dopamine and an increase in activity level. The "hypersensitivity" decreased after 3–4 weeks, thus simulating the clinical situation in humans where hyperactivity in ADD children diminishes spontaneously as they reached adolescence. Administration of amphetamine to hyperactive-treated rats led to a significant reduction in activity levels, mimicking its effect seen in ADD children. It was suggested that the results could be explained by postulating that the DA system acts as a modulator of excitatory activity (mediated by NE). It must be cautioned, however, that models explaining hyperactivity may not explain attentional deficits—although the DA system may be deficient in both.

Other models have been proposed, attempting to relate selective attention to one or another neurotransmitter. Mason (1980), in reviewing the literature on noradrenaline and attention, concluded that lesions in the NE-mediated dorsal bundle led to a "failure to ignore irrelevant stimuli." On the other hand, Matthysse (1977) argues for a relationship between DA and selective attention, noting the fixation of attention common in amphetamine overdose and the counteraction of disturbances in involuntary attention by neuroleptics.

Such an approach would fit in with the observations, noted in previous sections, that many nuclei are involved in processes that we feel fundamental to ADD: selective attention, vigilance and, via various limbic nuclei and the hypothalamus, reward and punishment. For example, the hippocampus has many different areas supplied by different afferents. Areas CA_1 and CA_3, which were centrally important in the "informational circuit" and the "regulatory circuit" of Vinogradova (1975), are not only different architectonically but are also activated by different nerve groups—the dorsal tegmental bundle (DTB) originating in the locus ceruleus (LC) and the median forebrain bundle (MFB) originating in the substantia nigra (SN) (Lindvall and Björklund, 1974). (Cf. Swanson, 1979.) The former is believed to be noradrenergic in function and the latter dopaminergic (see Figure 12). Thus, both neurotransmitter systems may be crucial to the behavioral manifestation called "attention." (Cf. also Davis and Berger, 1978).

---

*Cf. Dr. Kløve's discussion of this chapter, this volume.

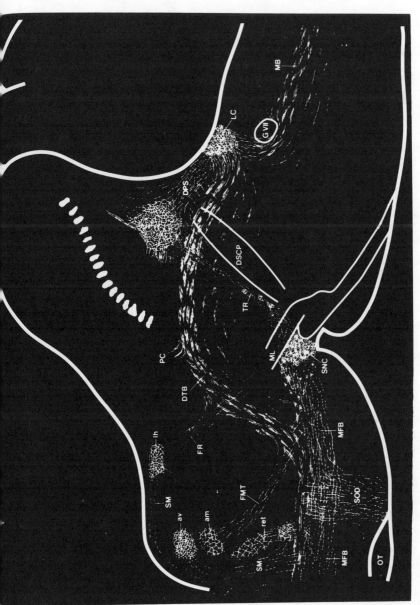

Figure 12. Semidiagrammatic representation of the ascending CA fiber system of the dorsal tegmental bundle (DTB), originating in the locus ceruleus (LC), and its projections in the diencephalon. The medial part of the medial forebrain bundle (MFB) and cells in the medial part of the pars compacta of the substantia nigra (SN) are also included. Composite drawing representing slightly different sagittal planes. Other abbreviations appear in Index. Reprinted with permission from Lindvall, O. and Björklund, A.: The organization of the ascending catecholamine neuron systems in the rat brain. Acta Physiol. Scand. Supplementum 412. Lund, Sweden, 1974, p. 7.

Kostowski (1980) stated:

> There is evidence that brain NA (NE) systems are interconnected with other monoaminergic neurons. The interaction between NA (NE) neurons and other systems seems to play an important role in brain function as well as in active mechanisms of psychotropic drugs. Recently the possible interactions among various catecholamine neurons has been explored. Fuxe, et al. (1974) have suggested that NA (NE) cells of the LC receive a tonic inhibitory input from other brain-stem catecholamine neurons.

He also states:

> It is currently believed that both NA (NE) and DA systems of the brain play an important role in the regulation of motor activity . . . data suggest that increased activity of NA (NE) neurons may enhance responses to DA receptor stimulation in the brain.

Antelman and Caggiula (1977) have related NE/DA interactions to stress.
    Recently, Paul (1983) discussed the interdependency of NE, 5HT, and DA on each other because of the neuronal interconnections between the SN (substantia nigra) and LC (locus ceruleus). Coyle, Price, and DeLong (1983) have identified the cholinergic neuronal cell bodies located in the nucleus basalis of Meynert, the diagonal band of Broca, and the medial septal nucleus as sending axons that innervate the entire neocortex, as well as the hippocampal formation.
    The search for the neurotransmitter is further complicated by the fact that the metabolism of NE and DA are interrelated. It has even been suggested in some studies that "the activity produced by DA is due to its conversion to or displacement of NE after being taken up by noradrenergic neurons" (Iversen, 1977), and that "increased activity of NE neurons may enhance responses to DA receptor stimulation in the brain" (Kostowski, 1980).
    Further data on bruising and platelet functioning in ADD suggest that "membrane secretion defects are not specific to the granular contents but to the membrane release mechanism" (Mueller, Koire, Rao, Christine, and Holmsen, 1981). The defect was reversed by methylphenidate and pemoline but not by dextroamphetamine, suggesting different modes of action of these drugs. It may be then hypothesized that methylphenidate alters membrane release of dopamine, whereas dextroamphetamine acts more as a direct dopamine agonist.
    With further studies it may be possible better to define neurotransmitter functions such as release and storage, to study differential drug actions, and to tailor medications to specific deficits. Patients with storage problems might respond to direct agonists, whereas those with release deficits might respond to medication acting on the membrane.

Studies of the neurophysiology of brain reward systems (Wise, 1980) can perhaps shed further light on this complex subject. As with ADD, there is much evidence pointing to DA systems being involved in a major way and, as with attentional disorders, brain areas such as the hippocampus, dorsal noradrenergic bundle, locus ceruleus, and median forebrain bundle are implicated. Moreover, anhedonia and deficits in response to rewards have been hypothesized to be critical aspects of the ADD syndrome (Wender, 1978). It is tempting, then, to assume interrelated processes between attentional and reward deficits in ADD. In this regard a locus ceruleus-endorphin derangement theory also deserves careful study. While the work of the Iversens as well as of Mason and Iversen and Iversen (1975) have focused on the NE dorsal bundle emanating from the locus ceruleus, it should be noted that this nucleus also sends DA fibers to the hippocampus and surrounding nuclei. (See Figure 13.)

Wise (1980) has postulated that both DA and NE mechanisms may be involved in reward mechanisms, DA in a direct fashion and NE indirectly, with NE neurons inhibiting reward mechanism. Thus, one could enhance reward characteristics by direct DA stimulation and also by NE suppression leading to a disinhibition of the DA mechanism. (Cf. discussion of reward by Virginia Douglas, this volume.) The important point is that multiple systems may influence reward and that the search for a single involved neurotransmitter may need to be replaced by a systems approach. (Cf. C. K. Conners' "The Psychophysiology of Stimulant Drug Response in Hyperkinetic Children," this volume.)

According to Gottfries (1980): "It is generally assumed that dysfunction in the brain arises from an imbalance between different transmitter systems." This may explain the findings that many patients do well with stimulant medication plus neuroleptic medication (Corboz, 1980) or neuroleptic (thioridazine) alone (Gittleman-Klein, Klein, Katz, Saraf, et al., 1976).

Recent work from Robertson's laboratory ". . . suggests a convergence of information from nonprimary sensory systems with information from the classical limbic system" (Robertson and Kaitz, 1981; Kaitz and Robertson, 1981; Robertson, Kaitz, and Robards, 1980). These studies are of interest concerning the aspect of motivation in ADD, discussed in Kinsbourne's chapter and Douglas's chapter in this volume.

The rapid accumulation of information about neurotransmitters, species differences in the function of the hippocampus, as demonstrated by Bennett (1975), and the impossibility of obtaining data from specific nuclei and neural tracts in the human brain with current methodology suggest that we probably must await the development of positron emission tomography (PET), BEAM, and other new noninvasive techniques before we can state with precision which neurotransmitters and what anatomical sites of the human brain are implicated in ADD. We hope that we have suggested fruitful lines of inquiry into areas of the brain, the hippocampus especially, for future research in ADD.

DISCUSSIONS

Marcel Kinsbourne

Many attempts have been made to formulate a model of hyperactivity and attentiveness, both at the behavioral level and at the brain level. None of them have achieved consensus. The authors are doing us a service by not defining for us which brain mechanism is responsible for this entity of interest but instead giving us a choice of possibilities. A reviewer or discussant should, if he is competent, do two things with respect to these suggestions: First, review the neurophysiological and neuropharmacological evidence in its own right, critically appraising the conclusions drawn by the investigators from their studies, and then review the behavioral manifestations that the authors regard as relevant to ADD and that correspond to those neurophysiological mechanisms.

When one deals with findings outside one's own field of expertise, one is inclined to believe what one is told. But given that, in one's own field, some 90% of what one is told is incorrect, one can assume that this is also the case in physiology and pharmacology. Which is the correct 10 percent?

Let us proceed to the behavioral level and first make the obvious point that attention, as a word, is such a general label that by virtue of the phenomenon of acquired equivalence of cues, one is tempted to include all sorts of diverse phenomena under this heading. A basic distinction, which I am sure hasn't escaped the authors, is between the intensive aspect of attention—the amount of mental effort that can be deployed—and its selective aspect. When one talks about dopaminergic mechanisms, one cannot include mental capacity. This appears to involve norepinephrinergic mechanisms, in relation to ascending alerting mechanisms. One should discuss the selective aspect of attention; that at least has a fighting chance of having dopamine involved in it.

The authors nominate a number of behaviors as representative of ADD. The first one is amnesia. They mention the well-known effects of bilateral hippocampal lesions on long-term memory in humans and wonder whether that long-term memory deficit has something to tell us about memory difficulties in ADD children.* We have worked intensively on the amnesic syndrome in adults, and so have many others, and we see no resemblance whatsoever in any aspect of that syndrome to anything that's ever been observed in ADD. Curiously enough, the suggestion has been made recently by Warrington and

---

*According to Squire (1980), "The brain structures involved in amnesia are not the sites of memory storage, but ... they are reqiuired for memory to be established in an enduring and usable way." Squire feels that the structures involved include the amygdala, cingulate gyrus, entorhinal cortex, medial frontal cortex, and perirhinal cortex, but he still reserves "a pre-eminent role for the hippocampal formation in memory functions" (p. 54)—Editor.

Weiskrantz (in press) that hippocampal lesions and amnesia are at the root of infantile autism. But if you are going to include amnesia someplace, it's at the other end of the spectrum of degree of sustained attention, where the autists are.

The second point addresses the orienting response (OR). There have been many studies of the OR and its habituation in ADD children. We have performed one study (Conte and Kinsbourne, in preparation) in which we found, in the resting state, no abnormality of the orienting response. If the OR is abnormal in these children, that is not a primary nor basic abnormality. We should not look there for a key to this syndrome. Of course, any syndrome may involve a number of systems to *some* extent.

Moving along to the third point in the paper, the suggestion is made that the rhythmic function that is attributable to the hippocampus may have to do with state-dependent memory. It is an interesting idea, but I suspect that the actual periodicity of state-dependence is at a much slower rate, over many hours, than the repetition rate of these rhythms.* However, if state-dependence in relation to stimulant therapy of hyperactive children (Swanson and Kinsbourne, 1979) could be modeled in preparations in which corresponding changes in hippocampal theta could be observed, this would be interesting. More important is the issue of selective attention, of the filtering of the relevant information. That is something that Dr. Douglas has reviewed authoritatively (Douglas and Peters, 1979). She concludes that nothing is the matter with the selective attention of ADD children, with their immediate attention to things, their inability to filter out the irrelevant and concentrate on relevant features. Stimulants change the findings in ADD children, but they do so equally in any child. We must look beyond selective attention for our valid behavioral model.

With respect to locomotor behavior, hippocampectomized rates locomote a lot and one can, in addition, point to the impressive stereotypical locomotion of rats who are overdosed with amphetamines. But everybody now recognizes that is not a matter of how much these kids move but of when and how they do, and animals also can show different movement patterns. Unfortunately, the animal models that have invoked increased locomotor behavior manifest rhythmic pacing rather than the unpredictable reorienting and locomoting to perpetually changing targets that we would prefer to see in our animal models of ADD. Locomotor behavior relative to changes of caudate function also is more valid as a model for stereotypical behavior, manneristic behavior, and repetitive behavior than it is for the restlessness of ADD children. Akathisia, mentioned by Dr. Davies, is seen in many normal people, when it is called *restless legs*, or *jittery legs*, or Ekbom's syndrome. The relevant thing

---

*The point made was that of phase, rather than frequency, as suggested in Figure 6. See page 45.–Editor.

about akathisia and restless legs is that they involve the legs, but not the rest of the person. This restlessness consists of a sudden need to move and jerk the leg, which comes on in the evening with fatigue and during sedentary activity, such as the playing of bridge. It is characterized by a subjective change which is known in Swedish as a *kryppening* in the legs. A person who feels this creeping, crawling sensation in his legs is impelled to jerk them. He gets up and pretends to be looking at his partner's hand. To my knowledge, ADD kids don't feel *kryppening*, and in ADD it isn't just legs.

The final point is the possibility of an abnormal reward system, suggested by Dr. Wender in 1971. This still remains an excellent candidate and one that I address to some extent in Chapter 7. With regard to neurotransmitter systems, I would like to point out the poignancy of the present situation relative to my introductory comment that we model, based on our best understanding of what the neuropharmacologists tell us, and then they change their story. There has been a sudden proliferation of neurotransmitters. Until a little while ago we had four or five to play with, now we have dozens of them. That's too many. As far as I am concerned, all bets are now off as to which neurotransmitter does what, where, and under the influence of which agent. A point made, which is very important, is that the search for a single involved neurotransmitter may need to be replaced by a systems approach (cf. Conners, Chapter 11). The brain is connected up and when one of the parts changes, others also do.* There will be a variety of metabolic rearrangements and a variety of neurotransmitter changes and we are not yet close to being able to figure those out.

Hallgrim Kløve

This interesting paper focuses on the problem of developing a model of ADD/MBD that makes sense both neurologically and psychologically. The last few years have seen the emergence of a number of biochemical, neurological, and neuropsychological correlates of ADD/MBD, but these studies have not significantly advanced our understanding of the mechanisms underlying the particular behavioral deficits with which we are concerned.

The goal must be to develop a model that makes both neurological, neuropsychological, and psychological sense. But the question is whether or not development of a model with a focus only on ADD/MBD is the best approach. The question is to what extent the ADD/MBD research should also be concerned with, for example, the abnormality in attention associated with childhood

---

*Cf. Kinsbourne (1974). Kinsbourne elaborates on the role of the right cerebral hemisphere in selective attention—Editor.

autism. Some evidence indicates that the abnormal findings with which we are concerned may be found on a continuum, where we may see Attention Deficit Disorder at one extreme and other types of attention problems at the other extreme of the continuum.

In our own laboratory, we have been interested in the question of serotonin level in ADD/MBD children. A study was undertaken to see how these variables would interact with administration of Ritalin. An experimental group was composed of children who were referred for neuropsychological evaluation because of unspecified behavior problems. Thus, the patients were not "prediagnosed" as hyperactive children. Based on anamnestic, observational, and clinical data, determination was made whether or not a child met a series of criteria for inclusion in the experimental group. The control group was selected on the basis of several comparison variables including absence of complaints regarding behavior problems in school, appropriate age, and intelligence within a normal range. An analysis of blood platelet serotonin determined that 80% of the hyperkinetic children had a serotonin level below the mean of the normal controls. There was no statistical difference between the normal controls, the hypoactive group (cerebral palsy), and the "other behavior pathology" group. The "other behavior pathology" group and the hyperactive group were given Ritalin for between 3–4 months, the average dose being 30 mg daily. A repetition of the serotonin studies indicated that the serotonin levels had increased significantly for the hyperactive group but were essentially unchanged in the "other behavior pathology" group (Table 1).

The significance of the differences in serotonin levels in the two groups is uncertain. It would, of course, be of considerable interest to do a similar study looking at the serotonin in the cerebrospinal fluid.

In another study, 56 of 62 children with the diagnosis of hyperkinetic behavior showed significant hyporeactivity of autonomic functions as reflected in skin conductance recordings. We have shown that marked hypoactivity in autonomic functions is normalized after administration of relatively small

Table 1. Blood Serotonin (Thrombocytes) in Various Groups

Group	N	Before Ritalin, mean (μg/ml)	After Ritalin for 3–4 months, mean (μg/ml)
Normal control	6	0.110	—
Hyperactive	31	0.066	0.087[a]
Hypoactive	9	0.160	—
Other behavior pathology	19	0.119	0.111[b]

[a]$p<0.01$.
[b]n.s.

dosages of Ritalin. This central hypoarousal state was not seen in another group of 12 children with the diagnosis of "behavior pathology" or in 10 normal children.

The autonomically hypoactive children were also characterized by marked deviations in intrauterine development, such as dysmaturity, high rates of pregnancy and delivery problems, an increased rate of minor physical abnormalities, and other developmental deviations both psychological and neurological.

We have also evaluated the relationship between autonomic variables and blood serotonin, but have been unable to demonstrate any relationship between the basal conductance level and the level of blood serotonin.

It is of interest that our findings related to blood serotonin seem to be similar to findings in the United States. Our finding that hyperactive children tend to have a hyporeactive autonomic nervous system that is normalized after administration of Ritalin would at least tend to throw doubt upon the concept of the central stimulant's "paradoxical" effect. Our finding that the hyperactive, hypoaroused group is characterized by a high degree of early developmental deviations would also tend to emphasize the viewpoint that the hyperkinetic syndrome seems to reflect a more serious condition than just a "developmental lag." In reviewing this stimulating chapter, I notice with interest that the viewpoints, the hypotheses, and the orientation of the studies reported are quite similar to what is going on in our own group.

REFERENCES

American Psychiatric Association. *Diagnostic and statistical manual of mental disorders* (3rd ed.). Washington, D.C., 1980, pp. 41–50.

Antelman, S. M. and Caggiula, A. R. Norepinephrine-dopamine interactions and behavior. *Science*, 1977, *195*:646–653.

Bannister, R. *Brain's clinical neurology*. (4th ed.) London: Oxford University Press, 1973.

Bennett, E. L. Electrical activity of the hippocampus and processes of attention. In R. L. Isaacson, and K. H. Pribram (Eds.), *The hippocampus*, Vol. 2. New York: Plenum Press, 1975, pp. 71–97.

Bloomingdale, L. M. and Bloomingdale, E. C. Minimal brain dysfunction: a new screening test and theoretical considerations. *Psychiatr. J. Univ. Ottawa*, 1980, *5*:295–306.

Brown, G., *Attention Deficit Disorder*, volume 2. New York: Spectrum Publications, in preparation.

Carpenter, M. B. *Human neuroanatomy*. (8th ed.) Baltimore: Williams and Wilkins, 1982.

Coleman, M., Steinberg, G., Tippett, J., Bhagavan, H. N., Coursin, D B., Gross, M., Lewis, C. and DeVeau, L. A preliminary study of the effect of pyridoxine administration in a subgroup of hyperkinetic children: a double-blind crossover comparison with methylphenidate. *Biological Psychiatry*, 1979, *4*:741–751.

Conners, C. K., and Rothschild, G. Drugs and learning in children. In J. Hellmuth (Ed.), *Learning disorders*, Vol. 3. Seattle: Special Child Publications, 1968.

Corboz, R. J. Psychiatry of early childhood minimal brain dysfunction. *Psychiat. J. Univ. Ottawa*, 1980, *5*:307–314.

Coyle, J. T., Price, D. L., and DeLong, M. R. Alzheimer's disease: a disorder of cortical cholinergic innervation. *Science*, 1983, *219*:1184–1190.

Davis, K. L., and Berger, P. A. Pharmacological investigations of the cholinergic imbalance hypotheses of movement disorders and psychosis. *Biol. Psychiatry*, 1978, *13*:23–49.

Deadwyler, S. A., West, M. O., and Robinson, J. H. Entorhinal and septal inputs differentially control sensory-evoked responses in the rate dentate gyrus. *Science*, 1981, *211*:1181–1183.

Douglas, V. I. and Peters, K. G. Toward a clearer definition of the attentional deficit of hyperactive children. In G. A. Hale and M. Lewis (Eds.), *Attention and the development of cognitive skills*. New York: Plenum Press, 1979.

Duffy, F. H., Denckla, M. B., Bartles, P. H., and Sandini, G. Dyslexia: regional differences in brain electrical activity by topographic mapping. *Ann. Neurol.*, 1980, *7*:412–420.

Dykman, R. A., Ackerman, P. T., Clements, S. D. and Peters, J. E. Specific learning disabilities: an attentional deficit syndrome. In H. Myklebust (Ed.), *Progress in learning disabilities* (Vol. 2). New York: Grune and Stratton, 1971.

Essman, W. B. (Ed.). *Neurotransmitters, receptors and drug action*. New York: Spectrum Publications, 1980.

Ferguson, H. B. and Pappas, B. A. (1979): Evaluation of psychophysiological, neurochemical, and animal models of hyperactivity. In R. L. Trites (Ed.), *Hyperactivity in children*. Baltimore: University Park Press, 1979. Table 1, p. 63.

Fuster, J. M. and Jervey, J. P. Inferotemporal neurons distinguish and retain behaviorally relevant features of visual stimuli. *Science*, 1981, *212*:952–954.

Fuxe, K., Lidbrink, P., Hökfelt, T., Bolme, P. and Goldstein, M. Effects of piperoxane on sleep and waking in the rat. *Acta Physiol. Scand.*, 1974, *91*:566–576.

Gittelman-Klein, R. and Klein, D. F. Methylphenidate effect in learning disabilities. 1. Psychometrics, *Arch. Gen. Psychiatry*, 1976, *33*:655–664.

Gittelman-Klein, R., Klein, D. F., Katz, S., Saraf, K., and Pollack, E. Comparative effects of methylphenidate and thioridazine in hyperkinetic children. *Arch. Gen. Psychiatry*, 1976, *33*:1217–1231.

Goldberg, J. O. and Konstantareas, M. M. Vigilance in hyperactive and normal children on a self-paced operant task. *J. Child Psychol. Psychiat.*, 1981, *22*:55–63.

Gottfries, C. G. Biochemistry of dementia and normal aging. *TINS*, 1981, *3*:55–57.

Gray, J. A. *The neuropsychology of anxiety: An enquiry into the functions of the septo-hippocampal system*. New York: Oxford University Press, 1982.

Hanley, J. and Sklar, B. (1976): Electroencephalographic correlates of developmental reading dyslexias: computer analyses of records from normal and dyslexic children. In G. Leisman (Ed.), *Basic visual processes and learning disability*. Springfield, Ill.: Thomas, 1976, pp. 217–243.

Iversen, S. D. and Iversen, L. L. Central neurotransmitters and the regulation of behaviour. In M. S. Gazzaniga and C. Blakemore, eds. *Handbook of psychobiology*. New York: Academic Press, 1975, 153–200.

Irwin, M., Belundink, K., McClosker, K., and Freedman, D. X. Tryptophan metabolism in children with attention deficit disorder. *Amer. J. Psychiat.*, 1981, *138*:1082–1085.

Iversen, S. D. Brain dopamine and behavior. In L. L. Iversen, S. D. Iversen and S. H. Snyder, eds. *Handbook of psychopharmacology*, vol. 8. New York: Plenum Press, 1977:333–384.

Kahn, E., and Cohen, L. H. Organic drivenness, *NEJM*, 1934, *210*:748–756.

Kaitz, S. S., and Robertson, R. T. Thalamic connections with limbic cortex. II. Corticothalamic projections. *J. Comparative Neurology*, 1981, *195*:527–545.

Khan, A. U. and Dekirmenjian, H. Urinary excretion of catecholamine metabolites in hyperkinetic child syndrome. *Amer. J. Psychiat.*, 1981, *138*: 108–110.

Kinsbourne, M. and Smith W. L. *Hemispheric Disconnections and Cerebral Function*. Springfield, Ill.: Charles C. Thomas, 1974, pp. 271–279.

Kostowski, W. Noradrenergic interactions among central neurotransmitters. In W. B. Essman, (Ed.), *Neurotransmitters, receptors and drug action*. New York: Spectrum Publications, 1980, pp. 47–65.

Lindvall, O. and Björklund, A. The organization of the ascending catecholamine neuron systems in the rat brain. *Acta Physiologica Scandinavica*, 1974. Supplementum 412, pp. 4–47.

Looker, A. and Conners, C. K. Diphenylhydantoin in children with severe temper tantrums. *Arch. Gen. Psychiat.*, 1970, *23*:80.

Luria, A. R. *The working brain*. New York: Basic Books, 1973, p. 256.

Mairlot, F. E. (1977): Approche pathogenique, sur base clinique et therapeutique, du syndrome de dysfoctionnement cerebral minime. *Congrés Organisé par la Société de Neurologie Infantile*, Marseille, France, 1977.

Mason, S. T. Noradrenaline and behaviour. *TINS*, 1979, *2*:82–84.

Mason, S. T. Noradrenaline and selective attention: A review of the model and the evidence. *Life Sciences*, 1980, *27*:617–631.

Mason, S. T. and Iversen F. D. Learning in absence of forebrain noradrenaline. *Nature*, 1975, *258*:422–424.

Matthysse, S. Dopamine and selective attention. In E. Costa and G. L. Gessa (Eds.), *Advances in biochemical psychopharmacology* (Vol. 16). New York: Raven Press, 1977, pp. 667–669.

Mueller, P. S., Koire, K., Rao, A. K., Christine, G., and Holmsen, H. A platelet secretion defect in attention deficit disorder. Presented at the American Psychosomatic Society Meeting, Cambridge, Massachusetts, 1981.

Munetz, M. R. and Cornes, C. L. Akathisia, pseudoakathisia and tardive dyskinesia: clinical examples. *Comprehensive Psychiat.*, 1982, *23*:345–352.

Nooteboom, W. E. *Some psychological aspects of the choreatiform syndrome*. Assen, The Netherlands, Van Gorcum and Co., 1967.

Owen, F. W., Adams, P. A., Forrest, T., Stolz, L. M., and Fisher, S. (1971): *Learning disorders in children: Sibling studies*. Monographs of the Society for Research in Child development, Serial No. 144, 1971, p. 34.

Nauta, W. J. H. and Feirtag, M. The organization of the brain. *Scientific American*, 1971, *241*:88–111.

Ojemann, R. G. Correlations between specific human brain lesions and memory changes. *Neurosciences Research Program Bulletin*, 1966, *4*:1–70, p. 20.

O'Keefe, J. and Nadel, L. *The hippocampus as a cognitive map.* London: Oxford University Press, 1978.

Paul, S. Neurotransmitter receptor plasticity. Presented at the 15th Annual Taylor Manor Hospital Psychiatric Symposium. Ellicott City, Maryland, 1983.

Pearson, D. E., Teicher, M. H., Shaywitz, B. A., Cohen, D. J., Young, J. G., and Anderson, G. M. Environmental influences on body weight and behavior in developing rats after neonatal 6-hydroxydopamine. *Science,* 1980, *209*:715–717.

Powell, E. M. and Hines, G. Septohippocampal interface. In R. L. Isaacson, and K. H. Pribram, (Eds.), *The hippocampus.* (Vol. 1). New York: Plenum Press, 1975.

Prechtl, H. F. R. and Stemmer, C. J. Ein Choreatiformes Syndrom bei Kindern, *Wiener Med. Wochenschr.,* 1959, *109*:22.

Robertson, R. T., Kaitz, S. S., and Robards, M. J. A subcortical pathway links sensory and limbic systems of the forebrain. *Neuroscience Letters,* 1980, *17*:161-165.

Robertson, R. T. and Kaitz, S. S. Thalamic connections with limbic cortex. I. Thalamocortical projections. *J. Comparative Neurology,* 1981, *195*: 501-525.

Scoville, W. B. and Milner, B. Loss of recent memory after bilateral hippocampal lesions. *J. Neurol. Neurosurg. Psychiatr.,* 1957, *20*:11–21.

Shaywitz, B. A., Klopper, J. H., Yager, R. D., and Gordon, J. W. Paradoxical response to amphetamine in developing rats treated with 6-hydroxydopamine. *Nature,* 1976, *261*:153–155.

Shaywitz, B. A., Yager, R. D. and Klopper, J. H. Selective Brain dopamine depletion in developing rats. *Science,* 1976, *191*:305–308.

Shaywitz, B. A., Cohen, D. J., and Bowers, M. B. CSF monoamine metabolites in children with MBD evidence for alteration of brain dopamine. *J. Pediatr.,* 1977, *90*:67–71.

Shekim, W. O., Dekirmenjian, H., and Chapel, J. L. Urinary MHPG excretion in minimal brain dysfunction and its modification by d-amphetamine. *Am. J. Psychiat.,* 1979, *136*:667–671.

Squire, L. R. The anatomy of amnesia. *TINS,* 1980, *3*:52–54.

Stamm, J. S. and Kreder, S. V. Minimal brain dysfunction: Psychological and neurophysiological disorders in hyperkinetic children. In M. S. Gazzaniga, (ed.), *Handbook of behavioral neurobiology* (Vol. 2). New York: Plenum Press, 1979, pp. 119–146.

Swanson, L. W. The hippocampus—new anatomical insights. *TINS,* 1979, *2*:9–12.

Swanson, J. M. and Kinsbourne, M. State-dependent learning and retrieval: methodological cautions and theoretical considerations. In J. F. Kihlstrom and F. J. Evans, (Eds.), *Functional disorders of memory.* New York: John Wiley, 1979, pp. 275–299.

Sykes, D. H., Douglas, V. I., Weiss, G., and Minde, K. K. Attention in hyperactive children and the effect of methylphenidate (ritalin). *J. Child Psychol. Psychiat.,* 1971, *12*:129–139.

Van Putten, T. The many faces of akathisia. *Comprehensive Psychiatry,* 1975, *16*:43–47.

Vinogradova, O. S. Functional organization of the limbic system in the process of registration of information: facts and hypotheses. In R. L. Isaacson and

K. H. Pribram (Eds.), *The hippocampus* (Vol. 2). New York: Plenum Press, 1975, pp. 3–60.

Wender, P. H. *Minimal brain dysfunction in children*. New York: John Wiley, 1971.

Wender, P. H. Minimal brain dysfunction: an overview. In M. A. Lipton, A. DiMascio, and K. F. Killam (Eds.), *Psychopharmacology*. New York: Raven Press, 1978, pp. 1429–1435.

Wise, R. A. Action of drugs of abuse on brain reward systems. *Pharmacol. Biochem. and Behav.*, 1980, *13*:213–223.

4

Remarks on the
Neurotransmitter Hypothesis

PAUL H. WENDER

EDITOR'S COMMENTS

In this chapter, several features in favor of the dopamine hypothesis are discussed. The different effects of methylphenidate, pemoline, and amphetamine are described. In addition to the dopamine hypothesis, a phenethylamine hypothesis is raised.

In Dr. Wender's presentation the specific hypotheses are capable of being tested directly, as opposed to "metaneuropharmacology," wherein no data can be obtained that will either confirm or negate the hypotheses.

Dr. Wender describes experiments with high-avoidant and low-avoidant rats and the study of the effects of various neurotransmitters. In addition, the dopamine response to amphetamine in hyperactive dogs shows that these animals have lower levels of dopamine and lower levels of dopamine turnover.

Neurotransmitter metabolite values of the spinal fluid of hyperactive adults are described. Molecular diagrams of dopamine, phenylalanine, phenethylamine, and phenylacetic acid are included and their structure is compared to that of amphetamine. Current research is being conducted on the precursor, phenylalanine, and principle metabolite, phenylacetic acid, of phenethylamine, that is, demethylated amphetamine.

*   *   *

It is indeed the case that the pharmacodynamics of the active drugs have not been fully worked out and our partial knowledge can lead the eager experimenter astray. For instance, Sol Snyder formulated the hypothesis that d- and l-amphetamine had strikingly differential effects on dopamine and norepinephrine. Based on that erroneous conclusion, Keith McCloskey, Gene Arnold, and I did a double-blind crossover study of d- and l-amphetamine and placebo.

Those of you who have attempted to maintain a 4^+ hyperactive child on placebo for three weeks will know what incredible psychological skills we had to exercise merely to complete this inconclusive experiment.

What is relevant to my ghastly statement about our partial knowledge of pharmacodynamics is that, after the completion of our experiment, Sol reversed his views. Nine weeks and thirteen angry mothers (from the three weeks the children were on placebo) later, we discovered we had been wasting our time.

The dopamine hypothesis has several features in its favor. First of all, waiving my statement that the pharmacodynamics of these drugs are not completely explicated, it is clearly the case that tricyclics don't work well in children with ADD. Dr. Garfinkel and I have shown that they don't work very well and others have found that when they do work, children develop tolerance. This is circumstantial evidence. Since the current evidence is that the tricyclic antidepressants work by increasing the activity of noradrenergic and serotoninergic systems, we can assume tentatively (based, as I have said, upon our slippery knowledge of pharmacodynamics) that noradrenalin and serotonin are not playing a significant role in the pathogenesis of ADD.

My current speculation is that a substantial number of individuals with ADD suffer from their problems because of decreased dopaminergic—or possibly phenethylaminergic—activity. To the best of my knowledge, methylphenidate and pemoline are interesting in that they are indirect dopamine agonists, i.e., unlike amphetamine, which is a very "dirty" drug, these two drugs simply act by releasing dopamine from storage granules.* Amphetamine is an MAO inhibitor, a direct agonist which causes the release from storage of NE, 5-HT, DA, so that, it is compounded, like a doctor's prescription, to have a threefold activity.

What ways are there of subjecting the dopamine hypothesis to a test? The best hypothesis is not necessarily the most explanatory. The scientific philosopher Carl Popper has stated that a good hypothesis does more than explain the observed facts. A good hypothesis should provide a rationale for the observed facts, but it should do more. It should suggest experiments or tests that can invalidate or support it. From a hypothesis, you draw inferences, each of which is susceptible to disproof, and the harder the time you have disproving them, the happier you feel.

What are the data relevant in particular to the dopamine and the phenethylamine hypothesis?

---

*Fischer and Cho (1979) recently showed that amphetamine causes release of cytoplasmic dopamine through the axonal membrane, rather than producing release of dopamine from dopamine from storage granules (neurotransmitter vesicles)—Editor.

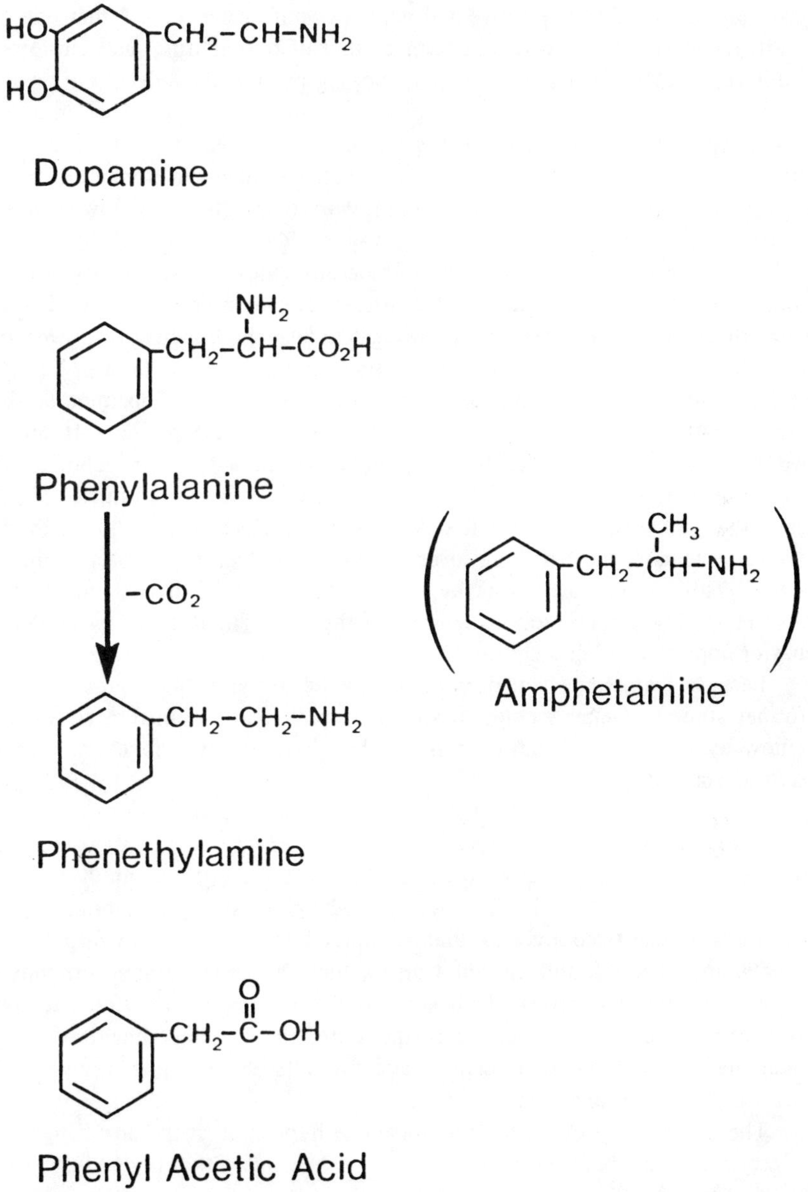

Figure 1. Precursors and metabolite of PEA (phenethylamine) compared to amphetamine.

In *Minimal Brain Dysfunction in Children*, I advanced the hypothesis that many of the symptoms of MBD could be interpreted as relative refractoriness to social conditioning (both positive and negative reinforcement) and that one of the effects of stimulants could be seen as that of potentiating such reinforcement (Wender, 1971). I reasoned that, looking at animal models, one would expect that animals who condition poorly would have deficiencies in their dopaminergic systems. Back in 1971, I imported to the NIMH, at considerable expense and nuisance, two strains of rats, that we called the Roman (because they came from Rome) High-Avoiders and Low-Avoiders (high- and low-avoiders because of their performance in a two-way avoidance test). The little low-avoidant creatures were of great interest because they showed a magnificent response to amphetamine: when administered amphetamine, they avoided as well as their cousins. Whereupon, we brought to bear the full analytic powers of the NIMH and came up with some interesting findings. Joe Coyle, Ann Lipsky, and I looked at dopamine turnover, dopamine synthesis vs. dopamine levels: the high- and low-avoiders were exactly the same in these respects. It subsequently turned out that the low-avoiding rats had very active cholinergic systems. If you think about this in terms of current neurotransmitter hypotheses, this makes sense: rather than having underactive "central sympathetic nervous systems," they had an overactivity of a "central parasympathetic system." This would lead to the hypothesis that they would respond to centrally active parasympathetolytic agents and they did. The Roman low-avoiders' behavior improved on scopolamine.

Because I am somewhat perseverative, I did not give up. I had converted a former student, Gene Arnold, to stimulantophilia, and he in turn convinced a fellow by the name of Sam Corson, at Ohio State, to try amphetamine on a bizarre strain of dogs.

These dogs are interesting, hyperactive Telomian-beagle hybrids and difficult to condition, the latter being what I regard as one of the major critical attributes of ADD hyperactive people. These little creatures, about half of them, got better on "speed." This was picked up by an Italian group, led by Bargetti, who sacrificed hybrids that responded to and failed to respond to amphetamine. They found, as did Corson, that the amphetamine responders not only became less active, which is a trivial attribute of the syndrome, but also became docile and obedient; furthermore, the amphetamine-responding animals had lower levels of dopamine and lower levels of dopamine turnover. Score 1 for my delusional system!

The second way of testing the dopamine hypothesis is invasive. One simply inserts a needle between two adjacent vertebra and withdraws CSF. One of the difficulties with children is that you can't get informed consent for non-therapeutic procedures. Accordingly, we addressed our attention to adults with residual ADD, an interesting group in themselves, who can give informed consent. The collaborators were myself, Fred Reimherr, Dave Wood, Len Jarko and K. C. Wong, the Chairman of Anesthesiology. Dr. Wong was particularly helpful. He and his residents used gauge 40 needles to extract volumes of fluid which were then sent by overnight service to the NIMH to be analyzed by our NIMH collaborator Michael Ebert. Our hypothesis was, of course, that adults with ADD (ADD, Residual Type or ADD, RT) who responded to methylphenidate, would, as compared to controls, have low levels of the principal metabolite of dopamine, HVA. This was undoubtedly the case with women. In the case of the men, there were two outliers (low HVA) who were among the controls so that parametric tests did not statistically distinguish between the two groups, although nonparametric tests did and in the predicted direction.

What we must now do is to enlarge the size of our control group to strengthen (or retest) our findings. One other finding was consistent with our hypothesis, of interest, and a surprise. In the case of the men, those subjects who became worse on methylphenidate had much higher HVA levels than the normals and the drug responders. From what I have said, you can see that there are a number of data, both from animal experiments and the human experiments my colleagues and I are conducting, that are consonant with the dopamine hypothesis.

Another technique of testing a monoamine hypothesis is to administer a "load" of the amino acid which is a precursor of the neurotransmitter. For dopamine, the amino acid is L-dopa. We did administer L-dopa to our patients and, much to our surprise, all our patients became duller, sleepy, and couldn't concentrate very well. Since I'm also an expert neurometapsychopharmacologist, there was no difficulty in explaining that. The beauty of neurometapsychopharmacology is that it predicts any outcome and cannot be invalidated by any findings. However, there are other precursors which we must try; one is tyrosine, which goes to form dopamine, NE and tyramine; there is the amino acid phenylalanine, which may play a role by being decarboxylated to a current sexy candidate, phenethylamine (PEA). PEA is amphetamine without the methyl group and might be "endogenous amphetamine." In certain schizophrenic circles PEA is of considerable interest as a compound that may be in excess in paranoid schizophrenia. Our hypothesis would be, based on my 1971 observation (Wender, 1971) that some MBD children have "congenital hypoamphetaminemia"; that, if anything, individuals with ADD should have low PEA and PEA metabolites. We are exploring the PEA hypothesis now in two ways: (1) by administering phenylalanine, the amino acid precursor of PEA, to patients with ADD, RT; and (2) by measuring the amounts of PEAA, the principle metabolite of PEA in the urine and blood, of patients with ADD, RT, and matched controls.

In summary, we are making specific hypotheses that can be directly tested. To test our theories, we might prefer to examine brain slices from our patients, as has been done with the Telomian-beagle dogs. Because we have a very tough human experimentation committee in that regard, and because many people refuse to have brain biopsies, we are forced to use these chemical methods that make direct predictions which will be testable.

REFERENCES

Fischer, J. F., and Cho, A. K. Chemical release of dopamine from striatal homogenates: evidence for an exchange diffusion model. *J. Pharm. and Exp. Therapeutics*, 1979, *208*:203–209.

Wender, Ph. L. *Minimal brain dysfuction in children.* New York: John Wiley, 1971.

5

A Neuropediatric and Neuropsychological Prospective Study of Learning Disorders: A Three-Year Follow-up

GUY WILLEMS, RAYMONDE BERTE-DEPUYDT,
NICOLE DE LEVAL, ANDRÉ BOUCKAERT, ANDRÉ NOEL,
AND PHILIPPE EVRARD

A homogeneous group of 281 Caucasian boys were assessed at 5½ to 6¼ years of age and reassessed at 8½ to 9¼ years, using a comprehensive examination of personality, social status, neurological functions, cortical functions, psychometric evaluation, and academic achievement. The social status was average to high. The results (continuous distributions) on the academic achievement test at 9 years can be predicted with confidence at 6 years by Finger Agnosia, Total I.Q., and Sequential Organization. Dyslexia and dyscalculia at 9 years can be predicted at 6 years with reasonable confidence by Verbal Sequential Memory, Finger Discrimination, Picture Naming (verbal), Similarities, Finger Agnosia, Dysgraphesthesia, Visual Discrimination (+), and Auditory Discrimination.

The authors gratefully acknowledge the constructive criticism of M. Kinsbourne, P. Satz, and D. Bakker in the early preparation of this work. This research was supported in part by funds from the Belgian Ministère de la Santé Publique (Dr. Claus, Dr. Francois), the Loterie Nationale, and the Fondation Roi Baudouin.

INTRODUCTION

The setting up of a battery for the predictive examination or the early identification of children at high risk for learning disabilities is a difficult scientific task, which should be addressed with great caution. A critical review of current literature on early identification shows that a number of problems tend to limit the validity of these examinations (Keogh and Becker, 1973; Satz and Fletcher, 1979; Lindsay and Wedell, 1982).

Problems in Early Identification

In the first place, little is known about the prevalence of reading disabilities with regard to a differentiation between backward readers and children with specific reading retardation (Yule and Rutter, 1976; Rutter, 1978). Furthermore, this prevalence varies with the child's age, sex, and with the cultural background in which the study is conducted.

Definitions of learning disabilities tend to differ (Celdic Report 1970, page 51). There are confusions between screening and diagnostic examinations and between early identification and prediction examinations (Cross, 1977). Measuring instruments and tests are quite often inadequate (Coles, 1978; Satz and Fletcher, 1979; Schery, 1980).

The setting up of an early identification or of a prediction system would require systems of classification of learning disabilities into subgroups, and also thereafter a knowledge of their specific predictors.

There is often a close connection between identification procedures and remediation or treatment programs (Strag, 1972; Muehl and Forell, 1973); however, there is much controversy on remediation programs and therapeutic interventions (Zigmond, 1978). Premature labeling as *learning-disabled* can have noxious consequences (Rosenthal and Jacobson, 1968).

Another problem in early identification stems from the child himself: the so-called "within-child factors." It can be assumed, or presupposed, that the development of certain cortical functions follows a chronological order that is thus predictable and implies continuity in the child's development. These assumptions require a better understanding of the natural course of the development and evolution of learning disabilities over time. Various studies have evinced the variability over time of the child's academic achievement and indicate that this is probably related to the child's capacity for putting compensating abilities into play (Keogh, 1974; Wedell, 1980), or, possibly also, to the inconsistency of the scholastic performances of children who are experiencing problems at school (Keogh and Smith, 1968; Feshbach, Adelman, and Fuller, 1977; Belmont and Belmont, 1978; Hall and Keogh, 1978).

Yet another series of problems are due to "extra-child factors." These external factors—belonging to the school and home environment, to the person of the teacher or to the educational system—can impair the validity of early identification (Adelman, 1971).

The predictive accuracy of an examination varies as a function of language, cultural background, socioeconomic status, and the child's previous experience in those environments (Sbordone and Keogh, 1975; Oakland, 1978; Pollack, 1980).

Methodology and Statistics

Other problems are related to the methodology and statistical instruments. The predictive power of the variables used in the examination varies with the nature and number of the variables chosen and with the statistical method applied. Our choice of the predictive variables is subject to rapid change as our understanding of the neurolinguistic and cognitive mechanisms of learning to read improves.

Certain methodological criteria should be applied when developing a predictive examination battery. First of all, the detection battery must be validated. There should be a sufficiently long temporal separation between the administration of the identification test battery and the diagnostic assessment of specific learning disorders (test-criterion interval). We suggest a time lapse of at least three years.

The study should be based at the outset on a total population, rather than on a selected sample of subjects at risk. Follow-up should take place in the framework of a longitudinal prospective study. The population selected should be, in our opinion, as homogeneous as possible, by considering "extra-child" factors, for instance, and maybe, in a first stage, by selecting solely boys.

Utilization of multiple cross-validation groups seems useful also (Satz and Friel, 1974). In the latter area, it would be good to apply total "hit-rate" analysis, which includes matrix analysis, and to study true and false positives and negatives (Meehl and Rosen, 1955; Mercer, Algozzine and Trifiletti, 1979). It seems also necessary to resort to a study of conditional probabilities (Feshbach, Adelman, and Fuller, 1974; Deruiter, Ferrel and Kass, 1975; Wissinik, Kass and Ferrel, 1975) as well as to a multivariate statistical analysis of the results (Satz and Fletcher, 1979).

OBJECTIVES AND DESIGN OF THE BRUSSELS STUDY

Objective

Our purpose was to identify and predict specific learning disabilities through a neuropediatric and neuropsychological examination. This, of course, implied that only "within-child" factors were considered. This modest objective, limited in scope, was based on the critical review of the literature that we presented in the preceding section. We endeavored in our research to select a standardized sample wherein the influence of "extra-child" factors was kept to a minimum. Accordingly, we aimed at obtaining a population as homogeneous as possible with respect to social, linguistic, cultural, environmental, and educational background. All these areas have already been discussed in numerous studies, especially in Europe and more specifically in the French school.

Subject Selection

Our selection of subjects was based upon the defining criteria of learning disabilities as set out in the Common Law of the United States.

Using intelligence tests (WISC), a sample of normally intelligent children was extracted and, on the basis of medical anamnesis and physical examination (by the school doctor), only children in good health and free of any severe auditory or visual problems where retained. In order to reduce as much as possible the effects of "extra-child" factors, we selected a unilingual population (to the exclusion of bilingual children) of Belgian nationality and with a socioeconomic status average to high. The children were enrolled in 19 different schools distributed over Brussels and attended school regularly.

In this way, and by applying the above criteria, 281 normal children were retained out of an originally much larger sample. At the beginning of the study, the subjects' ages ranged from 5 years and 6 months to 6 years and 3 months (5½ to 6¼ years), average 5; 10 (5 years and 10 months). Our decision to study a male cohort stemmed from the fact that a number of studies have demonstrated that there is 3-to-1 to 7-to-1 male predominance in the area of specific learning disabilities or dyslexia (Money, 1966; Benton, 1975; Hier, 1979). Lovell, Shapton, and Warren (1964) reported that the predominance of dyslexic boys increases with higher I.Q. scores. Witelson's studies (1976) on hemispheric specialization, "Sex and the Single Hemisphere," tend to indicate that dyslexia in boys is related to a different brain organization than in girls.

The data were collected from April to November 1977; the subjects were tested individually for four hours by a team of physicians and psychologists, who carried out all assessments in school so as not to interfere with the natural scholastic setting (Yule and Rutter, 1977). The children were followed up for a period of three years; they were assessed for reading and math levels in grades two and three. This was a sufficiently long temporal separation between testing and criterion follow-up (test-criterion interval). As a matter of fact, according to the definition of dyslexia adopted by the World Federation of Neurology, there must be a lag of at least two years in reading skill before the concept of dyslexia can meaningfully be applied. A three-year follow-up was long enough to avoid scores being affected by labile or momentary learning disorders. Eventually, a stepwise multiple regression and a stepwise discriminant analysis elicited the predictor variables by a procedure that will be explained later.

Choice of Predictor Variables

The test battery administered at the age of 5 years and 10 months included a neuropediatric examination (27 variables) (Willems, Noel and Evrard, 1979), a neuropsychological examination (11 variables) (Willems, Berte-Depuydt, and de Leval, 1982), an intelligence test (WISC, 9 variables, de Leval, Berte-Depuydt, Bouckaert, and Willems, 1982), and a personality test (one variable). The intelligence test was a short-form WISC test composed of the following subtests: arithmetic, similarities, vocabulary, picture arrangement, block design, and coding, proposed by Berte-Depuydt (1981a), giving the best approximation of the I.Q. level at this age. A total of 45 variables were assessed and 183 data were obtained on each child. The variables had been chosen among those retained for their predictive power by authors such as: Kinsbourne (1963, 1975); Jansky and de Hirsch (1972); Silver and Hagin (1975); Satz and Friel (1973); Martin Bax (1973, in his study of the Isle of Wight) and many others (Zazzo , Ajuriaguerra, Borel-Maisonny, et al., 1952; Van Wayenberghe, 1959; Burion, 1960; Frostig and Maslow, 1973; Inizan, 1965; Borel-Maisonny, 1956; Santucci and Pechaux, 1967; Dehant, 1968; Limbosch, Luminet-Jasinski and Dierkens-Dopchie, 1968; Zazzo, 1969; Debray-Ritzen and Badrig Mélekian, 1970; Sand et al., 1974; Klees, 1979; Estienne, 1977).

The rationale was to compare the predictive power of certain variables such as: (1) specific neurological signs (the "soft signs" of English-speaking authors; psychomotor or neuromotor disorders of the French school or sensory-integration of the English-speaking school); (2) the psychometric tests derived from WISC subtests or personality tests; (3) the various pediatric neuropsychological examinations.

Testing was administered to a homogeneous group of boys with a mean age of 6 years to 6 years and 3 months (average 5 years, 10 months).

Three-Year Follow-Up Study

In order to identify the population of children performing poorly in reading or in math or in both skills, we administered in grades 2 and 3 academic tests similar to the WRAT, using the criteria discussed by Satz and Fletcher (1979), Doehring, Hoshko, and Bryans (1979) and others. The test batteries used were: the "Poucet" (Simon, 1954), an expressive reading test; the California reading test (Tiegs and Clark, 1967; Claes and Gille, 1967; Dehant, 1968) a receptive or semantic reading test; and a math achievement test (Bonboir, 1969).

Our purpose was to identify all cases of poor academic achievement, regardless of their causes (truancy, psychiatric problems, teacher's disability or incompetence, incorrect teaching methods, etc. In this well-defined sample, we intend in future to isolate the various dyslexia or dyscalculia subgroups, by means of another neurolinguistic battery, and by using a statistical method of cluster analysis.

This method had the following advantages: (1) it was not biased by such subjective elements as school reports and teachers' evaluation; (2) it permitted us to examine a cohort of normal children on the basis of objective reading tests administered to a total, homogeneous population; (3) it enabled us to identify, by two types of reading tests, an expressive one and a receptive one (semantic or comprehension), the predictor variables related to these two aspects of reading.

The method's limitation was that it lacked diagnostic accuracy and failed to isolate subgroups of specific learning disabilities and pure dyslexia (i.e., to differentiate between backward readers and children with specific reading retardation, on the basis of the analysis of types of errors examined in a neurolinguistic approach). As already stated, this is the object of a study underway at the University of Louvain.

METHODOLOGY

Three major prediction types are proposed in this chapter. The first two involved "mixed" subjects, that is to say, subjects who may be at the same time poor readers and dyscalculics. The third prediction method was by exclusion, in which case the subjects studied were "pure" cases (e.g., dyscalculia without associated dyslexia, or vice versa). The advantage in selecting "pure" cases was, on the one hand, that it refined the predictive instruments and, on the other hand, that it led to an understanding of the natural history of the development of these "pure" subgroups.

The construction of the three predictive instruments was aimed at two major objectives. The purpose of the first method was to forecast the scores on a pedagogical criterion test of reading or math achievement (stepwise multiple regression) after a test-criterion interval of at least three years; the two other predictive methods attempted to forecast to which subgroup of poor or good readers (or calculators) the subjects would belong, our purpose being here effectively to predict dyslexia (Type I or Type II and/or dyscalculia (stepwise discriminant analysis).

With respect to the statistical method used in stepwise multiple regression, the question we raised was the following: considering that scores obtained on the criterion tests administered at the elementary school are regarded as following normal distribution curves, can the value of those performances be predicted on the sole basis of an examination at grade K (that is, three years previously)?

The method aimed at defining a predictive function based on predictors observable at grade K that, provided the degree of accuracy was satisfactory, would permit forecast of the child's performance on an expressive reading level test (Poucet), or on a receptive reading test (California), or on a math achievement test (Bonboir) three years later. We furthermore endeavored to achieve the greatest possible predictive accuracy obtainable when using a minimal number of predictive factors. This could be achieved by applying stepwise multiple regression analysis to each of the three tests.

The statistical method of stepwise discriminant analysis aimed at forecasting, with an error rate as low as possible, the position, with respect to a given acceptability threshold level (chosen cut-off scores), of the scores that would be obtained on the reading level and math achievement criterion tests. The sample of children re-examined at the elementary school was divided into two groups according to a performance criterion. This amounted to predicting which subjects would belong, respectively, to one of the following subgroups:

(a) *In the "Mixed" Cases*: M1 (Good expressive readers); M2 (Type I dyslexia, poor expressive readers); C1 (Good receptive readers); C2 (Type II dyslexia, poor receptive readers); B1 (Good calculators); B2 (Dyscalculia or poor calculators); MCB2 (Learning disorders associated with overall deficit);

(b) *In the "Pure" Cases*: Po (No failure); P4 (Type I dyslexia, poor readers in expressive reading only); P2 (Type II dyslexia, poor readers in receptive reading only); P1 (Dyscalculia, poor calculators failing in math only).

The question we approach in using the stepwise discriminant analysis is whether the evaluation performed at grade K enables us to forecast to which subgroup a subject will belong.

PREDICTORS OF PERFORMANCES ON CRITERION TESTS

In this chapter, we attempted to define, on the basis of examinations and tests administered to children aged 5 years 10 months (grade K), a predictive function that should enable us (provided we worked with adequate accuracy) to forecast the scores they would obtain three years later on the follow-up tests; these criterion tests were an expressive reading level test (Poucet), a receptive reading level test (California), and a math achievement test (Bonboir).

We furthermore endeavored to achieve a maximal predictive value on the basis of a minimal number of predictive factors. The statistical method used to this end was stepwise multiple regression analysis applied to each of the three tests.

Table 1. Predictors of Performance on Tests[a]

Expressive reading level test

Predictor	Coefficient
1 Predictor M. Corr. Coeff. = 0.608	
Finger agnosia (R)	
5 Predictors M. Corr. Coeff. = 0.721	
Finger agnosia (R)	+3.7320
Verbal sequential memory	-3.5579
Dysdiadochokinesis (R)	-3.0968
Sequential organization	+1.0820
Auditory discrimination	-4.1400
10 Predictors M. Corr. Coeff. = 0.777	
Finger agnosia (R)	+3.6636
Verbal sequential memory	-3.5117
Dysdiadochokinesis (R)	-3.4341
Sequential organization	+1.1134
Auditory discrimination	-4.9146
Simultanagnosia	-0.7198
Block design	-0.7409
Embedded F. T.	+0.1221
Nystagmus	+2.4562
Dysgraphaesthesia (R)	+0.4403

Constant = 50.313

Receptive reading level test

Predictor	Coefficient
1 Predictor M. Corr. Coeff. = 0.458	
Total IQ	
5 Predictors M. Corr. Coeff. = 0.664	
Total IQ	+0.1198
Verbal sequential memory	-9.099
Spatial discrimination	+3.884
Vocabulary	+0.2129
Finger agnosia (left)	+2.5899
10 Predictors M. Corr. Coeff. = 0.742	
Total IQ	+0.0578
Verbal sequential memory	-9.1450
Spatial discrimination	+3.3773
Vocabulary	+0.1834
Finger agnosia (L)	+1.8662
Simultanagnosia	-1.2550
Jump on one foot (R)	-4.4596
Finger praxia (L)	+3.5784
Picture naming (verbal)	+0.2282
Koch	-0.8680

Constant = 33.838

Math achievement test

Predictor	Coefficient
1 Predictor M. Corr. Coeff. = 0.446	
Sequential organization	
18 Predictors M. Corr. Coeff. = 0.720	
Sequential organization	+3.1439
Block design	+0.0387
Finger discrimination (R)	-6.1594
Sequential memory	-5.4516
Perseveration	-7.6183
Sentence Memory	+0.3491
Astereognosis	-7.3445
Performance IQ	+0.3857
Picture naming	-0.4383
Finger praxia (L)	-6.3990
Finger praxia (R)	+3.8174
Imitation of gestures	+1.1032
Finger agnosia (L)	+1.5045
Coding	-0.1332
Spatial discrimination	+1.7010
Jump on one foot (R)	-2.0430
Dysgraphaesthesia (L)	-1.4783
Dysgraphaesthesia (R)	+1.2000

Constant = 33.056

[a]Stepwise Multiple Regression Analysis

Prediction of Performances on the Expressive Reading Level Criterion Test

Finger agnosia (right) was the predictive test that correlated highest with the scores on the expressive reading level criterion-test, with a simple correlation coefficient of 0.608 and a standard error of 7.65 (Table 1.). Predictive accuracy could be improved by including additional predictive factors. With five test results, for instance, the multiple correlation coefficient increased to 0.721, with a standard error of 6.82.

The performances on the expressive reading criterion level test were predicted by means of an equation using the following predictive tests: (1) Finger agnosia (right); (2) Verbal sequential memory; (3) Dysdiadochokinesis (right); (4) Sequential organization; and (5) Auditory discrimination.

If we now wish to interpret these results, we should proceed very cautiously, since predictive factors should obviously not be confused with etiology. The association of the performances on the finger agnosia test with those obtained on the expressive reading level test suggested that identical cerebral functions might be involved. In both tasks, for instance, it is the expressive aspect of reading that is put into play, namely, with sequentially presented verbal material.

It should be noted here that the only variables that proved to have predictive value were the neuropsychological variables, whereas the psychological variables and the soft neurological signs appeared to be of little value as predictors of performances on the selected criterion reading tests.

The block design test (WISC) ranked only seventh, far behind the neuropsychological variables. It had, furthermore, a negative sign, which indicated that good performances on the block design test were registered in this equation as predicting a slight decrease of the subject's performances on the expressive reading level test, which was paradoxical.

The same remark can be addressed to the examination of soft neurological signs such as dysdiadochokinesis (right), which was negatively correlated with the performances on the reading test.

With 10 predictors, the multiple correlation coefficient increased to 0.777 with a standard error of 6.37. The expression of the equation is:

Predictors of Performance on Tests, Stepwise Multiple Regression Analysis

$$\text{Predicted Test Result} = \text{Constant} + \Sigma_i \left[(\text{Coefficient of Predictor i}) \times (\text{Result of Test i})\right]$$

The predictive value of the equation can still be increased at this stage by including more variables, but the resulting increase of the multiple correlation coefficient is insignificant.

Beyond the tenth variable, the equation admits successively the following predictors: dysgraphaesthesia (left), picture arrangement, digit span, visual discrimination.

It can be observed in the above equation that the predictive power of the conventional psychological tests was low as compared with that of the neurological and neuropsychological tests; Koch's test ranked only 19th and verbal I.Q. 25th.

Prediction of Performances on the Receptive Reading Level Test

The predictive test administered at the age of 5 years and 10 months, the performances on which correlated highest with those obtained on the California criterion test, was the total IQ, with a multiple correlation coefficient of 0.458 and a standard error of 12.32 (see Table 1). A possible interpretation of this outcome would be that there is a closer relation between intelligence tests and receptive reading (comprehension of the text read) than there is between intelligence and expressive reading.

Combining the 5 most predictive measures for the receptive reading level test, a multiple correlation coefficient of 0.664 was obtained, with a standard error decreasing to 10.597. With 10 predictors, the figures become 0.742 and 9.769 respectively; at this stage, the predictive function includes the items shown in Table 1.

Clearly, performances on the receptive reading test (California) were more markedly affected by the conventional psychological variables (e.g., I.Q.).

Prediction of Performances on the Math Achievement Test

Regarding the predictive tests administered at the age of 5 years and 10 months, the performance that correlated highest with the scores on the math achievement criterion test administered at the age of 8 years and 6 months (grade 3, elementary school) was the sequential organization test, but with a multiple correlation coefficient of 0.446 and a standard error of 14.882. There was a definite correlation between performances in math and the ability to organize a task sequentially, especially during the early stages of learning math.

To obtain a multiple correlation coefficient of 0.72, no less than 18 predictor variables had to be taken into the predictive equation. In this case, the equation was composed of the items shown in Table 1. Note that the arithmetic subtest (WISC) is lacking in the list.

Summary

We compared the students' performances in grade 3 on (1) the expressive reading level test (Poucet), (2) the receptive reading level test (California), and (3) the math achievement test (Bonboir) with the students' earlier performance in kindergarten on neuropediatric examinations, neuropsychologic examinations, intelligence tests, and personality tests. The best predictors of later performance were shown to be as follows: (1) for the expressive reading level test, finger agnosia (right); (2) for the receptive reading level test, total I.Q.; (3) for the math achievement test, sequential organization.

The use of the statistical method of stepwise multiple regression analysis permitted us to establish, on the basis of a minimal number of predictor variables, the prediction of the global performance on a criterion test.

The method had, however, the limitation that it predicted success rather than failure on the academic criterion tests three years later, because there was, within our normal total population, a lower incidence of cases of failure than of cases of success. That the prediction that the subject would belong to the group of poor readers (rather than to that of good readers) seems more readily usable in clinical practice. This is a subject we will discuss in the following section.

PREDICTION OF THE CRITERION SUBGROUP TO WHICH A SUBJECT WILL BELONG

While the stepwise multiple regression analysis, utilized in the preceding section, aimed at predicting as accurately as possible the scores that would be made on later tests, stepwise discriminant analysis aimed at predicting, with the lowest possible error rate, what the *position* would be of subject's scores on the expressive reading level, receptive reading level, and math achievement level criterion tests, with respect to an acceptability threshold. (Would his scores be below or above the cut-off scores?) This amounted to predicting, for instance, that the subject would belong respectively to one of the following criterion subgroups: expressive reading dyslexics, defined as type I dyslexia (Poucet reading test); receptive reading dyslexics, defined as type II dyslexia (California reading test); dyscalculics (Bonboir math achievement test, 1961, 1969).

The criteria applied in defining these subgroups at the elementary school (grade 3) were the objective performances on reading and math achievement criterion tests and not the teacher's subjective ratings (school reports).

The reading tests were the Poucet (Simon, 1954; Burion, 1956) investigation of the expressive aspect of reading and the California (Tiegs and Clark, 1967; Claes and Gille, 1967; Dehant, 1968) investigation of the receptive aspect of reading.

Pupils scoring higher than 51 on the Poucet test constituted subgroup M2 (Type I dyslexia), the others formed subgroup M1 (Good expressive readers). Pupils whose scores on the California reading test were lower than 34 constituted subgroup C2 (Type II dyslexia), the others formed subgroup C1 (Good receptive readers). Lastly, pupils scoring lower than 8 on the Bonboir math achievement test constituted subgroup B2 (Dyscalculia), the others formed subgroup B1 (Good calculators).

Obviously the subgroups defined as M2, C2, B2 provided a tentative quantified substratum for the concepts of dyslexia (Type I, Type II) and dyscalculia. The merits of such an attempt will be discussed later. In using the method of stepwise discriminant analysis, our purpose was to predict the criterion subgroups the subjects would respectively belong to: M1 or M2; C1 or C2; B1 or B2. We aimed in addition at predicting which subjects would have to be classified at the intersection of subgroups MCB2, where the overall deficits apparently formed a subgroup that we defined as the subgroup of "overall learning disabilities."

Let us point out that in this section we will discuss pathological cases identified as Type I or Type II dyslexia, or as dyscalculia, that were so-called "mixed" cases, since they could belong simultaneously, e.g., to the type II dyslexia subgroup and to the dyscalculia subgroup.

In the next section, "Prediction of Isolated or "Pure" Criterion Subgroup of Learning Disorders," we considered "pure" cases only.

Prediction of Type I Dyslexia, Poor Expressive Readers, "Mixed" Cases

Prediction of the Criterion Subgroup to which a subject will belong, Stepwise Discrimination Analysis

The prediction equation is:

Index of Predicted Subgroup Membership =
Constant + Σ_i [(Coefficient of Item i) (Result Item i)]

Positive results constituted a prediction of Type I dyslexia. Twelve percent of cases were found in subgroup M2 and were regarded as Type I dyslexia.

Sequential organization of digits emerged as the best predictor (see Table 2); its sign, however, was negative, hence the correlation was also negative. Verbal sequential memory (sentence memory) appeared to be one of the best predictors of Type I dyslexia (positive sign). Let us emphasize here that predictive factors should not be interpreted in terms of causes of explanations of dyslexia.

Table 2. Prediction of the Criterion Subgroup to Which a Subject Will Belong ("Mixed" Cases)[a]

Dyslexia Type I	Coefficient	Dyslexia Type II	Coefficient	Dyscalculia	Coefficient
Sequential organization	-0.3437	Sequential organization	-0.2368	Finger agnosia (R)	-0.0737
				Total IQ	-0.0315
Verbal sequential memory	+0.8735	Finger agnosia (L)	-0.9117	Sequential organization	-0.5304
				Picture naming (verbal)	+0.0761
Finger agnosia (L)	-0.1751	Finger discrimination (L)	+0.3973	Dysgraphaesthesia (R)	-0.2392
				Visual discrimination	+0.0383
Similarities	+0.1560	Vocabulary	-0.2290	Koch	+0.2288
				Crossing mid-line	+0.1017
Embedded F. T.	-0.0288	Embedded F. T.	-0.2740	Auditory integration	+0.0222
				Embedded F. T.	-0.0431
Dysdiadochokinesis (L)	+1.0439	Simultanagnosia	+0.1494	Coding	-0.0094
				Block design	+0.0107
Dysgraphaesthesia (R)	-0.3601	Verbal sequential memory	+0.7347	Picture arrangement	-0.0178
				Jump on one foot	+0.3994
Dysgraphaesthesia (L)	+0.2244	Dysdiadochokinesis (R)	+0.4086	Verbal sequential memory	+0.5141
				Dysdiadokinesis (R)	0.3233
Auditory discrimination	+0.9047	Astereognosis	+0.5227	Digit span	+0.0199
				Bender gestalt	+0.0215
Coding	-0.0102	Lamb chop test	-0.2190	Finger praxia (L)	+0.6426
				Finger praxia (R)	-0.3875
Schilder arm ext. T.	-0.5337	Visual discrimination	+0.0298	Astereagnosis	+0.5393
				Finger agnosia (L)	-0.3938
Dysdiadochokinesis (R)	-0.6904	Auditory discrimination	+0.6378	Finger discrimination (L)	+0.2262
				Dysgraphaesthesia (L)	
Astereognosis	+0.5951	Finger agnosia (R)	+0.5750		
		Dysgraphaesthesia (L)	+0.1161		
(Positive score) Constant = -0.1659		(Positive score) Constant = -2.789		(Positive score) Constant = -0.9248	

[a] Stepwise Discriminant Analysis

In the case of poor expressive readers, however, the analysis of the neuro-psychological functions showed that it was probably not sequential organization of digits that was important but that it was much more the memorization of *verbal* sequential material (in this case words tapped in sentence memory; positive correlation).

Binet's sentence memory is regarded by J. Jansky (Jansky and de Hirsch, 1972) as a predictor variable but, in our opinion, it is a predictor not with respect to short-term memory of syntactic structures but where there is a disturbance in the short-term memory of sequential structures.

Prediction of Type II Dyslexia, Poor Receptive Readers, "Mixed" Cases

The incidence rate of cases belonging to this subgroup was 11%. The predictive equation is:

Index of Predicted Subgroup Membership =
Constant + Σ_i [(Coefficient of Item i) (Result Item i)]

Positive scores constituted a prediction of Type II dyslexia. We defined the poor reader on the basis of the subject's performance on a reading test that assessed his understanding of what he was reading (a poor reader was thus defined on terms of his performance on the receptive—or semantic—reading test).

The best two predictors were sequential organization and finger agnosia (left); both, however, have a negative sign (see Table 2), so that the correlation also was negative. The next best predictor was finger discrimination (left), which has a positive sign; the next best predictor was simultanagnosia, followed by verbal sequential memory.

In the case of poor receptive readers, the analysis of the neuropsychological functions evinces not only the subject's ability to organize *nonverbal* material in memory (an ability that is tapped in the finger discrimination) but also his ability to organize and memorize *verbal* sequential material (in this case, words in a sentence memory test). Dirk Bakker's research work (1972) on "Temporal Order in Disturbed Reading" and that of Benton (1959), Kinsbourne and Warrington (1963), Willems, Peeters-Frenay and Berte-Depuydt (1980) on "Sequential Memory in Finger Discrimination" confirm the significance of these functions for poor readers. In his predictive study, Paul Satz (Satz, Taylor, Fried, and Fletcher, 1978) showed that the best predictor is finger discrimination, but it should be pointed out that in our study this holds only for the semantic aspects of reading.

Prediction of Dyscalculia, "Mixed" Cases

In this case the predictive equation needs to include more variables in order to reach the same value of the multiple correlation coefficient as obtained for dyslexia, that it had in stepwise multiple regression analysis (see preceding section):

Prediction of "Pure" Learning Disorders, Stepwise Discriminant Analysis

Index of Predicted Subgroup Membership =
Constant + Σ_i [(Coefficient of Item i) (Result Item i)]

The incidence rate of cases belonging to this subgroup was 17%. The best predictors were finger agnosia (right), total IQ and sequential organization of digits, but their sign was negative (see Table 2).

The best predictor with a positive sign was picture-naming (verbal). Whereas several authors, such as J. Jansky (Jansky and de Hirsch, 1972) and P. Satz (1978), suggested that picture-naming is a predictor of learning disabilities, our study tends to show that picture-naming is predictive of dyscalculia only and nonpredictive of Type I or Type II dyslexia. It should be noted again that the prediction of dyscalculia is apparently more complex than that of dyslexia; 24 tests were required to obtain a satisfactory predictive function.

Here again, if we may make a cautious interpretation, we observe that the subjects at risk of becoming dyscalculic later on were those who had scored highest on the total IQ test. This tended to confirm the currently accepted idea that learning dysfunction may be found with subjects with a normal intelligence and, sometimes, even with subjects of superior intelligence. In connection herewith, Levell, Shapton, and Warren (1964) reported that the predominance of dyslexic boys increases with higher I.Q. scores. The IQ distribution among "pure" learning disabilities subgroup will be discussed in the next section.

Prediction of Learning Disabilities (Overall Type)

The overall type of learning disabilities was defined here as the disabilities evidenced by those subjects whose cases belong to the intersection of subgroups M2, C2 and B2 (who present simultaneously Type I and Type II dyslexia and dyscalculia, MCB2).

The predictive function is:

Index of Predicted Subgroup Membership =
Constant + Σ_i [(Coefficient of Item i) (Result Item i)]

Table 3. Prediction of the Criterion Subgroup to Which a Subject
Will Belong ("Mixed" Cases)[a]

Learning disorders (overall type)

	Coefficient		*Coefficient*
Finger agnosia (L)	−0.4300	Lamb chop test	+1.8700
Bender gestalt	−0.0421	Sentence memory	−0.0327
Verbal sequential memory	+0.9128	Embedded F. T.	−0.0305
Auditory discrimination	+0.5856	Digit span	+0.0409
Simultanagnosia	+0.1200	Crossing the mid-line T.	−0.1093
Vocabulary	−0.0317	Finger agnosia (R)	−0.4041
Total IQ	+0.0526	Schilder arm ext. T.	−0.4729
Coding	−0.0279	Sequential organization	−0.1617
Dysdiadochokinesis (R)	+0.5363	Spatial discrimination	+0.2000
Astereognosis	+0.7888		

(Positive score)
Constant = −1.8777

[a]Stepwise Discriminant Analysis

Positive results constituted a prediction of learning disabilities (overall type).

The best predictive signs (see Table 3) were finger agnosia (left) and Bender-Gestalt; both, however, have a negative sign (negative correlation). Hence the best predictor with a positive sign was verbal sequential memory (as it was also for Type I Dyslexia, poor expressive readers).

Summary

The outcome of the predictions, on the basis of predictive tests administered at the age of 5 years and 10 months, that some subjects will belong, at the age of 8 years and 10 months, to the criterion subgroup of Type I or Type II Dyslexia or Dyscalculia, showed that the best predictors were: Type I dyslexia, verbal sequential memory; Type II dyslexia, finger discrimination; dyscalculia, picture-naming (verbal). As to overall learning disabilities, the best predictor was verbal sequential memory. The method of stepwise discriminant analysis permitted us to forecast which subjects would belong to the dyslexic or to the dyscalculic criterion subgroups, defined as such on the basis of their failure on a test of their academic level, administered at the age of 8 years and 10 months.

The methodology proposed above presented, however, limitations in that some subjects could well have failed simultaneously in two areas, because they were, for instance, at the same time Type I dyslexic and also dyscalculic. They were therefore "mixed" cases.

We *circumvent* this difficulty by attempting to establish a way to predict "pure" cases.

PREDICTION OF "ISOLATED" OR "PURE" CRITERION SUBGROUPS OF LEARNING DISORDERS

As we mentioned in the introduction, if prediction was our objective, this necessitated, in our opinion, a knowledge of the delineation of subgroups in learning disabilities as well as a knowledge of the specific predictors of each subgroup. This amounted, in short, to a knowledge of the natural history of the clinical development of these subgroups of learning disabilities. Current research, indeed, has not led, so far, to an understanding of the natural history of these subgroups, for the simple reason that the knowledge of learning disability subgroups is quite recent (Denckla, 1972, 1979; Boder, 1973; Kinsbourne and Warrington, 1966; Kinsbourne, 1975; Mattis, French and Rapin, 1975; Mattis, 1978; Doehrin,, Hoshko, and Bryans, 1979; Petrauskas and Rourke, 1979; Satz and Morris, 1980).

The working hypothesis that there are specific predictors for each subgroup entails that some credit should be given to the theory that the child's development evolves in a sequential and chronological order, certain aspects of which are then predictable. This hypothesis should, however, be tempered by our awareness of how variable development can be, not only with normal children, but even more with children "at risk." For the reasons mentioned above, we defined as "pure" subgroups those subjects who failed in one area only.

Definitions

A failure on one of these three tests (the Poucet expressive reading level test, the California receptive reading level test, or the Bonboir math achievement test) accompanied by success on the other two tests, was regarded in this connection as an isolated or "pure" disability.

For the purpose of this prediction, our sample was classified in 8 subgroups: Po = no failure; P1 = failure solely on Bonboir math achievement test or "pure" dyscalculia (4% of cases); P2 = failure solely on the California receptive reading test or "pure" Type II dyslexia (8% of cases); P3 = failure on the California receptive reading level test and on the Bonboir math achievement, with success on the Poucet expressive reading level test (4% of cases); P4 = failure solely on the Poucet expressive reading level test, or "pure" Type I dyslexia (4% of cases); P5 = failure on the Poucet expressive reading level test and the Bonboir math achievement test, success on the California receptive reading level test (1% of cases); P6 = failure on both reading level tests and success on the

Bonboir math achievement test (3% of cases); P7 = failure on all three tests, dyscalculia with Type I dyslexia, with Type II dyslexia (21% of cases).

Prediction of "Pure" Type I Dyslexia

The prediction was established by discriminating between Po and P4 on the basis of stepwise discriminant analysis. When the sign of the coefficient was positive, Type I dyslexia was predicted. The variables selected are shown, in descending order of importance, in Table 4. The predictive score on one of these tests was obtained by multiplying the raw score by the coefficient corresponding to that particular test and adding the constant -0.992 to the result.

The best predictor was the similarities subtest of the WISC, followed by picture naming, but both had a negative sign; then came, with a positive sign, finger agnosia (right), simultanagnosia, verbal sequential memory, and lamb chop test.

If one ventures a cautious interpretation of these predictors, while remaining aware that a prediction does not imply causality of deficits, one observes that the cerebral functions, put into play in the similarities test (WISC) at the age of 5 years and 6 months, are analogies; these analogies implied, according to Guilford's model (1967), such structural components of intellect as evaluation of semantic relation and an associative fluency (Meeker, 1969; Berte-Depuydt, 1982).

J. Jansky (Jansky and de Hirsch, 1972), too, regards the picture-naming test as one of the most powerful predictors. On the neuropsychological level, the mental functions involved in reading tasks (as in e.g., picture-naming) require ready elicitation of spoken equivalents or the ability to retrieve from memory verbal symbols. The poor reader frequently "gropes miserably for the words represented by the printed verbal symbols he sees on the page before him" (Jansky and de Hirsch, 1972, page 58).

The predictors with a positive sign ranking next were (Table 4): Finger agnosia (right), simultanagnosia, verbal sequential memory and the lamb chop test. It is worthy of note, on the neuropsychological level, that two major types of functions were involved in failure on these tests. Among these functions, attention and memory, either in encoding or in decoding, were probably the most important at the age of 5 years and 10 months.

In the finger agnosia test of our examination battery, the task assigned implied verbal denomination (i.e., naming the number corresponding to the finger touched by the tester; this implied retrieving in memory the exact number) and, moreover, mental representation (body schema) of the sequence of the fingers. There is ample evidence that finger agnosia is not unitary disability but rather a collective term covering diverse, complex types of defective performance related to finger identification (Schilder, 1931; Benton, 1959;

Table 4. Prediction of "Pure" Learning Disorders[a]

Dyslexia Type I	Coefficient	Dyslexia Type II	Coefficient	Dyscalculia	Coefficient
Similarities	+0.037	Verbal sequential memory	-1.917	Visual discrimination	+0.082
Picture naming (verbal)	-0.077	Picture naming (verbal)	+0.075	Astereognosis	+0.823
Finger agnosia (R)	+0.812	Dysgraphaesthesia (L)	-0.308	Finger discrimination (right)	+0.365
Bender gestalt	-0.037	Finger discrimination (L)	-0.669	Picture arrangement	+0.021
Simultanagnosia	+0.132	Dysdiadochokinesis (R)	-0.897	Auditory discrimination	-0.050
Verbal sequential memory	+1.518	Koch	+0.162	Total IQ	+0.892
Lamb chop test	+0.449	Astereognosis	+0.638	Jump on one foot (R)	-0.485
Jump on one foot (L)	+0.931	Similarities	-0.019	Picture naming	-0.050
Coding	-0.020	Perseveration	-0.638	Dysgraphaesthesia (R)	+0.177
Visual discrimination	-0.038	Finger agnosia (L)	+1.390	Sentence memory	-0.032
Dysdiadochokinesis (R)	-0.620	Finger agnosia (R)	-1.366	Crossing middle line	-0.086
Koch	-0.147	Vocabulary	+0.019	Finger praxia (L)	-1.107
		Simultangnosia	-0.171	Finger praxia (R)	+0.694
		Jump on one foot (R)	-0.475	Lamb chop test	-0.207
		Finger praxia (L)	+0.350	Verbal IQ	-0.046
				Verbal sequential memory	-1.000
				Finger discrimination (L)	-0.531
				Perseveration	-1.030
				Finger agnosia (L)	+0.322
				Block design	-0.014
(Positive score) Constant = -0.992		(Negative score) Constant = +3.185		(Negative score) Constant = -3.220	

[a]Stepwise Discriminant Analysis

Kinsbourne and Warrington, 1963; Critchley, 1966; Wllems, Peeters-Frenay, and Berte-Depuydt, 1980). These performances can be classified along a number of dimensions, e.g., whether the stimulus to be represented is verbal, visual, or tactile, or whether the required response is verbal or nonverbal (Benton, 1979). Stone and Robinson (1968), and Lindgren (1978) demonstrated in their studies that there are also indications that the verbal encoding of sensory information may play a significant role in the performances of young school children.

Here again we would like to stress the significance, in our view, of sequential verbal memory (which is present, in part, in our examination battery, in the finger agnosia test and, also, in the verbal sequential memory test).

The significance of sequential organization in dyslexia has been stressed by several authors: Bakker (1972), Benton (1975), Kinsbourne (1975), and Gaddes (1978). Poor expressive readers probably have a deficit in this function, since, as we know, the expressive aspect of reading implies an ability to use articulatory and phonemic sequences.

The quality of attention is probably one of the major functions measured by simultanagnosia and by the lamb chop test. As a matter of fact, the lamb chop test, a spatial orientation test proposed by Wechsler and Hagin (1964), is, as Kinsbourne (1970) has shown, not merely a spatial orientation test, but also a test of selective attention. In such a complex function as simultanagnosia, which involves double stimuli perception, certain attentional deficits might play a part in the failure on this task at the age of 5 years and 10 months.

Prediction of "Pure" Type II Dyslexia

The predictor variables selected are shown in descending order in Table 4. They were the outcome, on the basis of stepwise discriminant analysis, of discrimination between Po and P2. When the sign of the coefficient was negative, Type II Dyslexia was predicted. The predictive score on one of these tests was obtained by multiplying the raw score by the coefficient corresponding to that particular test and adding the constant +3.185.

The best three predictors with a negative sign were: verbal sequential memory, graphaesthesia (left) and finger discrimination.

If we venture a cautious interpretation of these results, it appears that Type II dyslexia (i.e., the inability to understand the text read) could perhaps be related to a difficulty in organizing verbal material (verbal sequential memory) or nonverbal material in memory (finger discrimination). This is probably a faculty requisite for ordering elements sequentially according to priority, in order to attain the ordered classification or the information-processing required to understand the text read.

Other factors may also be related to poor receptive reading. In dysgraphaesthesia, for instance, information-processing disturbances could be due, in part,

to selective attention deficit, as inferred from confusion in the recall of morphologically similar digits (e.g., 5/3; 1/7; 5/2). From these initial phenomena
of attention deficit, originate, perhaps, the first difficulties in sensing the verbal
material that is probably necessary for the first stage of understanding.

Prediction of "Pure" Dyscalculia

The discriminant function was constructed on the basis of the discrimination
between subgroups Po and P1. The incidence rate of "pure" dyscalculia in our
population was 4%. The predictor variables retained in the statistical method of
stepwise discriminant analysis are shown in descending order in Table 4. The
predictive score on one of these tests was obtained by multiplying the raw score
by the coefficient corresponding to that particular test and adding the constant
−3.220 to the result. A negative score obtained in this way corresponded to a
prediction of dyscalculia.

The best predictor with a positive sign was visual discrimination, a test
involving the functions of attention and visual discrimination, insofar as the task,
assigned at the age of 5 years and 10 months, consisted in recognizing two identical words presented in a group of four morphologically similar words.

Again, the significance of sequential organization should be noted; it inter-
venes here in two tests: Verbal sequential memory and picture-arrangement. As
with "mixed" cases, one notes the importance of total I.Q.; but, again, as with
"mixed" cases, the absence of the arithmetic subtest of WISC (this can be explained by different cognitive functions the child needed to achieve those two
tasks, i.e., arithmetic subtest and Bonboir math achievement test, Berte-
Depuydt, 1982) points to the fact that it is from a child's high score on total
I.Q. (WISC) that one can predict that he will perhaps exhibit dyscalculia at the
age of 8 years and 10 months. This needs further research.

Predictor variables with a negative sign were: auditory discrimination,
jump on one foot, picture-naming and sentence memory.

Low scores on these tests could be an indication that complex functions
intervene, possibly both in auditory verbal encoding and in auditory verbal
decoding, and that a failure on these tests is predictive of dyscalculia three years
later on. The higher degree of complexity of the cortical functions coming into
play in dyscalculia could explain why a larger number of predictors (20 in this
case) than in the various types of dyslexia were required to obtain a satisfactory
predictive function.

The Intelligence Quotient in the "Pure" Subgroups

The results of the I.Q. measurements are shown in Table 5 and are only indicative, as they were calculated on small subgroups.

Table 5.   Average IQ in "Pure" Subgroups of Learning Disorders

	Control group (N = 100)	"Pure" Dyslexia, Type I (N = 6)	"Pure" Dyslexia, Type II (N = 12)	"Pure" Dyscalculia (N = 6)
Total IQ	112.73 ± 13.71	115 ± 8	107.75	95.50 ± 10.15
Performance IQ	116.15 ± 14.61	115.2 ± 10.9	113.61	96.50 ± 11.96
Verbal IQ	107.31 ± 15.94	112.8 ± 6.5	100	95.33 ± 14.99

What first appears is that there was little or no difference between the total I.Q. scores obtained by the control group and those obtained by dyslexics. Dyscalculics, however, had a slightly lower total I.Q. than the control group and than dyslexics. In this case, also, our study did not indicate any significant difference between verbal I.Q. and performance I.Q. for any of the subgroups. This problem is discussed by de Leval, Berte-Depuydt, Bouckaert, and Willems (1982).

It seems, thus, that one can justifiably state, on the basis of these results, that dyslexia and dyscalculia also occur with normally intelligent subjects, which is a possible partial explanation of the low validity of WISC subtests as predictors of learning disabilities. (See previous two sections of this chapter.) On the other hand, while total I.Q., verbal I.Q., performance I.Q., and WISC subtests were nonpredictive of failure in reading or math, total I.Q. appeared to be a predictor of success in reading, particularly when one aimed at forecasting adequate results on a test assessing comprehension of a text read (see earlier discussion of prediction by means of stepwise multiple regression analysis of receptive reading).

Summary

With the definition of "pure" subgroups (that is to say, subgroups composed solely of subjects evidencing an "isolated" or "pure" disability), while succeeding in the other areas (e.g., dyscalculia without dyslexia), we were able to improve significantly our knowledge of the specific predictors of each subgroup.

The best two predictors were similarities and finger agnosia (right) for "pure" Type I dyslexia; verbal sequential memory and dysgraphaesthesia (left) for "pure" Type II dyslexia; visual discrimination (+) and auditory discrimination (-) for "pure" dyscalculia.

Prediction of dyscalculia seems more complex than prediction of dyslexia; out of an initial total of 183 variables introduced in this study, the predictive function was established with 12 variables for "pure" Type I dyslexia, 15 for "pure" Type II dyslexia, and 20 for "pure" dyscalculia. Scores on intelligence tests showed that the subgroups of dyslexics and dyscalculics did not differ significantly from the control group. This could perhaps explain in part the low validity of intelligence tests for the prediction of learning disorders.

DIAGNOSTIC VALUE OF TESTS

Definitions: Statistical Principles of Diagnostic Testing

The following terms are used to describe the performance of a diagnostic test (Vecchio, 1966; Galen and Gambino, 1975; Armitage, 1973).

True Positive (TP) denotes a diseased person in whom a positive test result is obtained. *False Negative* (FN) denotes a diseased person in whom a negative test result occurs. The total number of diseased persons is the sum of TP + FN.

True Negative (TN) denotes a nondiseased person in whom a negative test result is found.

False Positive (FP) denotes a nondiseased person in whom a positive test result occurs. The total number of nondiseased persons is the sum of TN + FP.

Sensitivity refers to the rate of correct identification of diseased persons by the test and is expressed as:

$$\text{Percent sensitivity} = \frac{TP}{TP + FN} \times 100.$$

Specificity refers to the rate of correct identification of nondiseased persons and is expressed as:

$$\text{Percent specificity} = \frac{TN}{TN + FP} \times 100.$$

Predictive value of a positive test result (PV$^+$) refers to the proportion of all positive test results which are *True Positives*, and is expressed as:

$$(\%) \, PV^+ = \frac{TP}{TP + FP} \times 100.$$

Similarly, the *Predictive Value of a negative test result* (PV$^-$) refers to the proportion of all negative test results which are *True Negatives* and is expressed as:

$$(\%) \, PV^- = \frac{TN}{TN + FN} \times 100.$$

The PV results are the most important criteria for the performance of a predictive test battery since, unlike the sensitivity and specificity results, they allow for the prevalence of the disease (i.e., dyslexia, dyscalculia) in the population being tested, because they are calculated from the absolute numbers of TP, FP, TN, and FN subjects, whereas the sensitivity results ignore the frequency of FP subjects, and the specificity results ignore the frequency of FN subjects.

Results of Our Predictive Study

If one's purpose is to construct an examination to predict a deficit occurring after three years, based on an original total population of normal children aged 5 years and 10 months, validation of the diagnostic value of the tests is essential. Only a few studies to date have performed such a check utilizing the concept of "hits" and "misses" (Meehl and Rosen, 1955). In other words, few studies established a computation of correct classification, specificity, and sensitivity, as well as determined the rate of valid or false positives and negatives. Even studies using probability statistics (e.g., Feshbach et al., 1974) made use only of overall efficiency rather than examining the differential efficiency for the children predicted to pass or fail at a later stage, by criterion measures (Lindsay and Wendell, 1982).

The overall efficiency (correct classification) of our examination battery was, for "mixed" cases: 85.39% for type I dyslexia, 84% for type II dyslexia, 90.48% for dyscalculia, and 98.56% for overall learning disability (Table 6); for "pure" type cases: 83.3% for "pure" type I dyslexia, 81.3% for "pure" type II dyslexia, and 96% for "pure" dyscalculia (Table 7).

In the "mixed" cases our examination battery had a specificity of 89% with dyslexics (type I or type II) and 92% for "pure" dyscalculia (Table 7). On the other hand, its sensitivity with poor expressive readers was 61%, 58% with poor receptive readers, and 80% with dyscalculics. In the "pure" cases, we obtain approximately the same results (Table 7).

The problem of valid and false positives is complex, and varies to a considerable extent according to whether the follow-up is performed after one year or, as in our study, after three years. In his study, Lindgren (1975), for instance, examined children at the end of kindergarten and reexamined them for a follow-up at the end of the first year of the elementary school. In this case, and thanks to his use of stepwise discriminant analysis, he obtained: overall accuracy, 91%; valid positives rate, 79%; and only 4% of false positives. The low rate of false positives seems mainly due to the follow-up having occurred after an extremely short time lapse (less than one year).

The same criticism could, perhaps, be addressed to the "Search" predictive battery of Silver and Hagin (1975), who also performed follow-up after one year and, moreover, had given part of the population early remediation for perceptual deficits that, in our opinion, could have biased the outcome of the prediction.

In J. Jansky and de Hirsch's study (1972), the rate of false positives after a two-year follow-up increased to 25%. In their screening tests, these authors correctly identified 76% of the children, 79% of the poor readers (valid positives), but they misclassified 25% of the good readers (false positives).

In their reanalysis of the Feshbach et al. (1974) data, Satz and Fletcher (1979) demonstrated that the overall efficiency (total hits) of the Student Rating

Table 6. Diagnostic Value of Tests in "Mixed" Subgroups in Percent

	Dyslexia, Type I	Dyslexia, Type II	Dyscalculia	Learning disorders (overall type)
Correct classification	85.39	84	90.48	98.56
Specificity	89	89	92	100
Sensitivity	61	58	80	71
Prevalence	12	11	17	5.3

Table 7. Diagnostic Value of Tests in "Pure" Subgroups in Percent

	"Pure" Dyslexia, Type I	"Pure" Dyslexia, Type II	"Pure" Dyscalculia
Correct classification	83.3	81.3	96
Specificity	84.84	85.71	95.74
Sensitivity	66.6	58.3	100
Prevalence	4	8	4

Scale (S.R.S.) was 77%. Further analysis revealed, however, that the S.R.S. yielded the following rates: valid positives, 30%; false negatives, 70%; false positives, 3%; and valid negatives, 97%. Thus, even though the overall efficiency was high (77%), 70% of the children who later failed had been missed by the screening test (Lindsay and Wedell, 1982).

Similar findings are reported by Lindsay (1979) for the Infant Rating Scale. As with the S.R.S., overall efficiency is high (80%), but true positive rate is only moderately high for cognitive factors (language, 47.7%; early learning, 45.5%) and low for behavioral factors (behavior, 13.6%; social integration, 13.6).

On the other hand, the rate of true negatives is high (language, 81.4%; early learning, 80.6%; behavior, 87.8%; social integration, 92.3%), which means that this examination does predict very correctly, indeed, which subjects will be normal, but, even when using the best factor score results, the Infant Rating Scale misses over 50% of the children who will later fail reading (Lindsay and Wedell, 1982).

Paul Satz et al. (1978), in their excellent study, obtained, thanks to a longer follow-up, results in which the false positive incidence rate was lowered to a virtual minimum. In fact, only 12 of the 258 good readers were misclassified, which reflects an overall false positive rate of only 4.6%. The authors ascribed this low rate to the fact that these predictive outcomes which are, in summary, even higher than those obtained in the three year follow-up (grade 2), are due largely to the marked reduction of the false positive rate over time. However, whereas the false positive rate is low, the valid positives in the tests proposed by Satz et al. correctly predicted only 52 of the 90 severe cases (PV^+ = 58%), and only 19 of the 94 mild cases (PV^+ = 20%). For valid negatives, on the other hand, the tests correctly predicted 157 of the 168 average readers (PV^- = 94%), and 89 of the 90 superior readers (PV^- = 99%).

Here again, it is worthy of note that the predictive test proposed by Satz et al. was nonpredictive for 42% of the severe cases, and for 80% of the mild cases (false negatives), while it predicted very correctly which subjects would become good readers (valid negatives). The results of our study are shown in Tables 6 through 14.

With the "mixed" cases, the overall efficiency (correct classification) was 85.39%; 84% for type I dyslexia, 90.48% for type II dyslexia, and 98.56% for overall learning disabilities. Note that efficiency was higher for dyscalculia and learning disabilities than for dyslexia.

The specificity of our predictive examination battery was high, since we obtain, respectively, 89%, 89%, 92%, and 100% (Table 6). With *"pure" cases* our results were similar: The overall efficiency if 83.3% for "pure" type I dyslexia; 81.3% for "pure" type II dyslexia, and for dyscalculia, 96% (Table 7).

With *"mixed" cases* we obtained 61% valid positives for type I dyslexia, 58% for type II dyslexia, and 80% for dyscalculia. The valid negative rates were, respectively, 89%, 89%, 92% of the cases (see Tables 8, 9, 10).

Table 8. Diagnostic Value of Test, Dyslexia Type I "Mixed" Cases

	Early identification criterion. Predictive battery (5 Y. 10 M.) N = 178	
Later achievement criterion (8 Y. 10 M.)	Normal N = 147	"At risk" N = 31
Normal N = 155	138 TN = 89%	17 FP = 10%
Dyslexics (Type I) N = 23	9 FN = 39%	14 TP = 61%

Specificity $= \dfrac{138}{155} = 89\%$

Sensitivity $= \dfrac{14}{23} = 61\%$

"Hits" (correct classifications) = 85.4%

"Misses" = 14.6%

Table 9. Diagnostic Value of Test, Dyslexia Type II "Mixed" Cases

Later achievement criterion (8 Y. 10 M.)	Early identification criterion. Predictive battery (5 Y. 10 M.) N = 169	
	Normal N = 137	"At risk" N = 32
Normal N = 140	125 TN = 89%	15 FP = 11%
Dyslexics (Type II) N = 29	12 FN = 42%	17 TP = 59%

Specificity = $\dfrac{125}{140}$ = 89%

Sensitivity = $\dfrac{17}{29}$ = 59%

"Hits" (correct classifications) = 84%

"Misses" = 16%

Table 10. Diagnostic Value of Test, Dyscalculia "Mixed" Cases

		Early identification criterion. Predictive battery (5 Y. 10 M.) N = 168	
		Normal N = 137	"At risk" N = 31
Later achievement criterion (8 Y. 10 M.)	Normal N = 143	132 TN = 92%	11 FP = 8%
	Dyscalculics N = 25	5 FN = 20%	20 TP = 80%

Specificity = $\dfrac{132}{143}$ = 92%

Sensitivity = $\dfrac{20}{25}$ = 80%

"Hits" (correct classifications) = 90.5%

"Misses" = 9.5%

Table 11. Predictive Value of Tests ("Mixed" Subgroups) in Percent

	Dyslexia, Type I	Dyslexia, Type II	Dyscalculia
Predictive value of a positive test			
True positives			
$PV_{TP} = \dfrac{TP}{TP + FP} \times 100$	45	53	64
False positives			
$PV_{FP} = \dfrac{FP}{FP + TP} \times 100$	55	47	35
Predictive value of a negative test			
True negatives			
$PV_{TN} = \dfrac{TN}{TN + FN} \times 100$	94	91	96
False negatives			
$PV_{FN} = \dfrac{FN}{TN + FN} \times 100$	6	9	4

The predictive value of a positive test (PV^+) was, for "mixed" cases, 45%, 53%, and 64%, respectively. The predictive value of a negative test (PV^-) in these cases was 94%, 91%, and 96% (Table 11). False negative rates [(FN/(TN + FN) × 100] were only 6%, 9%, and 3.6%. Our 81–98% range of correct classification rates demonstrates the accuracy of our predictive screening. The limitations of such a predictive approach could be due not only to the considerable variability of performances of normal children but even more of children "at risk" and also to the children's compensating ability. Wedell (1980) argues that children can and do compensate for their deficiencies.

On the other hand, our knowledge of the specific predictors of each sub-group of learning disabilities has improved considerably since we were able to show in our study that there are distinct predictors for dyscalculia, dyslexia, and cases of disability defined as "pure" or "mixed."

Footnotes on False Positive Rates

Computation of predictive classification, resulting in a knowledge of the incidence of false positives and of false negatives, depends on a number of factors, including:

1. Choice of the cut-off scores of the test on both the early identification instrument and the criterion measure. (Poor results on a test are determined with respect to minus one standard deviation or minus two standard deviations from the mean.)
2. Nature and type of the (presumably) predictive tests chosen.
3. Choice of the original constant term. [The incidence of false positives and false negatives will vary considerably, according to whether the likelihood of becoming a poor reader has been estimated at 0.5 (50%) in a philosophy of screening, or at 0.2 (20%) as a result of epidemiological studies claiming that prevalence of dyslexia is between 15 and 20%.]
4. Incidence of false positives that can change spontaneously over time. [For instance, certain false positives may change into true positives (a normal child becoming dyslexic) and other false positives may become normal (true negatives) as a result of an appropriate teaching method, when follow-up is pursued beyond a test-criterion interval of three years.]

As a rule true positives and true negatives should not be compared as long as the real prevalence figures are not known. Each procedure should be assessed on the basis of its specificity and sensitivity. Screening implies knowledge of the relationships between sensitivity and specificity. The prerequisite to attaining a good definition of a "risk" population is obviously to avoid "missed" cases (i.e., false negatives).

CONCLUSIONS

On the basis of a total population of 281 normal children aged 5 years and 10 months, who were reexamined after three years, we attempted to isolate the predictor variables of simple reading retardation (backward readers) and dyscalculia.

Our first objective was to ascertain the importance of certain variables in the prediction of learning disabilities, such as (1) specific neurological signs (the "soft signs" of the British literature, "troubles psychomoteurs" or "troubles instrumentaux" of the French school, or sensory-integration of some American authors); (2) psychometric tests derived from the WISC subtests or personality tests; (3) various pediatric neuropsychological examinations.

To achieve our goal, we selected a homogeneous population of boys and reduced to a minimum the importance of "extra-child" factors (while remaining conscious of the fact that they should not be ignored). What we proposed with our study was essentially to evaluate the part that "within child" factors can play in originating, or in permitting, the prediction of reading and mathematics backwardness three years later.

A first delineation of subgroups in our selected sample was obtained by means of a definition of expressive dyslexia (type I dyslexia), receptive dyslexia (type II dyslexia), and dyscalculia. Another refining approach, with a view to delineate subgroups further by means of a neurolinguistic analysis of reading errors, and by means of a study of the type of information processing involved in dyscalculia, is currently in progress. Our study, however, has already elicited a number of elements toward answering the question raised by the necessity of a knowledge of the specific predictors of each subgroup, thanks to the definition of "mixed" versus "pure" subgroups. ("Pure" subgroups are defined as comprising solely of subjects exhibiting only one "isolated" aspect of disability in expressive or receptive reading, or in mathematics.)

Prediction was based on two statistical methods, stepwise multiple regression and stepwise discriminant analysis; the latter, recently proposed in the literature, permits very precise knowledge of the specific predictors, not only of *success* in reading and mathematics, but also, in "pure" or "mixed" cases, of *failure* in the same skills (i.e., type I dyslexia, type II dyslexia, and dyscalculia). Few studies to date have attained these objectives.

The results of our study show the high significance of neuropediatric and neuropsychological predictors [success: finger agnosia, total IQ, sequential organization; failure: verbal sequential memory, finger discrimination, picture naming (verbal), similarities, finger agnosia, dysgraphaesthesia, visual discrimination (+), auditory discrimination (-)], and the lesser importance, for instance, of soft neurological signs, and also of other items that were presumed to be predictive in some studies.

Of the 183 variables obtained on each child, 13 or 12 were needed for predicting type I dyslexia, 14 or 15 for predicting type II dyslexia, and 24 or 20 for predicting dyscalculia, respectively, for "mixed" and "pure" subgroups.

The advantage of our study resided also in that it did not attempt to make a prediction on the basis of the whole ready-made package of a standardized test battery, but by utilizing a selection of items that are held as predictive by the authors of recent studies in Europe and in English-speaking countries, and by comparing their predictive powers. This comparison was performed through a longitudinal study, with an adequate test-criterion interval (three years), that permitted us virtually to preclude a great number of the children who would have exhibited a transient developmental variability occurring between, for instance, the ages of 5 years and 10 months and 7–10 years (with a subsequent, temporary, and simple learning retardation).

Validation of the "diagnostic accuracy" of the test battery (diagnostic value of the test) has shown that the predictors proposed in our study yielded a high overall efficiency (85% to 90%), a very good specificity (89% to 96%), and sensitivity (58% to 80%). (See Tables 12–14.)

Our study has enabled us to propose a predictive examination based on the best predictors (Willems et al., 1979; Willems et al., 1982) that can be performed in approximately half an hour.

It is also worthy of note that the number of false negatives in our study was remarkably low (3.6 to 5%), which means that very few cases "at risk" were missed by our predictive examination.

Clearly, this kind of predictive examination should not be interpreted in terms of causation of academic failure that may originate in a variety of causes, that can be linked with "within-child" or "extra-child" factors (such as socio-economic status, family background, emotional problems, etc.). Best results are obtained when this type of predictive examination is applied within its precise limitations; that is, when the physician, the psychologist, and the teacher are provided with a neuropsychological profile of the child at the age of 5 years and 10±4 months enabling them to isolate and to realize better the significance of certain "within-child" factors in the group of children "at risk."

By using a predictive examination involving an original screening with a view to a possibly more elaborate diagnosis and, maybe, a subsequent early intervention (screening → diagnosis → intervention), the professional may be better able to fill his responsibilities to the child.

Table 12. Diagnostic Value of Test, Dyslexia Type I "Pure" Cases

Later achievement criterion (8 Y. 10 M.)	Early identification criterion. Predictive battery (5 Y. 10 M.) N = 72	
	Normal N = 58	"At risk" N = 14
Normal N = 66	56 TN = 84.84%	10 FP = 15.16%
Dyslexics (Type I) N = 6	2 FN = 13.4%	4 TP = 66.6%

Specificity = $\dfrac{56}{66}$ = 84.84%

Sensitivity = $\dfrac{4}{6}$ = 66.6%

"Hits" (correct classifications) = 83.3%

"Misses" = 16.7%

Table 13. Diagnostic Value of Test, Dyslexia Type II "Pure" Cases

		Early identification criterion. Predictive battery (5 Y. 10 M.) N = 75	
		Normal N = 59	"At risk" N = 16
Later achievement criterion (8 Y. 10 M.)	Normal N = 63	54 TN = 85.71%	9 FP = 14.3%
	Dyslexics (Type II) N = 12	5 FN = 41.7%	7 TP = 58.3%

"Hits" (correct classifications) = 81.3%

"Misses" = 18.7%

Specificity = $\dfrac{54}{63}$ = 85.71%

Sensitivity = $\dfrac{7}{12}$ = 58.3%

Table 14. Diagnostic Value of Test, Dyscalculia "Pure" Cases

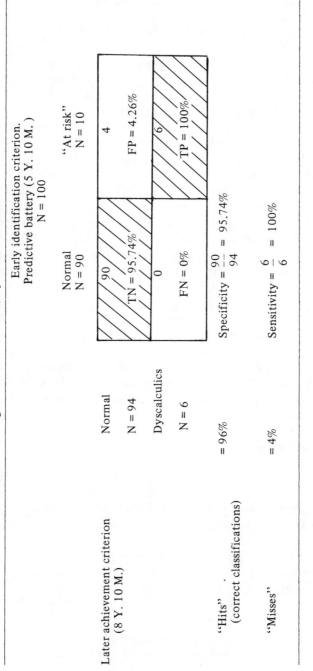

DISCUSSIONS

Virginia I. Douglas

First, let me commend Dr. Willems and his colleagues on the great amount of effort that obviously went into planning and carrying out this massive three-year prospective study. His attempt to arrive at predictors of *subgroups* within the learning disability population is impressive.

I attended the first meeting organized by Dr. Keogh of a representative group of researchers in this area.* It was a humbling experience. I am afraid that it contributed to a growing concern I have had that the "learning disability" label is rapidly replacing "minimal brain dysfunction" as a "wastebasket" diagnosis to be used for children who do not fit any of our other diagnostic categories but who, nevertheless, are failing in school for reasons we do not understand. Dr. Keogh and her colleagues had undertaken an extensive review of subject selection procedures and assessment techniques used in published learning disability studies over the past several years. The facts and figures they assembled made obvious the need for acceptance of common "marker variables" that would make it possible to compare the work of different investigators in the field. They also revealed, however, that a mind-boggling variety of psychological, neurological, and psychoneurological tests are being used by different investigators to assess an almost equally mind-boggling number of hypothesized defective processes.

Furthermore, as Dr. Willems has stated, the reliability and validity of most of these tests is far from established. Particularly troubling to me was the fact that informal discussions among the assembled "experts" at the meeting revealed little agreement on what the various tests measured, that is, our opinions on what psychological or psychoneurological processes were assessed, even by some of the most widely used instruments.

I also had difficulty with Dr. Willems' interpretation of some of the findings. It appears that he has chosen to set aside a number of the "best predictors" from his analyses because they had negative signs. It was my understanding that there is no statistical rationale for ignoring negative findings that happen to be counterintuitive when an investigator is using multiple-regression and discriminant analysis techniques.

I am particularly intrigued, for example, about why the Finger Agnosia Test (particularly *right* finger agnosia) should have emerged as one of the better predictors of performance on expressive reading.

---

*Marker Variable Project Conference. January 29–31, 1979. Held at the University of California, Los Angeles. Project Director: Barbara K. Keogh.

General Discussion

Dr. Kinsbourne: We must clarify the point on finger agnosia. It is correct that left-sided finger agnosia predicted the reading disturbance and right-sided finger agnosia predicted dyscalculia?

Dr. Willems: Left-sided finger agnosia ought to predict a right-brain deficit.

Dr. Kinsbourne: I don't personally recognize such a thing as either left or right finger agnosia. Finger agnosia is a high-level deficit which, by definition, has to be across both hands if it is to be properly diagnosed. If it occurs in one hand only, then one has not excluded some sensorimotor problems which might have to do with performance on the test.

The point about finger agnosia as opposed to low sensitivity in two-point discrimination tests is that it should be superordinate to that level of processing. So, if one were to think of finger agnosia in the cognitive sense, one should think of it as a left parietal manifestation. Then, one would, indeed, expect finger agnosia to be present in a subset of children with language and reading problems, as Lou Lavent and I showed 20 years ago and, indeed, also related to dyscalculia that is part of that syndrome. However, it would do so across both hands.

Now, if you have a subset of children who have only a lateralized right or left problem, and regard this as a marker for lateralized brain damage, then it might well be the case that children in whom poor performance on the finger test that I wouldn't call finger agnosia but poor performance of finger test lateralized to one hand, had a contralateral hemisphere deficit, that then relates to a scholastic problem. So it may be interesting to look back at the data in that sense, subdividing those children into those who have a bilateral problem and see if they fit into the subtype of dyslexia with dyscalculia, as we described, and certainly to look at those in whom the problem is strictly unilateral.

Dr. Conners: What test did you use in the finger testing?

Dr. Willems: We used the finger discrimination test described by Marcel Kinsbourne. The other one is the finger agnosia, the child had just to say the number of the finger touched with his eyes closed.

Dr. Douglas: These other tests are also in-between tests, in which we don't understand the discriminatory one-finger, two-finger, touching test. It seems to lateralize the right and left more with the in-between being the right. But that is just a guess.

Dr. Willems: The problem is also that it must be just a learning deficit. We start with finger discrimination, or finger agnosia, with the right hand, and then if we have that preserved on the left hand, it's just reason or just an indication that the child didn't learn.

Dr. Douglas: You may not be specific enough at the time of the test and you don't have enough data behind this.

Dr. Willems: There is a countdown between sides, order, and administration: we need to do more work.

REFERENCES

Adelman, H. The not-so-specific learning disability population. *Exceptional Children*, 1971, *37*:528–533.

Armitage, P. (Ed.), *Statistical methods in medical research.* New York: John Wiley, 1973.

Bakker, D. J. *Temporal order in disturbed reading: Development and neuropsychological aspects in normal and reading-retarded children.* Rotterdam: Rotterdam University Press, 1972.

Bax, M., and Whitmore, K. Neurodevelopmental screening in the school entrant medical examination. *Lancet*, 18 Aug., 1973, *2*:368–370.

Belmont, I., and Belmont, L. Stability or change in reading achievement over time: Developmental and educational implications. *Journal of Learning Disabilities*, 1978, *11*:80–88.

Benton, A. L. *Right-left discrimination and finger localization: Development and pathology.* New York: Hoeber-Harper, 1959.

Benton, A. L. Developmental dyslexia: Neurological aspects. In W. J. Friedlander (Ed.), *Current reviews of higher nervous system dysfunction.* New York: Raven Press, 1975.

Benton, A. L. Body schema disturbances: Finger agnosia and right-left disorientation. In K. M. Heilman and E. Valenstein (Eds.), *Clinical neuropsychology.* New York: Oxford University Press, 1979.

Berte-Depuydt, R. Manuel pour l'application clinique du WISC; Etude d'une forme abrégée. Working Paper, n° 2. Faculté de Psychologie et de Sciences de l'Education, Unité de Psychodiagnostic, 1981(a).

Berte-Depuydt, R. Test de l'Arbre: Une grille d'indices émotionnels permettant de classer les réponses en termes d'un score global de "maturité affective" sur une échelle de 10 classes. Working Paper, n° 5, 1981(b), Centre de Recherche Psychodiagnostique et de Consultation Psychologique Voie du Roman Pays, 20. 1348 Louvain-La-Neuve, Belgium. Berte-Depuydt, 1982.

Binet, A. *The development of intelligence in children.* Baltimore: Williams and Wilkins, 1916.

Boder, E. Developmental dyslexia: A diagnostic approach based on three atypical reading-spelling patterns. *Developmental Medicine and Child Neurology*, 1973, *15*, 663–687.

Bonboir, A. Test pour la mesure de l'acquis arithmétique en fin de scolarité primaire. Document n° 10 du C. N. R. P. S., Vaillant-Carmanne (Ed.), 1961. Laboratoire de Psychométrie, Voie du Roman Pays, 20 1348 Louvain-La-Neuve, Belgium.

Bonboir, A. Test d'arithmétique. Ecole Primaire. Commission Consultative Universitaires de Pédagogie. Ministère Belge de l'Education Nationale et de la Culture. Edition: Laboratoire de Pédagogie Expérimentale, Université Catholique de Louvain, Belgium, 1969.

Borel-Maisonny, S. Dyslexie et dysorthographie. Rev. Française d'Hygiène et Médecine Scolaire et Universitaire, 9, n° 1, Paris, 15–24, 1956.

Burion, J. Une épreuve de lecture orale. "Le Courrier de la Recherche Pédagogique", n° 5, 3–14, 1956, Faculté de Pédagogie, Université de Mons, Belgium.

Burion, J. Test de la lecture orale: "EMILE"; Inst. Sup. de Pedagogie du Hainaut, Morlanwez, 1960.

"California" Adaptation française du California reading test. M. Claes, Laboratoire de Pédagogie Expérimentale de l'Université de Louvain, Belgium. (Prof. A. Gille). Editest, 1967.

Celdic Report, One million children: A national study of Canadian children with emotional and learning disorders. Toronto, Ontario, Canada: L. Crainford, 1970.

Claes and Gille, 1967. (MS307) (MS315).

Coles, G. S. The learning disabilities test battery: Empirical and social issues. Harvard Educational Review, 1978, 48:313–340.

Critchley, M. The enigma of Gerstmann's syndrome. Brain, 1966, 89:183–198.

Cross, L. An introduction. In L. Cross and K. W. Goin (Eds.), Identifying handicapped children: A guide to casefinding screening, diagnosis, assessment and evaluation. New York: Walker and Co., 1977.

Debray-Ritzen, P., and Badrig Mélékian. La dyslexie de l'enfant. Casterman Edit., 1970.

de Leval, N., Berte-Depuydt, R., Bouckaert, A., and Willems, G. Abridged study of the WISC test on 281 preschool aged boys. Its interest and limitation in a neuropsychological evaluation of learning disability. Revue de Neuropsychiatrie Infantile et d'Hygiène Mentale de l'Enfant (France). In Press, 1982.

Dehant, A. La dyslexie. Orientation bibliographique. Cahiers de l'Institut des langues vivantes, n° 11, Université Catholique de Louvain, Belgium, 1968a.

Dehant, A. Etude experimentale de méthodes d'apprentissage de la lecture. Librairie Universitaire, Université Catholique de Louvain, Belgium, 1968b.

Denckla, M. B. Clinical syndromes in learning disabilities: The case for "splitting" vs. "lumping." Journal of Learning Disabilities, 1972, 5:401–406, 1972.

Denckla, M. B. Childhood learning disabilities. In K. Heilman and E. Valenstein (Eds.), Clinical neuropsychology. New York: Oxford University Press, 1979, pp. 535–573.

Deruiter, J. A., Ferrel, W. R., and Kass, C. E. Learning disability classification by Bayesian aggregation of test results. Journal of Learning Disabilities, 1975, 6:365–372.

Doehring, D. G., Hoshko, I. M. and Bryans,   . Statistical classification of children with reading problems. Journal of Clinical Neuropsychology, 1979, 1:5–16.

Estienne, F. *L'enfant et l'écriture*. J. P. delarge (Ed). Editions Universitaires, Paris, 1977.

Feshbach, S., Adelman, M., and Fuller, W. Early identification of children with high risk of reading failure. *Journal of Learning Disabilities*, 1974, 7:639–644.

Feshbach, S., Adelman, H., and Fuller, W. Prediction of reading and related academic problems. *Journal of Educational Psychology*, 1977, 69:299–308.

Frostig, M., and Maslow, P. *Learning problems in the classroom: Prevention and Remediation*. New York: Grune and Stratton, 1973.

Gaddes, W. H. A review of some research in the area of serial order behavior. Delivered at the International Academy for Research in Learning Disabilities. Amsterdam, May 17, 1978.

Hall, R. J., and Keogh, B. K. Qualitative characteristics of educationally high risk children. *Learning Disabilities Quarterly*, 1978, 1(2):62–68.

Hier, D. B. Sex differences in hemispheric specialization: Hypothesis for the excess of dyslexia in boys. *Bulletin of the Orton Society*, 1979, 29:74–83.

Inizan, A. *Le temps d'apprendre à lire*, Paris: Colin, 1965.

Jansky, I., and de Hirsch, K. *Preventing reading failure–Prediction, diagnosis, intervention*. New York: Harper and Row, 1972.

Keogh, B. K. A compensatory model for psychoeducational evaluation of children with learning disorders. *Journal of Learning Disabilities*, 1974, 4:544–548.

Keogh, B. K., and Becker, L. D. Early detection of learning problems: Questions, cautions and guidelines. *Exceptional Children*, 1973, 40(1):5–11.

Keogh, B. K., and Smith, C. E. Changes in the copying ability of young children. *Perceptual and Motor Skills*, 1968, 34:617–618.

Kinsbourne, M. The analysis of learning deficit with special reference to selective attention. In *Specific reading disability, advances in theory and method*. D. J. Bakker, and P. Satz (Eds.), Rotterdam University Press, 1970.

Kinsbourne, M. Cerebral dominance, learning and cognition. In H. R. Mykelbust (Ed.), *Progress in learning disabilities*, (Vol. 3). New York: Grune and Stratton, 1975.

Kinsbourne, M., and Warrington, E. K. The developmental Gerstmann syndrome. *Archives of Neurology*, 1963, 8, 490–501.

Kinsbourne, M., and Warrington, E. K. Developmental factors in reading and writing backwardness. In J. Money (Ed.), *The disabled reader: Education of the dyslexic child*. Baltimore: Johns Hopkins Press, 1966, 59–72.

Klees, 1976 (p. 307).

Klees, M. Figures ground perception and instrumental impairments. *Monographies Pédiatriques*, H. L. Vis (Ed.). Edition de l'Université Libre de Bruxelles, Belgium, 1979.

Limbosch, N., Luminet-Jasinski, A., and Dierkens-Dopchie, N. *Le dyslexie à l'école primaire: dépistage et prévention*. Edition de l'Institut de Sociologie de l'Université Libre de Bruxelles, Belgium, 1968.

Lindgren, S. D. Finger localization and the prediction of reading disability. *Cortex*, 1978, 14:87–101.

Lindsay, G. A., and Wedell, K. The early identification of educationally "at risk" children revisited. *Journal of Learning Disabilities*, 1982, 15: Number 4.

Lovell, K., Shapton, D., and Warren, N. S. A study of some cognitive and other disabilities in backward readers of average intelligence as assessed by a non-verbal test. *British J. of Educational Psychology,* 1964, *34*:58–64.

Mattis, S. Dyslexia syndromes: A working hypothesis that works. In A. L. Benton and D. Pearl (Eds.), *Dyslexia: An appraisal of current knowledge.* New York: Oxford University Press, 1978.

Mattis, S., Fench, J. H., and Rapin, T. Dyslexia in children and adults: Three independent neuropsychological syndromes. *Developmental Medicine and Child Neurology,* 1975, *17*:150–163.

Meehl, P., and Rosen, A. Antecedent probability and the efficiency of psychometric signs, patterns or cutting scores. *Psychological Bulletin,* 1955, *52*: 194–216.

Meeker, M. N. *The structure of intellect, its interpretation and uses.* Meeker, M. N., Newell C. Kephart (Eds.), Columbus, Ohio: Merrill,1969.

Mercer, C. D., Algozzine, B., and Trifiletti, J. J. Early identification: Issues and considerations. *Exceptional Children,* 1979, *46*:52–54.

Money, J. *The disabled reader, education of the dyslexic child.* Baltimore: John Hopkins Press, 1966.

Muehl, S., and Forell, E. R. A follow-up study of disabled readers: variables related to high school reading performance. *Reading Research Quarterly,* 1973, *9*:110–123.

Oakland, T. Predictive validity of readiness tests for middle and lower socioeconomic status Anglo, black and Mexican-American children. *Journal of Educational Psychology,* 1978, *70*:574–582.

Pollack, M. D. The effects of testwiseness language of test administration, and language competence level, Spanish-speaking children. Unpublished doctoral dissertation, University of California at Los Angeles, Los Angeles, California, 1980.

Petrauskas, R., and Rourke, B. Identification of subgroups of retarded readers: A neuropsychological multivariate approach. *Journal of Clinical Neuropsychology,* 1979, *1*:17–37.

Rosenthal, R., and Jacobson, L. *Pygmalion in the class-room.* New York: Holt, Rinehart and Winston, 1968.

Rutter, M. Prevalence and types of dyslexia. In A. L. Benton and D. Pearl (Eds.), *Dyslexia, an appraisal of current knowledge.* London: Oxford University Press, 1978, 5–28.

Sand, E., Emery-Hauzeur, C., Buki, H., Chauvin-Faures, C., Sand-Ghislain, J., and Smets, P. L'échec scolaire précoce; variables associées; prédiction. Laboratoire de Médecine Sociale. Ecole de Santé Publique et Laboratoire de Calcul Scientifique de la Faculté de Médecine, Faculté de Médecine de l'Université Libre de Bruxelles, Belgium, 1974.

Santucci, H., Pecheux, G. *Epreuve d'organisation grapho-perceptive, manuel pour l'examen psychologique de l'enfant.* Delachaux et Niestlé, 1967.

Satz, 1979 3 (see MS 304) and (307).

Satz, P., and Fletcher, J. Early screening tests: Some uses and abuses. *Journal of Learning Disabilities,* 1979, *12*:56–60.

Satz, P., and Friel, J. Some predictive antecedents of specific reading disability: A preliminary one year follow-up. In P. Satz and J. J. Ross (Eds.), *The Disabled learner: Early detection and intervention.* Rotterdam, University Press, 1973, pp. 79–98.

Satz, P., and Friel, J. Some predictive antecedents of specific reading disability: A preliminary two-year follow-up. *Journal of Learning Disabilities,* 1974, 7:437–444.

Satz, P., and Morris, R. The search for subtype classification in learning disabled children. In R. E. Tarter (Ed.), *The child at risk.* New York: Oxford University Press, 1980.

Satz, P., Taylor, H. G., Friel, J., and Fletcher, J. Some developmental and predictive precursors of reading disabilities: A six year follow-up. In A. L. Benton and D. Pearl (Eds.), *Dyslexia, and appraisal of current knowledge.* London: Oxford University Press, 1978.

Sbordone, M., and Keogh, B. Early identification of educationally high risk and high potential first grade children. Technical report, University of California, Los Angeles, 1975.

Schery, T. K. Correlates of language development in language disordered children: an archival study. Unpublished doctoral dissertation, Claremont Graduate School, Claremont, California, 1980.

Schilder, P. Fingeragnosie, fingerapraxie, fingeraphasie. *Nervenarzt,* 1931, 4: 625–629.

Silver, A. A., and Hagin, R. A. *Search: A scanning instrument for the identification of potential learning disability: Experimental edition.* New York: New York University Medical Center, 1975.

Simon, J. *Psychopedagogie de l'orthographe.* Paris: Ed. P.U.F., 1954.

Stone, F. B., and Robinson, D. The effect of response mode on finger localization errors. *Cortex,* 1968, 4:233–244.

Strag, G. A. Comparative behavioral ratings of parents with severe mentally retarded, special learning disability and normal children. *Journal of Learning Disabilities,* 1972, 5:52–56.

Tiegs, E. W., and Clark, W. W. *California reading test.* Monterey, California: California Test Bureau (Division McGraw-Hill Book Company), 1967.

Van Wayenberghe, M. A. *Test 6 ans, EPI.* Bruxelles, Belgium: Clerebaut, 1959.

Wechsler, D., and Hagin, R. A. The problem of axial rotation in reading disability. *Perceptual and Motor Skills,* 1964, pp. 319–326.

Wedell, K. Early identification and compensatory interaction. In R. Knights and D. Bakker (Eds.), *Treatment of hyperactive and learning disordered children: Current research.* Baltimore: University Press, 1980.

Willems, G., Berte-Depuydt, T., de Leval, N. A pediatric neuropsychological test for the prediction of learning disorders. Working Paper, University of Louvain, Belgium, 1982.

Willems, G., Noel, A., and Evrard, Ph. *Learning disabilities, neuropediatric examination of the learning functions of preschool-aged children.* Paris: Doin, 1979a.

Willems, G., Noel, A., and Evrard, Ph. Neuropediatric examination of the learning functions of preschool aged children. Revue Française d'Hygiène et de Médecine Scolaire et Universitaire, 1979b, 32:3–104.

Willems, G., Peeters-Frenay, M. C., and Berte-Depuydt, R. The significance of finger localisation test in the assessment of learning disability. *Revue "La Psychomotricité,"* (Vol. 4). Paris: Editions Masson, 1980.

Wissinik, J. F., Kass, C. E., and Ferrel, W. R. A Bayesian approach to the identification of children with learning disabilities. *Journal of Learning Disabilities,* 1975, 8:158–166.

Witelson, S. F. Sex and the single hemisphere: Specialization of the right hemisphere for spatial processing. *Science*, 1976, *193*:425–427.

Yule, W., and Rutter, M. The epidemiology and social implications of specific reading retardation. In R. Knights and D. J. Bakker (Eds.), *The neuropsychology of learning disorders: Theoretical approaches*. Proceedings of NATO Conference, Baltimore: University Park Press, 1976.

Yule, W., Rutter, M., and Graham, P. 1977. (MS 306).

Zazzo, R., Ajuriaguerra, J., Borel-Maisonny, S., Galifret-Granjon, N., Stambak, M., Simon, J., Chassagny, C. L'apprentissage de la lecture et ses troubles, *La psychologie scolaire*, numéro spécial, *Enfance*, Nov–Dec., 1952, 445–479.

Zazzo, R. *Manuel pour l'examen psychologique de l'enfant*. Delachaux et Niestlé, France, 1969.

Zigmond, N. Remediation of dyslexia: a discussion. In A. L. Benton and D. Pearl (Eds.), *Dyslexia, an appraisal of current knowledge*. London, Oxford University Press, 437–438, 1978.

SELECTED ADDITIONAL READINGS

Bakker, D. J. A set of brain for learning-to-read. Lecture given at the University of Louvain, Pediatric Neurology Department, St. Luke University Clinic, Brussels, 1978.

Benton, A. L. Development of finger-localization capacity in school children. *Child Dev.*, 1955, *26*:225–230.

Berte-Depuydt, R. Essai d'adaptation de l'échelle d'intelligence pour enfants de D. Wechsler (WISC) à des écoliers belges d'expression française. Document n° 8 du C. N. R. P. S. Imprimerie F. Clerebaut, S.A., 1961.

Dubois-Manne, R. La maladaptation scolaire, les médecins et les oeuvres de la première enfance. *L'enfant* n° 5, 377–422, 1981.

Galen, R. S., and Gambino, S. R. *Beyond normality: The predictive value and efficiency of medical diagnosis*. New York: John Wiley, 1975.

Gilly, M. Progression scolaire et apprentissage de la lecture chez des enfants de niveaux socio-culturels différents fréquentant les mêmes écoles. *Bulletin de l'Association Française de Psychologues Scolaires*, 1963, *3*:35–45.

Guilford, J. *The nature of human intelligence*. New York: McGraw-Hill, 1967.

Lindgren, S. D. The early identification of children at risk for reading disabilities: Finger localization ability, verbal skills and perceptual-motor performance in kindergarten children. Unpublished master's thesis, University of Iowa, 1975.

Lindsay, G. *The infant rating scale manual*. London: Hodder and Stoughton, 1981.

McLeod, J., and Greenough, P. The importance of sequencing as an aspect of short-term memory in good and poor spellers. *Journal of Learning Disabilities*, 1980, *13*:255–261.

Robinson, H. M., Vocabulary: Speaking, listening, reading and writing. In H. A. Robinson (Ed.), *Reading and the language arts*. Chicago: University of Chicago Press, 1963.

Rutter, M., Graham, P., and Yule, W. A. *Neuropsychiatry study in childhood. Clinic in developmental medicine*. London: Heinemann Medical Book, 1970.

Rutter, M., Tizard, J., and Whitmore, K. *Education, health and behavior.* London: Longmans, 1970.

Stambak, M. Le problème du rythme dans le développement de l'enfant et dans les dyslexies d'évolution. Enfance, Paris Tome IV, P.U.F.: pp. 480–502, 1951.

Szliwowski, H. B., Dopchie, N., and Klees-Delange, M. Mise au point de la notion de "lésions cérébrales à minima." *Acta Paediatrica Belgica,* 1970, *24*(3–4): 287–293.

Vecchio, T. J. Predictive value of a single diagnostic test in unselected population. *N. Engl. J. Med.* 1966, *274*:1171–1173.

Willems, G. Neuropediatric examination of the learning functions of preschool children carried out in Brussels. Annales du Congrès de Neurologie Infantile de Langue Française. Marseille, Dec. 1977.

Willems, G. Components of early identification. International Academy for Research in Learning Disabilities. *Thalamus,* 1980(a), *1*:29–36.

Willems, G. Sleep and learning disabilities. Lecture given at the University of Louvain (Belgium), Pediatric Neurology Dept., Cliniques Universitaires St Luc, May 1980(b).

6

A Critical Note on the Value of Attention Deficit as a Basis for a Clinical Syndrome

DAVID SHAFFER AND IRVIN SCHONFELD

EDITOR'S COMMENTS

In this chapter, "inattention" is analyzed and the inadequacy of the questions on commonly used rating scales for diagnosing this symptom are specified. The authors demonstrate the difficulties encountered in attempting to diagnose inattention as a cardinal symptom using the one relevant question on the Rutter Behaviour Questionnaire. Subsequently, the authors point out the limitations in the measurement of activity in children using various methods, both in a strict setting and a more naturalistic one.

David Shaffer then proceeds to discuss the analysis of his research sample of boys who were known to have neurological soft signs at the age of 7 compared with a matched control group known to have been without such signs. Problems in using teachers' and parents' rating scales of overactivity are explored. For instance, there were no significant correlations between scores on the parents' Motor Activity Checklist and the teachers' checklists of either activity or attention. It is suggested that there is a strong correlation between hyperkinetic and inattentive factors, rated by teachers, raising questions about their independence.

The authors conclude by submitting that "the definitional problems pertaining to the symptoms of hyperactivity and inattention are so considerable that it is premature to base any behaviorally defined psychiatric syndrome on their presence or absence."

*   *   *

William James wrote, "We all know what is meant by attention." Surely a warning note. The complexity of the behaviors that we loosely call *overactivity* and *inattention* has received critical attention elsewhere (see Cromwell, Baumeister and Hawkins, 1963; Martin and Powers, 1967; Shaffer and Greenhill, 1979; Douglas and Peters, 1979). The purpose of this chapter is to present some epidemiological and laboratory data that suggest that the problems of defining and hence measuring these behaviors are so considerable that they call into question the wisdom of basing a clinical syndrome on their presence or absence.

The term "inattention" is usually used to refer to off-task behavior. It is reasonable to suppose that this form of behavioral deviance could follow from a number of causes, including: the *inappropriateness* of the task, i.e., when the difficulty or interest level of the task does not match the chronological or mental age, or the cultural habits of the child; *inadequate motivation*, which could in turn follow from a disturbance of affect, variations in achievement motivation (a purported personality dimension); *inadequate or inappropriate reinforcement opportunities* associated with the task. or more specific *cognitive elements*, such as distractibility or impaired vigilance (an inability to sustain attention). It may also be that certain children who are called inattentive will on close examination show appropriate on-task behaviors but also inappropriate or annoying behaviors, which are better understood as denoting such dimensions as dependency, aggression, or anxiety. In the face of this complexity, the ways in which we most frequently ask about attentional behaviors are surprisingly naive. Table 1 lists the wording found in several commonly used behavior rating scales, which have been employed as the basis for subject definition in a large number of research studies.

If a statement that a child is inattentive cannot be relied upon to indicate a single psychological construct, we might expect that different children will be called inattentive or overactive for different reasons, that "inattention" used in this way will not be a particularly useful discriminant between normal and disturbed children nor between children with different clinical entities, and that different ways of measuring attention will not necessarily correlate well with each other.

It is possible to review the data collected from Rutter's epidemiological study on the Isle of Wight (Rutter, Tizard, and Whitmore, 1970) to examine some of these predictions. In that study, information about the presence of a variety of symptoms was obtained from a representative, population-based sample of nondisturbed 10- to 11-year-old children and from all the children of the same age who had a psychiatric disorder. The presence of disturbance was determined, not through an administrative procedure such as a history of clinic referral, but after screening and obtaining information from two informants (parents and teachers) and a direct assessment of the child. The advantage of that approach for this examination is that, in addition to studying patients with

Table 1. Inattention Scale Items in Commonly Used Behavior Inventories

Scale	Item
Quay, Peterson (1975)	Short attention span Daydreaming Distractibility
Conners (1969)	Inattentive; easily distracted Fails to finish things he started Short attention span Daydreaming Distractibility or attention span problem Easily frustrated in efforts
Achenbach (1981)	Fails to finish things he starts Can't concentrate, pay attention for long
Rutter, Tizard and Whitmore (1970)	Cannot settle for anything for more than a few moments

more severe problems, it allows us to compare the prevalence of behaviors such as inattention or overactivity in disturbed children who are not encumbered with a diagnostic label, with both normal children and children with relatively minor disorders who might not otherwise be seen at a clinic.

Table 2 shows the prevalence of behaviors that are regarded as pathognomonic of Attention Deficit Disorder in disturbed and nondisturbed children. The rates are derived from responses to the Rutter Behavior Questionnaires (1970), checklists similar in form and content to other commonly used inventories, such as the Conners Parent and Teacher Rating Scales (1969) and Achenbach's

Table 2. Features of the Attention Deficit Disorder
in Disturbed and Nondisturbed 10- to 11-Year-Old Boys, in Percent

Item	Source	General population (controls)	Psychiatric disturbance
Poor concentration	Parent scale	25.2	65
Poor concentration	Teacher scale	35.3	81.1
Overactivity	Parent scale	35	65
Overactivity	Teacher scale	16	55
Distractible	Psychiatric examination	10	28

From Rutter et al. (1970), *Education, Health and Behavior.*

Child Behavior Checklist (1981). It can be seen that the rates are significantly higher among the disturbed than among the nondisturbed on all measures. However, the point of interest is the very high base rate for these symptoms among normals. A simple calculation will convey the impact of these figures. The prevalence of psychiatric disorder in that population was approximately 7%. Therefore, in a population of 1,000 children there would be 70 disturbed and 930 nondisturbed children. If 35% of the nondisturbed children and 81% of the disturbed children are considered inattentive by their teachers, then the population of 1,000 will include a total of 382 children called *inattentive*, of whom only 52 (15%) will be disturbed. Clearly, this is a problem if inattention is to be regarded as a cardinal symptom in a clinical entity.

If we regard hyperactivity or inattention as symptoms of such specificity that a diagnostic entity can rest on their presence, which is certainly the implication of the DSM-III glossary (Spitzer, 1980), we would also anticipate that they would be differentially distributed in children with different clinical problems. However, a further examination of the Isle of Wight data (see Tables 3 and 4) shows that prevalence rates for inattention and overactivity are similar in three different diagnostic groups, regardless of the source of information. This is in spite of the very considerable differences in other types of symptomatology, family background, individual differences, and prognoses that are found in these groups of disturbed children. This could be explained if different types of behavior with different psychological meaning are being described in a similar nonspecific and ultimately confusing fashion.

Table 3. Poor Concentration in 10- to 11-Year-Old Boys
with Different Psychiatric Diagnoses, in Percent

	Neurotic disorder	Conduct disorder	Mixed neurotic conduct
Poor persistence (psychiatric examination)	34	43	54
Distractibility (psychiatric examination)	23	23	36
Poor concentration (teacher questionnaire)	75	85	78
Poor concentration (parent interview)	82	77	71

From Rutter et al. (1970), *Education, Health and Behavior.*

Table 4.   Overactivity in 10- to 11-Year-Old Boys
with Different Psychiatric Diagnoses (Teacher's Ratings), in Percent

Rating	Neurotic disorder	Conduct disorder	Mixed neurotic conduct
Overactive (teacher)	44	62	57
Fidgety (teacher)	50	62	70

From Rutter et al. (1970), *Education, Health and Behavior.*

What possible solutions are there to these problems of definition? One approach has been through the standardization of reporting and the use of formal behavior inventories. Data obtained in this way can be treated empirically to identify clusters of symptoms that are commonly found to be associated with each other. However, a "hyperactivity factor" derived in this way may be no freer of semantic muddle than the individual items from which it is constituted. In support of this we find high correlations between hyperactivity factors and other symptom groups within the same individual (Goyette, Conners, and Ulrich, 1978). We find poor correlations between items checked on inventories and observations made on the same children (McConnell, Cromwell, Bialer, and Son, 1964; Blunden, Spring, and Greenberg, 1974; Whalen and Hencker, 1976). We also find generally poor levels of interrater reliability when different raters use the same scale on the same child (Whalen and Hencker, 1976).

Yet another approach is to devise laboratory tests to obtain objective measurement of abnormal behaviors. Laboratory approaches to the measurement of activity include the use of ballistographs (Foshee, 1958); ultrasonics (Peacock and Williams, 1962); photoelectric cells arrayed in a free-activity area (Ellis and Pryor, 1959); pneumatic floor pads (Cromwell et al., 1963); pedometers (Stunkard, 1958); actometers (Schulman and Reisman, 1959; Colburn et al., 1976), and stabilimeters (Sprague and Toppe, 1966). The limitations on the measurement of activity level in children using some of these methods have been critiqued by Johnson (1972). Studies using multiple informants and analyzing activity in different locations (Stevens, Kupst, and Suran, 1978) show somewhat inconsistent relationships and the whole issue of the objective measurement of activity has been reviewed by Porrino, Rapoport, Behar et al., (1983). They conclude that measurement in very restricted settings may be misleading; they have gone on to study activity in a naturalistic rather than in a laboratory setting, an approach that presents considerable difficulties and expense when applied to the measurement of attention or "on-task" behavior.

**Table 5. Agreement between Parents and
Teachers on High Activity**

Conners checklist hyperactivity factor (teachers)	Motor activity checklist (parents)		
	Low	High	Total
Low	61	4	65
High	12	2	14
Total	73	6	79

In Table 5, data are presented from a study of 115 black male 7-year-olds who were being investigated as part of a systematic follow-up of children who had been enrolled in the Collaborative Perinatal Project (see Shaffer, Stockman, O'Connor, et al., 1983, for a full description of the sample). Half of the sample are adolescent boys who are known to have had neurological soft signs at the age of seven and the other half were known to have been without such signs. Behavioral ratings were obtained using the Conners Teachers Rating Scale (Conners, 1969, 1973) completed by three different teachers, and the Motor Activity Checklist (Werry and Sprague, 1970) in an interview with the parents. The checklist is made up of a series of systematic questions concerning gross motor activity, restlessness, and fine motor activity during everyday activities such as watching television, reading, playing a game, eating a meal, and during a social conversation. Both the Passive Inattentive Factor and the Hyperactivity Factor from the Conners Teachers Rating Scale have been used in our analyses. The direct examination carried out on these adolescents also included a number of laboratory measures of attention, including the Continuous Performance Test (Rosvold, Mirsky, Sarason, et al., 1956) and David's (1971) assessment method for hyperkinesis. The Continuous Performance Test uses a microprocessor continuously to monitor errors of omission and commission. A feedback system reduces the interstimulus interval and thereby increases the difficulty of the task as a function of the number of correct and appropriate responses. A brief interstimulus interval at the end of the ten-minute test therefore reflects an accurate and attentive performance, whereas a longer interval indicates a performance with more errors.

If the argument expressed above is correct, i.e., that attention and overactivity are poorly defined variables that may not be reported in a standardized fashion by observers, we should expect to find low correspondence between teachers' and parents' ratings and between laboratory measures such as the Continuous Performance Test, but good agreement between different behavior factors rated by the same individual.

Table 5 shows the relationship between parents' and teachers' evaluations of overactive behavior in 79 adolescents from whom sufficient data were available. A high teacher's score on the hyperactivity factor was taken as equal to or more than the mean plus one standard deviation for the sample (1.24). A similar statistical criterion was used to define a high overactive score on the parent's Motor Activity Checklist. If more than one teacher's rating had been obtained for each child, those ratings were averaged. Table 5 shows that approximately 18% of all children have a high score on the teacher's and 8% a high score on the parent checklist. The agreement between teachers and parents was highly unsatisfactory with only 2 out of the 18 adolescents noted to be hyperactive by both raters.

This finding of poor correspondence between teachers' and parents' evaluations of children's and adolescents' activity and attention has been found elsewhere (Sandberg, Rutter, and Taylor, 1978) and it has been suggested (Schachar, Rutter, and Smith, 1981) that it is only in cases where overactivity or inattention is clearly cross-situational and has been noted by both parents and teachers that the diagnosis of hyperactivity should be applied. It may well be that the reason for poor concordance between parents and teachers is the situation-specificity of the behaviors under examination; however, another explanation is a lack of agreement between raters on what constitutes overactive behavior. This might in turn be confused with a threshold effect, so that agreement only focuses where activity or attention is severe.

Table 6 demonstrates correlations between the parent-completed Motor Activity Checklist Scores and scores on the Conners' Teacher Scale Hyperactivity and Inattention factors and the final interstimulus interval obtained on the Continuous Performance Test.

Table 6. Correlation Between Different Measures of Inattention and Overactivity in 83-106 Black Male Adolescents

| | Conners factor scores | | |
	Hyperactivity	Inattention	Final I.S.I.[a]
Motor activity checklist (parent)	−.043	−.116	.143
Conners hyperactivity factor (teacher)	−	.582***	.417***
Conners inattentive factor (teacher)	−	−	.229*

[a]Interstimulus interval on continuous performance test.
*p < .05
***p < .001

Table 7. Correlation Between Different Measures of Inattention,
Overactivity, and I.Q. in 83-106 Black Male Adolescents

	Conners factor scores		
	Hyperactivity	Inattention	Final I.S.I.[a]
Full scale I.Q.	–.303***	–.307**	–.552***

[a]Interstimulus interval on continuous performance test.
  **p <.01
***p <.001

In the correlation matrix presented in Table 6, we can see that there are no significant correlations between scores on the parent-completed Motor Activity Checklist and the teacher checklists of either activity or attention. However, there is a strong correlation between the hyperkinetic factor and the inattentive factor completed by the teachers, which raises questions about their independence. The parent-completed Motor Activity Checklist score is unrelated to the final interstimulus interval measure of the Continuous Performance Test. This is reasonable because the parent Motor Activity Checklist is a report on gross and fine motor activity and does not focus on inattentive behaviors. However, when we look at the relationship between the teacher's hyperactivity and inattentive factors and the laboratory tests, we find a more confused situation. Both are significantly related to performance on the Continuous Performance Test, but all three of these measures are also related to I.Q. (see Table 7). If we examine partial correlations, taking out the effects of full-scale I.Q. (see Table 8), we find that a score on the Conners Inattentive Factor is no longer significantly related

Table 8. Partial Correlations Between Different Measures of Inattention and
Overactivity, Taking Account of I.Q., in 83–106 Black Male Adolescents

	Conners factor scores		
	Hyperactivity	Inattention	Final I.S.I.[a]
Motor activity checklist: (parent)	–.015	–.140	.059
Conners hyperactivity factor (teacher)	–	.590***	.333**
Conners inattentive factor (teacher)	–	–	.097

[a]Interstimulus interval on continuous performance test.
  **p <.01
***p <.001

to the laboratory measure of inattention, although the hyperactivity factor remains correlated to a somewhat lesser extent.

To summarize: A parent's rating of overactivity is unrelated to a teacher's rating of overactivity or to a teacher's or laboratory measure of inattention. A teacher's rating of overactivity is very strongly related to a teacher's rating of inattention and to a laboratory measure of inattention, even after taking into account I.Q.; however, a teacher's rating of inattention is unrelated to a laboratory measure of inattention after taking account of I.Q.

This argument has only dealt with the confusion that surrounds the various designations of attention and does not deal with the quite different problem concerning the differences between Attention Deficit Disorder and conduct disorders, which has been addressed elsewhere (see Shaffer and Greenhill, 1979).

In conclusion, we submit that the definitional problems pertaining to the symptoms of hyperactivity and inattention are so considerable that it is premature to base any behaviorally defined psychiatric syndrome on their presence or absence.

DISCUSSIONS

Dennis P. Cantwell

Dr. Cantwell: It is probably unfortunate that this disorder, by whatever name you want to call it, was given a name switching from *one symptom* (hyperactivity), to *another symptom* (inattention), with the implication that this is now the "central core" of the disorder. When DSM-III was being put together, early on, I think Paul [Wender] and I jointly suggested that this disorder should be called Hoffman's syndrome, named after Heinrich Hoffman, the pediatrician who, you are all aware, first described this condition in a German children's book called, *Der Strüwelpater*, in describing a little boy called "fidgety Phil." Now our suggestion was voted down at the time because it was decided there would be no eponyms in DSM-III. But I think it would have been much better to have a neutral name for our disorder, rather than assuming that something like attention, which has been pointed out by many people actually carries multiple connotations, really is the central core problem.

When different measures are used to measure what is supposedly the same thing, not surprisingly, you come up with different results. That indicates that not only do we need better theoretical looks at our constructs, but also better ways to measure them.

Now some specific comments on some of the main points. In the Isle of Wight study, as I remember, the final diagnosis of "disturbed" vs. "not disturbed" did include items from parent/teacher rating scale. So those were not mutually exclusive and it's not surprising that you find certain symptoms that are higher in a disturbed population, because it was on the basis of those symptoms that the diagnosis was made.

I also want to comment on something that Hans Huessy said regarding the use of high scores on teacher and parent rating scales and using them alone to indicate disturbance. Now, part of the idea of a psychiatric disorder is that it requires clinical judgment to decide whether the combination of symptoms that the child presents (evaluated from a variety of sources; parent, teacher, child himself, etc.) is really causing a significant disturbance and functional disability in the child's life. There are many numbers of people who might have had high scores on the Conners Rating Scale when they were young, and many who would have high scores right now. That is, they have not changed. But I would submit that a high score doesn't necessarily mean psychiatric diagnosis and I think that it is important to recognize that.

Number three: Often we are seeing that Parent and Teacher Rating Scales are being used alone in factor and cluster analysis to create subgroups of patients. There are several problems with that. If you look at the data from the Isle of Wight study, one of the most striking things is that if you take the disturbed group vs. the nondisturbed group, that the Parent and Teacher Rating Scales are equally good at picking out deviant children, but they pick out *different* children. So that if you use only the Parent or only the Teacher Rating Scale, to use that in a factor or cluster analysis, you're going to come up with clusters that I don't think necessarily have that much meaning.

Number four: There are items on the Rating Scale that *we* know what they mean. I mean, when Keith Conners wrote his rating scale, he knew what those items meant. I'm not so sure that the parent and teacher—*all parents and teachers*—know what those items mean in the same way. One of the items with which I consistently come across this is an item—it's on a rating scale we're using and it is probably on your scale and it's probably on the Achenbach scale—something like "obsessive ideas . . . can't get mind off certain thoughts." It is always checked by parents. When you ask them what that means, it means, "Well, when we go to Toys 'R Us and we won't buy him a toy, he won't shut up." Now that obviously does not mean obsessive ideas to us, but if you use that in a factor analysis, you're going to come up with a nice group of obsessive ideas over here that don't mean a clinical tinker's damn. So I think that that's important to recognize.

The question I would have with regard to your study has to do with CPT findings worse in the "soft" sign group and then the washing out with I.Q. Are the CPT findings related to the presence of later signs . . . at the age 17, when you saw them?

Dr. Shaffer: With children who had signs at age 17, there were also CPT differences; there were also I.Q. differences. Furthermore, the differences washed out when adjustment was made for the I.Q.

Dr. Cantwell: Is it related to later diagnosis at all?

Dr. Shaffer: No. The data really showed that they were reciprocally related to diagnosis in the "soft-sign-positive" group.

C. Keith Conners

It's not surprising to me that one would find that in the collaboratory paranatal study, those children with motor signs don't have attention deficits. In the same way, if you picked up a group of children with sensory signs, they wouldn't necessarily have motor deficits. It's not the same thing to have an attentional dysfunction in the brain as to have a motor dysfunction. There may be some slight overlap, but of course over that large period of time you wouldn't expect there to be much of an association.

With respect to parent and teacher evaluations of inattentiveness, one way to look at it is in terms of the correlation between the factors on the separate teacher and parent scores. If you look at our standardization example in Pittsburgh, you'll see that the correlations are something like 0.4—modest but highly significant. They're obviously significantly related but they wouldn't give you much more than a 16% overlap if you were to look at the shared variance. I think it's obvious that these factor symptom scores are not diagnostic devices. They are simply measures, in a very crude way, of somebody's impression of the presence of a class of symptoms; whether those symptoms represent a diagnostic entity or just normal variations of behavior isn't really addressed by these studies. There are data to show that teachers' measures on the symptom ratings in the classroom do correlate with other measures of attentiveness.

One might ask: which is really the valid measure? The CPT measures one kind of very specific laboratory activity and it would be a miracle if it were identical to a teacher's perception of restlessness and inattentiveness in the classroom. There may well be some overlap in the data, however. It's not very persuasive to me that children with a clinically defined disorder have a marginal performance on teacher ratings or CPT. In other words, I don't think you could reduplicate diagnosis by a single measure, particularly a gross measure. I think it's wrong to conclude from these low associations with teacher ratings that a carefully structured hyperkinetic group isn't inattentive or restless. What those symptom rating measures do is tell you what the major *dimensions* are in the symptom ratings. Whether those symptom ratings measure something pathological is an entirely different question.

I think that the dimension of "inattentiveness" that shows up on these measures is not necessarily a measure of brain information processing that could be picked up on laboratory measures. I don't think that you can dismiss the notion of an attention deficit because you don't find very high correlations with teacher or parent ratings, given that they will not pick up the momentary "tuning out" so characteristic—we believe—of ADD.

REFERENCES

Achenbach, T. M., and Edelbrock, C. S. Behavioral problems and competencies reported by parents of normal and disturbed children aged 4-16. *Monographs of the Society for Research in Child Development*, 1981, No. 188, Vol. 46, No. 1.

Blunden, D., Spring, C., Greenberg, L. M. Validation of the classroom behavior inventory. *Journal of Consulting and Clinical Psychiatry*, 1974, *42*:84-88.

Colburn, T. R., Smith, B. M., and Guarini, J. J. An ambulatory activity monitor with solid state memory. *ISA Trans.*, 1976, *15*:149-154.

Conners, C. K. A teacher rating scale for use in drug studies with children. *Am. J. Psychiat.*, 1969, *126*:884-888.

Conners, C. K. Rating scales for use in drug studies with children. *Psychopharmacology Bulletin* (Special Issue: Pharmacotherapy of Children), 1973, pp. 24-84.

Cromwell, R. L., Baumeister, A., and Hawkins, W. F. Research in activity level. In: N. R. Ellis (Ed.), *Handbook of mental deficiency*. New York, McGraw-Hill, 1963.

Davids, A. An objective instrument for assessing hyperkinesis in children. *Journal of Learning Disabilities*, 1971, *4*:35-37.

Douglas, V., and Peters, K. Toward a clearer definition of the attentional deficit of hyperactive children. In: G. A. Hale and M. Lewis (Eds.). *Attention and the development of cognitive skills*. New York: Plenum Press, 1979, pp. 173-247.

Ellis, N. R., and Pryer, R. S. Quantification of gross bodily activity in children with severe neuropathology. *Am. J. Ment. Def.*, 1959, *63*:1034-1037.

Foshee, J. G. Studies in activity level: 1. Simple and complex task performance in defectives. *Am. J. Ment. Def.*, 1958, *62*:882-886.

Goyette, C. H., Conners, C. K., and Ulrich, R. F. (1978). Normative data on Revised Conners Parent and Teacher Rating Scales. *Journal of Abnormal Child Psychology*, 1978, *6*:221-236.

Johnson, C. F. Limits on the measurement of activity level in children using ultrasound and photoelectric cells. *Am. J. Ment. Def.*, 1972, *77*:301-310.

McConnell, T. R., Jr., Cromwell, R. L., Bialer, I., and Son, C. D. Studies in activity level: VII. Effects of amphetamine drug administration on the activity level of retarded children. *Am. J. Ment. Def.*, 1964, *68*:647-651.

Martin, G. L., and Powers, R. B. Attention span: An operant conditioning analysis. *Exceptional Children,* 1967, *33*:565–570.

Peacock, L. J., and Williams, M. An ultrasonic device for recording activity. *Am. J. Psychol.,* 1962, *75*:648–652.

Porrino, L. J., Rapoport, J. L., Behar, D., et al., (1983). A naturalistic assessment of the motor activity of hyperactive boys. 1. Comparison with normal controls. *Arch. Gen. Psychiatry,* 1983, *40*:681–687.

Quay, H. C., and Peterson, D. R. Manual for the behavior problem checklist. Unpublished manuscript.

Rosvold, H. E., Mirsky, A. F., Sarason, I., Bransome, E. D., Jr., and Beck, L. H. A continuous performance test of brain damage. *Journal of Consulting Psychology,* 1956, *20*:343–350.

Rutter, M. L., Tizard, J., and Whitmore, K. *Education, health and behavior.* London: Longmans, 1970.

Sandberg, S. T., Rutter, M., and Taylor, E. Hyperkinetic disorder in psychiatric clinic attenders. *Dev. Med. Child. Neurol.,* 1978, *20*:279–299.

Schachar, R., Rutter, M., and Smith, A. The characteristics of situationally and pervasively hyperactive children: Implications for syndrome definition. *J. Child Psychol. Psychiat.,* 1981, *22*:375–392.

Schulman, J. L., and Reisman, J. M. An objective measure of hyperactivity. *Am. J. Ment. Def.,* 1959, *64*:455–456.

Shaffer, D., and Greenhill, L. A critical note on the predictive validity of the hyperkinetic syndrome. *J. Child Psychol. Psychiat.,* 1979, *20*:61–72.

Shaffer, D., Stockman, C. S., O'Connor, P. A., Shafer, S., Barmack, J., Hess, S., Spalten, D., and Schonfeld, I. S. (1983). Early soft neurological signs and later psychopathology. In: Erlenmeyer, N. Kimling, and B. S. Dohrenwend (Eds.), *Life span research on the prediction of psychopathology.* In press.

Spitzer, R. L. (Ed.), *Diagnostic and statistical manual of mental disorders.* 3rd ed. Washington, D.C.: American Psychiatric Association, 1980.

Sprague, R. L., and Toppe, L. K. Relationship between activity level and delay of reinforcement in the retarded. *Journal of Experimental Child Psychology,* 1966, *3*:390–397.

Stevens, Kupst, and Suran. *J. Abnorm. Child Psychol.,* 1978, *6*:163–173.

Stunkard, A. Physical activity, emotions and human obesity. *Psychosomatic Medicine,* 1958, *20*:366–372.

Werry, J. S., and Sprague, R. L. Hyperactivity. In: *Symptoms of Psychopathology.* G. G. Costello (Ed.), New York: John Wiley, 1970, pp. 397–417.

Whalen, C. K., and Hencker, B. Psychostimulants in children: A review and analysis. *Psychological Bulletin,* 1976, *82*:1113–1130.

7

Beyond Attention Deficit:
Search for the Disorder in ADD

MARCEL KINSBOURNE

EDITOR'S COMMENTS

Dr. Kinsbourne believes that if attention is at the core of ADD, vigilance (sustained attention) is the major focus for research. He points out that although experimental studies are necessarily conducted under circumstances that tend to mitigate the disturbed behavior of ADD children, results of such experiments may nevertheless be regarded as reliable.

Marcel Kinsbourne describes his experimental design and methods for measuring differences of various factors differentiating normal, ADD responders, and nonresponders and his subsequent research on what appeared to be the major distinction between index and control groups of children, their strategic approach to problem-solving.

The author depicts a model for reducing the area of uncertainty in order to arrive at a decision. He shows a diagram of the U-shaped curve for CNS arousal level: low (hyperactive), normal, and high (anxious). He then describes further experiments that he conducted with paired-associate learning and the effect of medication thereon. In addition, psychophysiological measurements of the children during tasks were made. Heart rate was not useful in revealing differences that would differentiate favorable from unfavorable responders to stimulant drugs. However, those children having lower comparable skin conductance before testing learn better on stimulant medication. Those who had higher levels before testing on drug learned worse with the stimulant but this was for all children and there was no significant difference in base levels of skin conductance between favorable and adverse responders.

Two more experiments are described, one with the Lykken maze and the other with a marble-dispensing machine. Kinsbourne found a striking difference between favorable and adverse responders interacting with the drug and placebo conditions, a difference that could not be related to attention but rather had to do with difference of response to reward and punishment, using the marble-dispensing machine. Dr. Kinsbourne reaches the following conclusion:

> The ADD child needs something solid and concrete or frequent and salient before he, too, can control his behavior the way the rest of us can under a much wider range of conditions. But then he can. The attention deficit in ADD is not invariant. The machinery for efficient behavioral control exists in the ADD child. Extra activation is needed, however, to enable it to participate consistently in controlling the way these children live.

*   *   *

Terms that presuppose an understanding of the mechanism of impulsivity and inattentiveness in *hyperactive, attention deficit disordered* children err by identifying one manifestation as primary, without knowing whether it is. However, to call it a no-name syndrome is not useful either. Those who claim to be dispassionate and atheoretical observers of the human condition (empiricists) delude themselves. They are theorists who just haven't bothered to formulate their preconceptions. Everybody has some construct about these children.

We can agree that motor restlessness is neither necessary nor sufficient to make the diagnosis. Is the attention deficit the fundamental disorder in ADD? Dr. Douglas and others have shown convincingly that if attention is at the core, it is not selective attention but sustained attention that we should incriminate; I concentrate on that area.

Our work for the last twelve years has been based on laboratory paradigms that use acute, double-blind, drug-placebo challenges. You will be reading about an elegant adaptation of this paradigm in the behavioral part of Barry Garfinkel's investigation. Note that when we measure our children's attention in the laboratory, we may not be tapping their typical attentional state, because the problem in ADD is both context-dependent and task-dependent. The children who are ordinarily hyperactive or attention-disordered may not exhibit their disorder in the laboratory. The novelty, structure, and individual attention in the laboratory may temporarily counteract the hyperactive state. In one study (Conte and Kinsbourne, in preparation), a sample of hyperactive children, when observed by their parents in the laboratory, were given a mean Conners' questionnaire score of 6, which is within the normal range. We counteract our own goal of analyzing hyperactive behavior in these studies by having to conduct them under circumstances that tend to mitigate that behavior. It does pertain that effects that emerge nonetheless can be regarded as reliable.

The attentional problems have mostly been characterized as impulsivity and inattentiveness. For measuring the first, the Matching Familiar Figures task (MFF—Kagan, 1965) or one of its variants is appropriate and for the second, continuous performance tasks like the Children's Check Test (Keough and Margolis, 1976) can be used. One MFF-like procedure that we have used was computerized (Flintoff, Barron, Swanson, et al., 1982). The child was given a target, a spiky figure (nonsense polygram), and an ensemble of figures, all similar but with only one identical to the model. The child's eye movements were recorded in terms both of location and latency. The ADD children on methylphenidate made more comparisons between items in the ensemble and the target before coming to a decision and also compared more variants with each other. Interestingly, they matched no more accurately on drug than on placebo. They used a different strategy but, in this situation, the strategic difference was not confounded with a performance difference.

Why didn't these children, who on our paired-associate task (which I will discuss later) were favorable drug-responders, show a drug-placebo performance difference? *Because it matters whether the task is simple or complex.* In this particular task, the children felt as if they were playing a computer game. Perhaps they attended relatively well because they found this an attractive task, and/or because they had the one-to-one attention of the examiner. Only a subtle difference in style emerged. In unpublished work (Kapelus, et al.) we also have continuous performance data on a tracking task. Both "favorable" and "adverse"

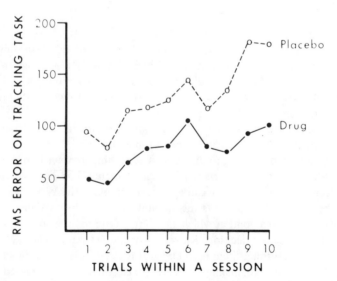

Figure 1. Performance on computer-controlled tracking task for 18 favorable responders to stimulant medication.

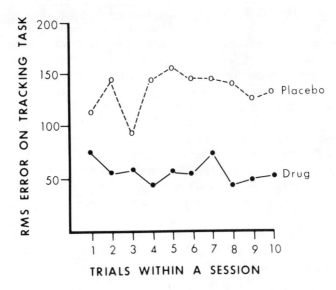

Figure 2. Performance on computer-controlled tracking task for 9 adverse responders to stimulant medication.

drug-responders did better on drug than on placebo. That is, all the children responded "favorably" on *this* test (see Figures 1 and 2). On a cognitively low-level performance test, we would expect both ADD children and control children, however sampled, to do better on stimulants. However, that is not the case on more complex and challenging tasks.

What kind of a model may we entertain in regard to the temporal dimension of ADD? Figure 3 presents a simple formulation.

A person who is trying to understand something in order to make a choice begins with an area of uncertainty, which in Figure 3 is represented by the surface area of the circle. As he gathers information and thinks about it (moving toward the center), he constricts the amount of uncertainty. When uncertainty has been reduced to a point at which an internal criterion for knowing enough is satisfied, he makes his decision. Knowing enough is by no means synonymous with knowing everything there is to know. It is rarely adaptive to run a problem into the ground before making a decision. By then, life has passed one by. Perhaps children with ADD tend to resolve uncertainty less before they make decisions. They are therefore hasty, impulsive, and less accurate because less uncertainty has been resolved.

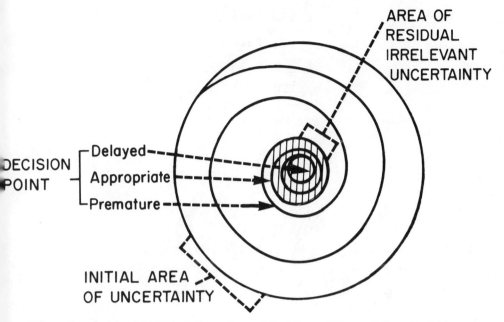

Figure 3. Model of temporal dimensions of decision-making and the effect of ADD on decision-making.

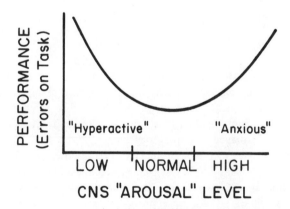

Figure 4. Diagram of postulated effect of stimulants on performances of hyperactive children.

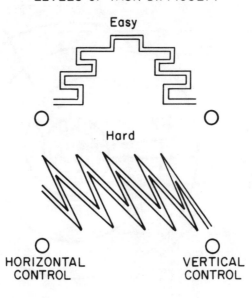

Figure 5. Etch-a-Sketch task. From T. Humphries, J. M. Swanson, M. Kins-bourne, and L. Yu, Stimulant effects on persistence of motor performance of hyperactive children. *Journal of Pediatric Psychology*, 1979:4, 55–56.

Figure 4 shows a further assumption. Some system in the brain is under-active in hyperactive children and, as a result, performance deteriorates rapidly over time. As its activation is increased, for instance by a psychoactive drug, performance is better maintained. If it is more active still, as when the drug is given in overdose, performance deteriorates again.

The next study gives a simple example (Humphries, Swanson, Kinsbourne, and Yu, 1979). In this case, we used the Etch-a-Sketch task. One draws a line on a surface, controlling it with two knobs. The child is asked to draw a line so as not to infringe the boundaries of a superimposed schema (see Figure 5). We time how long the child takes and we count the number of infringements. For the schema shown in Figure 6, we find that for the first two trials, 1 and 2, there is no differential number of infringements between the children on drug and on placebo, but for trials 3, 4, 5, and 6 there is. So, over time, a performance

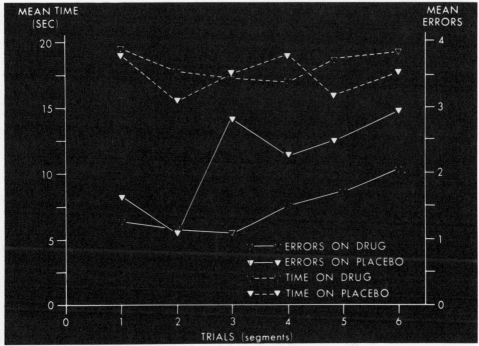

Figure 6. Persistence of performance (time and errors) for responders across trials on Maze II (Etch-a-Sketch). From T. Humphries, J. M. Swanson, M. Kinsbourne, and L. Yu, Stimulant effects on persistence of motor performance of hyperactive children. *Journal of Pediatric Psychology*, 1979: 4, 55–56.

discrepancy emerges and this, of course, exemplifies the typical pattern of failure to sustain attention seen in hyperactive children.

In the next two studies, we used paired-associate learning as one way of trying to delineate the nature of the difficulty experienced by ADD children and the effect of stimulants on that difficulty. Conners, Eisenberg and Sharp (1964) first showed that paired-associate learning is sensitive to stimulant effects in hyperactive children. One of our paradigms was designed within the context of Bugelski's (1962) total-time hypothesis. The hypothesis claims that how much one learns depends on how long one studies, regardless of how one distributes the study time across items. One may, given items to study, spend an nth of the time on each item, or half an nth on each item, but study each item twice. According to the hypothesis, such rearrangements make no difference.

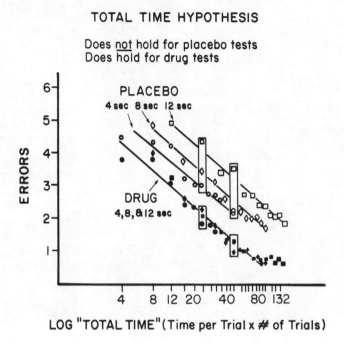

Figure 7. Placebo and drug groups' errors on paired-associate task testing total-time hypothesis.

We presented stimulus-response pairs, namely slides of animals in relation to simple verbal responses, at rates of 4 seconds a pair, 8 seconds a pair, or 12 seconds a pair (Dalby, Kinsbourne, Swanson, and Sobol, 1977). The hyperactive children on placebo violated the total-time hypothesis. They learned at a greater rate on the 4-second schedule than on the 8-second schedule, and at a greater rate on the 8-second schedule than on the 12-second schedule. These three curves are shown on the right of Figure 7. If you give the children medication, two things happen: They do better in an absolute sense in all three conditions (4-, 8-, and 12-second rates) as compared to the placebo group; and there is no longer a performance differential between the three rates of presentation—the total-time hypothesis now holds. The hyperactive children's performance is normalized by the drug in that it now conforms to the total-time principle. This fits well with our notion that hyperactive children have a diminished concentration span, as exemplified in the spiral explanatory device shown in Figure 3. They just did not concentrate on each item as long as it was on view. Therefore, particularly when the presentations were lengthy, they were not taking full advantage of their available study time.

However, another interpretation is also possible. Stimuli every 8 seconds constitute more events per unit time than stimuli every 12 seconds. Stimuli every 4 seconds generate a higher rate still. Maybe hyperactive children are stimulation-dependent and need a faster event rate to keep their flagging processing systems going.

We did some more studies to resolve the issue between those two explanations. With a computerized version of paired-associate learning (Conte and Kinsbourne, in preparation) we compared a 12-second-per-item rate with an 8-second-per-item rate. Again we found that stimulant-responsive subjects made fewer mistakes in the 8-second than the 12-second condition, holding total study time constant, replicating our previous findings; whereas the stimulant-unresponsive ones had the opposite pattern.

The next study attempts to deconfound the issue. We used a standard 8-second repetition rate, comparing it to what we call "split list," in which half of the items are presented for 8 seconds and half for 12. Any given pair, as it recurs, maintains its 8- or 12-second presentation time. The children on placebo did better on the standard than on the mixed list. That would fit either model. After medication, this difference disappeared. This too, would fit either model. The point of difference is that if concentration span was curtailed at the level of the individual item, the 8-second items within the split list should be better learned than the 12-second items within the split list; whereas if it is the ambient event rate that matters, there should be no difference. In fact, there was no difference. This supports the model of the overall event rate as controlling the amount of learning that the hyperactive children accomplished, rather than their attention span individually for each pair of associates. The difference between drug and placebo increases over time, as expected.

During one phase of these studies, we took certain psychophysiological measurements with rather complex results. One was resting heart rate: This did not differ between favorable and adverse responders. There was the expected cardiac acceleration on stimulant, but equally for both the stimulant-responsive and -unresponsive children, so that did not identify any biological difference between the two groups. The phasic heart rate (during the task performance) also increased on drug as compared to on placebo. It increased marginally significantly more for the stimulant-responsive children; I don't know what that means. During an 8-second trial, for stimulant-responsive and -unresponsive children on placebo, there is cardiac acceleration followed by deceleration, and this also occurs on drug. The base heart rate is elevated on drug, but the form of the heart rate response is the same as on placebo. During the first 8 seconds of 12-second trials, there is some initial cardiac deceleration instead. All the children's learned rate response differs during the 8- and the 12-second conditions, but does so similarly in both drug and placebo states.

In summary, heart rate did reveal a difference between the 8- and 12-second condition, but did not enlighten us as to why some children are and others are not favorably responsive to stimulant drugs. This study did not support the model of underarousal in ADD that Satterfield and others pioneered. Does it deserve support from measures of skin conductance? Comparing the drug with the placebo condition, those children who did better on the medication than on the placebo exhibited no change in skin conductance on the drug. Certainly in them, skin conductance did not go up, as would have been expected if the successful stimulant treatment had corrected underarousal as measured by that dependent variable. Those children who did worse on the medication than on the placebo experienced a rise in resting skin conductance (in proportion to the adverse drug response on learning rate). The rise in skin conductance began before the children were given the learning task. The rise was not a consequence of the learning. In other words, those children who had comparable skin conductance before testing in the two conditions learned better on drug. Those who had higher levels on stimulant learned worse on stimulant.

Complicated as this is, it does suggest that skin conductance measures something different than heart rate. Heart rate went up on drug and did not discriminate in relation to the drug-learning interaction. Skin conductance did discriminate. When stimulants are effective, they perhaps stabilize some specific system not indexed by psychophysiological concomitants of arousal and help learning proceed. When stimulants are ineffective, they increase general arousal, making the child more tense or for some other reason not as well able to learn. There was no significant difference in base levels of skin conductance between favorable responders and adverse responders. So, any underarousal would apply to a specific brain mechanism rather than to nonspecific reticular activating systems.

Further complicating the picture are the results of performing a median split for incidence of spontaneous skin potential responses. The children whose response was below the median showed the presentation rate effects. Those responding above the median did not.

Can we base an explanation of the full phenomenology of ADD on the disorder of an attentional variable? Probably not; I can illustrate this with two studies that examine ADD children's reaction to reward (Freeman and Kinsbourne, in preparation). In one, we adapted a paradigm used by Lykken (1957) with primary psychopaths. The Lykken maze is a display of 20 rows of locations, four locations in each row. The subject has to find the correct route through this maze. In each row, one location is "rewarded": it lights up. Two locations are neutral: nothing happening if they are touched. One location is "punished" by electric shock.

Lykken found that normal subjects not only "intentionally" learn the way through the maze according to instruction, but also in the course of trial

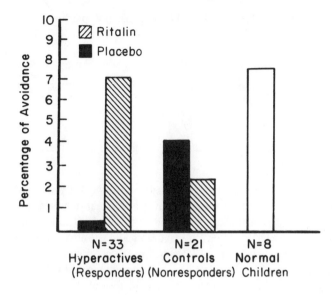

Figure 8.   Avoidance of aversive tones by hyperactive children and controls on and off Ritalin on the modified Lykken Maze.

and error "incidently" learn to avoid the punished locations. They would make fewer than the one-third mistakes on the punished locations expected on the basis of chance and more than the chance expected two-thirds mistakes on the two neutral locations. Lykken found that "primary psychopaths" did not show incidental avoidance learning. We adapted the method so as to use white noise delivered by headphones as "punishment." Figure 8 shows our results with hyperactive children on and off medication. Favorable responders on placebo made one-third punished mistakes. They showed no incidental avoidance learning at all. The same children on medication showed the normal avoidance learning. The adverse responders behaved unexpectedly in that they showed the normal avoidance learning on placebo but on drug they went up to one-third punished errors, like the favorable responders on placebo. Here is a double dissociation, which warrants further study. A simple model of defective sustained

144   ATTENTION DEFICIT DISORDER

Table 1. Results of Marble-Dispensing Experiment

Condition	Favorable responders		Adverse responders	
	Money	Shock	Money	Shock
Drug	15.000	3.607	14.750	4.313
	(11.4)	(5.96)	(6.3)	(4.45)
Placebo	14.321	9.750	16.750	4.750
	(6.54)	(9.52)	(9.48)	(7.43)

attention will not encompass these results. In the final study we used a marble-dispensing machine. The child pressed a lever and a marble was dispensed. Each marble was exchangeable for 2¢ at the end of the study. There were two conditions, two kinds of ADD children (the favorable and the adverse responders) and two states, drug and placebo. In one condition, the child was told he could press the lever as many times as he liked and each time he would get a marble, but if he pressed the lever once too often, he would lose all his marbles. Then the experimenter pressed the lever for demonstration purposes and all the marbles disappeared from sight. But the experimenter does not say how often "once too often" would be. In the other condition the experimenter again tells the child that he may press the level as often as he likes, but if he pressed that lever once too often, he will receive an electric shock. At this point, the experimenter pretends to give himself a shock; he has demonstrated the consequence of pressing the lever "once too often," again without specifying how often that would be. In the actual data-collection, nobody lost all his marbles and nobody was given a shock, but the manipulations were effective. The children limited the risk they would take in exchange for their reward. Table 1 shows the outcome.

In the "money" condition (threat of losing money), there was no significant difference between medication and placebo in either group. The money incentive did not differentiate our groups at all, nor the drug/placebo states. However, the "physical shock" did, enormously. The favorable responders were willing to press the lever some ten times on the average before they gave up, whereas the adverse responders would only press it five times. But the same group of children who pressed an average of ten times on placebo pressed fewer than four times on medication. So there we had a striking difference between favorable and adverse responders interacting with the drug and placebo conditions, a difference that cannot be conceptualized in attentional terms.

In our approach toward an adequate conceptual model for ADD problems, we consider the possibility that these are children whose attention requires a higher than usual event rate to keep it going. The events have to be compelling in their own right. For anybody to attend at a low event rate, certain reward-based behavioral control mechanisms may have to come into play. These mechanisms counteract the effects of progressive boredom, relying on internalized standards of expectation of long-term reward. We suspect that such a reward system is underactive in ADD children. Most of us are able to sustain attention even at low event rates under undramatic circumstances, given such intangibles as being asked to do so by the experimenter. The ADD child needs something solid and concrete or frequent and salient before he, too, can control his behavior the way the rest of us can under a much wider range of conditions. But then he can. The attention deficit in ADD is not invariant. The machinery for efficient behavioral control exists in the ADD child. Extra activation is needed, however, to enable it to participate consistently in controlling the way these children live.

REFERENCES

Bugelski, B. R. Presentation time, total-time, and mediation in paired-associate learning. *Journal of Experimental Psychology*, 1962, *63*:409–412.

Conners, C. K., Eisenberg, L., and Sharpe, L. Effects of methylphenidate (Ritalin) on paired associate learning and Porteus maze performance in emotionally disturbed children. *J. Consul. Psychol.*, 1964, *28*:14.

Conte, B. and Kinsbourne, M. in preparation.

Dalby, J. T., Kinsbourne, M., Swanson, J. J. and Sobol, M. P. Hyperactive children's underuse of learning time: correction by stimulant treatment. *Child Development*, 1977, *4*:1448–1453.

Flintoff, M., Barron, R., Swanson, J., Ledlow, A., and Kinsbourne, M. Methylphenidate increases selectivity in visual scanning. *Journal of Abnormal Child Psychology*, 1982, *10*:145–161.

Humphries, T., Swanson, J. M., Kinsbourne, M., and Yu, L. Stimulant effects on persistence of motor performance of hyperactive children. *Journal of Pediatric Psychology*, 1979, *4*:55–66.

Kagan, J. Individual differences in the resolution of response conflict. *J. Pers. Soc. Psychol.*, 1965, *2*:154–160.

Keough, B. K., and Margolis, J. S. A component analysis of attentional problems of educationally handicapped boys. *Journal of Abnormal Child Psychology*, 1976, *4*:349–359.

Lykken, D. A study of anxiety in the sociopathic personality. *J. Abn. Soc. Psychol.*, 1957, *55*:6.

8

The Psychological Processes Implicated in ADD

VIRGINIA A. DOUGLAS

EDITOR'S COMMENTS

In this chapter, Dr. Douglas presents her current working model of ADD. She believes there are four primary, related predispositions: (1) an unusually strong inclination to seek immediate gratification and/or stimulation; (2) an unusually weak inclination to invest attention and effort in demanding tasks; (3) an impaired ability to inhibit impulsive responding; and (4) an impaired ability to modulate arousal or alertness to meet situational demands.

Dr. Douglas points out that visual and auditory perception show no impairment in ADD children and that neuronal representation of the perception of visual and auditory stimuli persists over considerable periods of time, *provided* the children have concentrated sufficiently during the period when such stimuli were perceived. Their impairment does involve: (1) the maintenance of attention over time; (2) the extent to which attention is self-directed and organized; and (3) the amount of effort invested, the "intensive" aspect of attention.

Virginia Douglas agrees with Marcel Kinsbourne that ADD children are qualitatively different than normals in the mastering of problems involving complex memory, perceptual search, and problem-solving, even when the children are well-motivated. Their inferior perceptual and conceptual strategies are not ameliorated by either medication or reinforcement.

With regard to the reward system, Dr. Douglas concludes: (1) Both positive and negative reinforcement are effective, in some ways and under some conditions, in improving ADD children's task performance; (2) however, partial and noncontingent reinforcement lead to impaired performance and agitated, erratic behavior; (3) withdrawal of rewards during extinction seemed to affect ADD children more than normal controls; in addition, even positive, consistent feedback can increase impulsive responding because the children may be paying more attention to the reinforcers (or the person reinforcing) than to the behavior being evaluated.

Virginia Douglas concludes with a careful, critical analysis of some research reported by Marcel Kinsbourne published in the previous chapter of this volume, pointing out that different implications may be derived from Kinsbourne's data, using her basic axioms for ADD.

*   *   *

I present a brief description of the psychological model that evolved from our own work with ADD children. Fortunately, it is not too difficult to integrate a discussion of our own research at McGill with that of Dr. Kinsbourne's (see Chapter 7) because, as will become evident, our thinking has converged on a number of issues. This could simply mean, of course, that we share a common delusional system; however, I choose to find comfort in the fact that our ways of thinking about the disorder agree on a number of points.

This degree of consensus is, perhaps, even more reassuring when you consider that Dr. Kinsbourne's research team and my own have tended to favor two rather different research paradigms. As Dr. Kinsbourne explains, much of his work has involved comparisons between favorable and unfavorable responses to stimulant medication under drug and placebo conditions. Our group usually compares children meeting accepted criteria for a diagnosis of ADD with one or more control groups on several variables. As a second step, we sometimes use a cross-over drug-placebo design to study the effect of the stimulants on those variables in ADD children.

Lest I have lulled you into thinking that I am in total agreement with Dr. Kinsbourne, let me say that I also stress points on which there are rather significant differences in emphasis between our current conceptualizations. If I had time to be even more argumentative, I would have also liked to talk about the difficulty our team is experiencing in finding the clear-cut differences between favorable and unfavorable drug responders that Dr. Kinsbourne describes. Perhaps, however, we can reserve this topic for the Second High Point Hospital Symposium on ADD.*

A schematic representation of our current working model of ADD appears in Figure 1 (reproduced from Douglas, in press, b). I limit most of my discussion to evidence for the "more basic predispositions" appearing in the upper left-hand corner of Figure 1. I would caution, however, that any comprehensive theory of ADD will have to take account of the secondary and long-term cognitive, motivational, and behavioral consequences that must inevitably follow when a child begins life with the predispositions that I discuss. Thus, Figure 1 includes a schematic representation of the spiraling effect of these predispositions on the development of conceptual skills and on the child's ability and motivation to

---

*The Second High Point Symposium was held October 25–26, 1982, and the papers presented will appear as the second volume in this series.

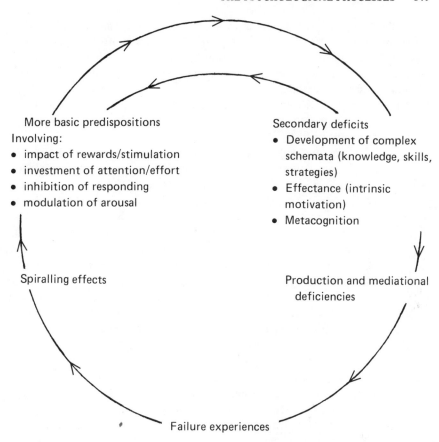

More basic predispositions
Involving:
- impact of rewards/stimulation
- investment of attention/effort
- inhibition of responding
- modulation of arousal

Spiralling effects

Secondary deficits
- Development of complex
  schemata (knowledge, skills,
  strategies)
- Effectance (intrinsic
  motivation)
- Metacognition

Production and mediational
deficiencies

Failure experiences

Figure 1. Model depicting spiraling effects of hypothesized predispositions.

undertake more subtle and demanding kinds of cognitive and social problem-solving. By the time the ADD youngster is referred to a physician or psychologist, many of these longer-term consequences have become part of the presenting problem and must be treated as such. The broken line with arrows pointing in the opposite direction is included as a reminder that therapeutic interventions directed at deficits appearing later in the causal chain can, hopefully, work toward reversing the process and thus help bring the original predispositions under better control. (For a more complete discussion of the model and its treatment implications, see Douglas and Peters, 1979; Douglas, 1980b; Douglas, in press, a; Douglas, in press, b).

As you can see (in Figure 1), I have postulated that the problems of ADD children develop out of four related predispositions. These include: (1) An unusually strong inclination to seek immediate gratification and/or stimulation; (2) an unusually weak inclination to invest attention and effort in demanding tasks; (3) an impaired ability to inhibit impulsive responding; and (4) an impaired ability to modulate arousal or alertness to meet situational demands. Although I suspect that these predispositions are constitutionally determined, there is every reason to believe that environmental factors, such as inconsistent parental discipline or a chaotic family situation, can have a profound effect on their development.

Before presenting evidence for each of the proposed predispositions, let me stress the extent of their interrelatedness. Indeed, depending on one's theoretical preference, it often is possible to attribute an observed deficit to any one of the four. If you are interested in underlying physiological mechanisms, this means that one or more of several mechanisms could be implicated in any particular deficit. For example, ADD children may perform poorly on dull, repetitive vigilance tasks because of: a defective facilatory mechanism that fails to keep their attention effortfully engaged in the task; a defective inhibitory mechanism that fails to prevent them from being seduced by other stimuli; a defective reward mechanism that makes them uninterested in situations not offering immediate gratification; or a defective arousal modulation mechanism that fails to keep them sufficiently alert in situations offering low stimulation. Similarly, improvement on vigilance task performance following stimulant medication can be—and indeed has been—attributed to the drug's effect on each of these postulated mechanisms (see Douglas, in press, b).

Consider another, rather sobering, implication of the close relationship among my hypothesized predispositions. In a situation in which we are attempting to predict an ADD child's behavior, a change that affects any one of the predispositions is likely to change the interaction among them. If, for example, a child is placed in the presence of a forbidden toy, several variables can come into play: these may include the reward value of the toy for the child, the level of arousal it elicits in him, and his capacity for resisting temptation. Consequently, a manipulation that influences one of these variables, such as making the forbidden object more desirable, stationing an authority figure in the room, or engaging the child in an exciting activity, is likely to influence the outcome.

It is possible that an explanation of this kind can account for the fact that Dr. Kinsbourne seems to have been successful in showing that hyperactive children benefit from a fast event-rate, whereas data from two of our studies provided only equivocal support for this hypothesis. The first study involved a concept-discovery task (Freibergs and Douglas, 1969) and the other a continuous-performance test (Sykes, Douglas, Weiss, and Minde, 1971). On both we compared the effects of a faster and a slower event-rate. In the case of the concept-discovery task, although eyeballing the data suggested that the hyperactives did slightly better at the fast intervals, the statistical analyses did not yield significant differences. One could conjecture that, in contrast to Dr. Kins-bourne's rather boring paired-associates task, our game-like apparatus, which delivered marbles for correct responses, was sufficiently stimulating and re-warding to hold the children's attention over the longer intervals. The continu-ous-performance test, on the other hand, was dull and repetitive. The findings here indicated that *both* subject groups made more correct responses when a slower presentation rate was used, probably reflecting the greater attentional demands imposed by briefly appearing stimuli. When error scores were con-sidered, however, one difference did emerge. Although hyperactives made about the same number of errors at the two interstimulus intervals and although hyper-actives and controls made a similar number of errors at the faster interval, the hyperactive group made more errors than the control group at the slower inter-val. Since errors on this task involve pushing to incorrect stimuli ("errors of commission"), we favored an explanation incorporating both an even rate and an impulsivity hypothesis. That is, we reasoned that it might be more difficult for hyperactives than for normal children to inhibit impulsive responding when they are dealing with dull, slowly paced stimuli.

To muddy already murky waters just a bit more, let me advance an alter-nate hypothesis for the findings Dr. Kinsbourne obtained in his paired-associates study. In several of our encounters with ADD children, we have remarked that they do not adjust to the demand qualities of a series of tasks item-by-item. What seems more often to happen is that a style that is more or less businesslike and reflective (usually less!) gets established and it spills over to influence their concentration throughout the series. I am suggesting, therefore, that the chil-dren's disorganized, uncritical approach to tasks might be responsible for Dr. Kinsbourne's failure to find differences between the 8- and 12-second items. Isolating the effects of the kinds of variables we are discussing is not going to be easy.

In view of these complex interrelationships, I have been reluctant, up to this time, to suggest that any one of my four hypothesized predispositions is more basic or fundamental than the others. Since the children's attentional prob-lems constitute only one of the four on my list, I strongly agree with others who have expressed concern that adoption of the new "Attention Deficit Disorder" label could result in an unnecessarily constricted conceptualization of the problem.

Further research will possibly help us assign a more dominant role to one of my hypothesized predispositions, but we probably are dealing with an inter-acting system that, ultimately, will be able to account for the variety of deficits I have conceptualized under all four. In the meantime, I prefer to study the chil-dren from all four perspectives.

You may be surprised to find the children's hypothesized inclination to seek immediate gratification at the top of my list. This was done partly to expand our horizons beyond attentional problems and partly because our own empirical and theoretical emphasis is currently focused on ADD children's response to reinforcement. This has been a recurring interest in our group since we undertook our first study of their response to partial reinforcement in the 1960s. As you are probably aware, this interest puts us in good company: Wender (1971; 1973) emphasized what he considered to be an abnormal *under-responsivity* to reinforcers in his early model; Kinsbourne has presented us with provocative findings that directed his attention toward the possibility that some aspect of the reward system is underactive in ADD children. I, on the other hand, have argued that the children may be *unusually responsive* to rewards. Thus, there are potentially important differences in the ways in which we conceptualize the nature of the reinforcement abnormality. I shall return to this issue, but I wish first, to review the evidence for my other three hypothesized predispositions.

In earlier papers (Douglas, 1980a; Douglas and Peters, 1979), I compiled a list of tasks on which the performance of hyperactive children has been shown to be impaired (this list is reproduced in Table 1). Equally important, tasks on which there are not significant differences between hyperactives and normal controls also were identified. I argued that the pattern of strengths and weaknesses emerging from this analysis pointed to a particular constellation of processes. Interestingly, although the defective processes are fairly circumscribed, their effect is very pervasive. They manifest themselves on a variety of tasks, ranging from the relatively simple to the highly complex. Several of the tasks listed in Table 1 have been mentioned by other speakers. They vary from vigilance and reaction-time tests, through the Matching Familiar Figures Test, to two problem-solving tasks that developmental psychologists have shown to require sophisticated cognitive strategies, and to a rather demanding version of the paired-associates paradigm.

I have summarized the demands of these tasks under two headings, "facilatory behaviors" and "inhibitory behaviors" (see Table 1). Although the "facilatory" category encompasses a variety of information-processing and problem-solving skills, they appear to be characterized by a need for good concentration, careful reflection, and an organized, planful approach. Typically, a reciprocal requirement for the inhibition of careless or impulsive responding also is present. Thus, it is relatively easy to argue that poor performance on the tasks results from a defective facilatory mechanism, a defective inhibitory mechanism, or both. As I suggested earlier, however, one might also hypothesize that the tasks do not offer ADD children sufficient reward or interest to motivate the amount of effort required; or, their difficulties could be attributed to a faulty arousal modulation mechanism that fails to generate sufficient arousal or alertness to enable them to cope with the tasks successfully.

I do not have time to discuss the tasks on which hyperactives do relatively well. These, I believe, effectively eliminate a number of other possibilities. A recent review of this literature led me to conclude that:

> In ruling out possible causes for hyperactive children's performance deficits it is important to stress that there are many indications that the children are capable of perceiving visual and auditory stimuli clearly and accurately. It also appears that neuronal representations of perceptual stimuli persist over considerable periods of time, *provided* the children have concentrated sufficiently during the period when neural traces of such images were being established (Douglas, in press, a).

I hope that by now it is becoming clear that if we are going to attribute attentional deficits to hyperactive children, the deficits must be of a very specific nature. As Dr. Kinsbourne mentioned, I have invested a good deal of effort in trying to convince other investigators that the youngsters' attentional problems cannot be explained by a defective filtering mechanism, an inability to discriminate between relevant and irrelevant stimuli, or an impaired ability to process information from different sources concurrently (Douglas and Peters, 1979; Douglas, in press, a; Douglas, in preparation). I have argued, rather, that their impairment involves: (1) the maintenance of attention over time; (2) the extent to which attention is self-directed and organized; and (3) the amount of effort that is invested (sometimes referred to as the "intensive" aspect of attention). There have been a surprising number of failures to prove that children are more "distractible" than normal controls (Douglas and Peters, 1979). Furthermore, in those cases where unusual distractability has been demonstrated, I have argued that it is readily attributable to one or another of the four more basic predispositions that I have posited (Douglas, in press, a; in preparation).

As you can see, there are obvious similarities between Dr. Kinsbourne's model depicting individual differences in the degree of information a person collects and considers before making a decision and what I have been saying. In a previous paper (Douglas and Peters, 1979), I referred to the "exploratory-vs.-search-strategy" differentiation made by developmental psychologists to help illuminate this disinclination of hyperactives to process beyond the most salient, novel, or reinforcement-related aspects of a situation. Let me also add that I thoroughly agree with another point made by Dr. Kinsbourne early in his chapter. As he pointed out, many of the children's problems do not become evident in the authoritarian atmosphere of our research laboratories. In fact, one of the most irritating aspects of their behavior is their failure to use information and abilities they are known to possess. Again, I have used terminology from cognitive psychology, "production and mediational deficiencies," to refer to this phenomenon (see Figure 1).

Table 1. Tasks on Which Hyperactives Perform Poorly

Task	Facilatory behaviors	Inhibitory behaviors
Continuous performance test: vigilance task (Anderson et al., 1971; Doyle et al., 1976; Dykman et al., 1971; Sykes, et al., 1973)	Establish response set for designated stimuli Concentrate on responding quickly Maintain response set (vigilance) over time	Inhibit responding to inappropriate stimuli
Reaction time tasks with pre-paratory interval (Cohen and Douglas, 1975; Parry, 1973; Zahn, et al., 1975)	Establish response readiness on basis of warning signals Concentrate on responding quickly to reaction signals Establish response readiness repeatedly over time	Inhibit responding at inappropriate times
Kagan's matching familiar figures test: reflection-impulsivity (Campbell, et al., 1971; Cohen, et al., 1972; Juliano, 1974; Parry, 1973; Peters, 1977; Schleifer, et al., 1975)	Concentrate on finding exact match to target picture Conduct exhaustive, organized search of all alternatives in a visual array Systematically compare standard and alternatives on critical perceptual features	Inhibit choosing pictures only superficially like standard
Embedded figures test: field dependence (Campbell, et al., 1971; Cohen, et al., 1972)	Concentrate on forming clear visual image of target figures Conduct exhaustive, organized search for correct figures embedded within a visual array	Ignore embedding context Inhibit responding to superficially similar figures
Porteus mazes (Parry, 1973)	Concentrate on finding safe route to goal Conduct careful search at critical points to discover consequences of taking alternate routes	Avoid entering blind alleys Inhibit cutting corners, crossing lines, etc.
Tests with multiple choice format (Hoy, et al., in press)	Concentrate on finding correct logical choice among several alternatives Conduct exhaustive logical search of all alternatives Note: Hyperactives did not show deficit when number of choices was limited to two	Inhibit responding to superficially correct answers

Task		
Wisconsin card sorting task (Parry, 1973)	Concentrate on finding all possible legitimate categories for sorting Systematically examine patterns on cards for common features Abstract class concepts from patterns (e.g., color, form, number) *Note:* Hyperactives have no problem with shifting set	Inhibit responding with salient but unacceptable categories Inhibit idiosyncratic responses
Matrix solution tasks (Tant, 1978)	Concentrate on finding strategies that will eliminate most cards Scan and analyze visual display Classify stimuli into groups and label each group Choose questions that will elicit most information Make correct deductions from feedback provided Remember which possibilities previous questions eliminated Coordinate a series of questions into a planful approach	Avoid being misled by salient but less informative cues
Rule learning tasks (Tant, 1978)	Concentrate on finding the rule connecting stimulus attributes that will enable correct sorting Conduct careful perceptual analysis of stimuli appearing on cards Code stimuli logically, depending on the presence or absence of key attributes Use feedback to assign classes of stimuli to positive and negative categories Remember logical implications of feedback	Avoid responding only to *perceptual* aspects of stimuli (as opposed to *logical* classes they represent)
Memory for paired associates: arbitrary associations (Benezra, Note 7)	Concentrate on finding best way of remembering paired associates Consider possible strategies, mnemonic devices Choose most effective strategy	Inhibit choosing readily available but less effective strategies
Story completion task: frustrating stories (Parry, 1973)	Concentrate on understanding a social situation from several perspectives Consider possible motives of frustrator Consider consequences of own behavior Consider possible substitutes for los object or event	Inhibit aggressive responses

From V. I. Douglas, Treatment approaches: Establishing inner or outer control? In C. K. Whalen and B. Henker (eds.), *Hyperactive Children: The Social Ecology of Identification and Treatment.* New York, Academic Press, 1980.

There is another point, however, to which both Dr. Kinsbourne and I must give more thought. As I stressed earlier, I have become convinced that, if we use sufficiently complex tasks, we will find that the children's more basic predispositions have prevented them from building the store of knowledge and sophisticated problem-solving strategies already mastered by peers of similar intellectual capacity. Recent studies in our laboratory assessing complex memory, perceptual search, and problem-solving skills (Ain, 1980; Benezra, 1980; Tant, 1978; Tant and Douglas, 1982) seem to be showing that, even when the children are well-motivated, inferior perceptual and conceptual strategies put them at a disadvantage. This is a problem that neither medication nor reinforcement, no matter how effective, can correct, unless there is a concomitant program to develop the missing skills. A similar point has been made by Weingartner and his colleagues (Weingartner, Rapoport, Buchsbaum, Bunney, Ebert, Mikkelsen and Caine, 1980).

Consequently, I would caution that Dr. Kinsbourne's argument that complex tasks must be used in order to differentiate favorable and unfavorable responders should not be pushed too far. In considering the findings Dr. Kinsbourne reported from his "MFF-like" task, for example, it seems possible that the improved "style of approach" that emerged when his drug responders were placed on methylphenidate was not sufficiently sophisticated and efficient to reduce their errors significantly below placebo levels. The children probably rated an "E" for effort, but previous failure to perfect perceptual search strategies may have set limits on how far their effort could take them. Thus, from this perspective, the task may have been too complex to show medication effects.

While I am on the topic of stimulant medication, let me advance a point of view that differs from that of several other investigators'. I was not surprised by recent findings that have shown a similar response to the stimulants in normal and hyperactive children; indeed I anticipated this outcome several years ago (Douglas, 1976a). Nor do I believe that these results undermine any of the notions about underlying mechanisms of ADD that I have discussed. I would simply argue that ADD youngsters have a greater need than normal children for the beneficial effects of the stimulants in order to function within acceptable limits. I do anticipate, however, that as we become more knowledgeable, we will discover more subtle ADD–normal differences in drug responsivity involving such variables as dosage level and task complexity [and, possibly, tolerance–Editor].

Since there have been numerous reviews of studies of the children's arousal patterns in the literature (e.g., Barkley and Jackson, 1977; Douglas, in press, a), let me touch upon this issue very briefly. I think that it is fair to say that investigators have come up with theories postulating just about every possible combination of excitatory or inhibitory relationship involving abnormally high or abnormally low levels of general or specific reactivity in cortical or subcortical brain centers! In my own attempt to understand the existing data (Douglas, in press, a), I have been impressed with two major facts: First, evidence from the rather dull, repetitive paradigms typically used in laboratory studies thus far has provided more support for a hypothesis of underreactivity to specific task stimuli than for a hypothesis involving either overarousal or underarousal in resting levels. Secondly, there is suggestive evidence that introducing rewards or novel stimuli into the laboratory situation may be associated, behaviorally, with impulsive responses and, physiologically, with supraoptimal arousal. It is because the evidence points toward suboptimal alertness in some situations and supraoptimal reactivity in others that I have been attracted by the notion of an impaired capacity for modulating arousal. I hasten to add, however, that much more research is needed to test this hypothesis.

Let us turn, finally, to the issue that has intrigued Dr. Wender, Dr. Kinsbourne, and myself: that of the children's response to reinforcement. Some years ago, Dr. Wender advanced the hypothesis that hyperactive children are less responsive than normal children to both positive and negative reinforcers (Wender, 1971; 1973). At about the same time (Freibergs, 1965; Freibergs and Douglas, 1969), we were evolving an hypothesis that at least appears to be just the opposite of Dr. Wender's: we thought that hyperactives might be unusually sensitive to rewards. This idea arose from a series of studies in our laboratory in which we investigated the children's response to a variety of reinforcement parameters while they were performing on several different tasks. The tasks studied have included a rather complex concept-discovery task, a simple reaction-time task, and a delayed reaction-time task. Reinforcement parameters that have been investigated include continuous vs. partial reinforcement, contingent vs. noncontingent reinforcement, positive vs. negative reinforcement, and withdrawal of rewards during extinction (for reviews see Douglas, in press a, in press b, in preparation; Douglas and Peters, 1979).

These studies led to a number of conclusions: First, both positive and negative reinforcement are effective, in some ways and under some conditions, in improving ADD children's task performance. This conclusion has been strengthened by reports from a number of behavior modifiers who have been successful in controlling disruptive behaviors and in producing modest improvements in academic performance. On the other hand, we also found that some reinforcement schedules, namely partial and noncontingent reinforcement, had some rather unique effects on our hyperactive subjects: They seemed to lead to impaired task performance and agitated, erratic behavior. Withdrawal of rewards during extinction also seemed to affect them more than it did normal controls. In addition, there was suggested evidence that even positive, consistent feedback can increase impulsive responding.

In summarizing possible reasons for these negative effects we suggested:

> . . . One reason seems to be that reinforcers become a highly salient aspect of the learning situation for the hyperactive child. Consequently, he may be paying more attention to the reinforcers themselves (or the reinforcing person) than to the particular behavior being reinforced, or to the specific stimuli associated with it. In addition, hyperactive children appear to be unusually sensitive to the loss of reinforcement and to the failure of expected reinforcers to appear (Douglas and Peters, 1979, p. 209).

In recent reviews (Douglas, in press a, in preparation), I have discussed further findings from other laboratories, which seem to support this interpretation. There are instances in the behavior modification literature, for example, where withdrawal of rewards during extinction appears to result in a kind of "rebound effect" in hyperactive children—that is, their behavior becomes even worse than it was during baseline. Also, the youngsters sometimes seem to be only superficially responding to task demands while giving the appearance of conforming to the reinforcement manipulations.

In addition, Gordon (1979) has recently reported results from his doctoral dissertation that, if replicated, could be most important. He found that hyperactive children show marked inferiority to normal children in coping with a "delayed reinforcement for low rate responding" (DRL) paradigm. To succeed on this task, subjects must learn to inhibit responding during arbitrarily set time intervals in order to obtain a reward. (Interestingly, in interpreting his results, Gordon places more emphasis on the children's impulsivity than on the valence of the rewards for them.)

Finally, there are the very tantalizing results that Dr. Kinsbourne has reported. Since the findings that he and Freeman (Freeman, 1978) obtained are complex and open to a number of interpretations, let me try to summarize them very briefly. They found that a group of favorable drug-responders failed to show adequate avoidance learning on the Lykken maze apparatus when they were receiving placebo, whereas placing them on stimulant medication seems to have alleviated the avoidance deficit. In addition, adverse responders showed normal avoidance learning while on placebo but avoided punishment less successfully when they were given medication. These findings suggest that the stimulant-responsive children have an "avoidance deficit" that is corrected by the medication.

But what could be causing this "avoidance deficit"? Are the children underresponsive to punishment, as many investigators in this area would conclude? Let's consider another possible hypothesis: although no one seems to have mentioned it, the Lykken apparatus is a rather compelling game. It involves a variety of colored lights, some of which light up when you push the right button and these help you find your way through the maze. Not so compelling as the current video games, perhaps, but of the same ilk! It seems to me, therefore, that the children may find the "manifest task" so stimulating that they do not pay sufficient attention to the "incidental task" to enable them to make the rather subtle observation that, in each row of the maze, a particular one of the three "wrong" lights is always associated with the loud noise. Or, if you like, they become too impulsive or too aroused to notice. The action that you attribute to the medication will depend, of course, on which of the explanations you choose.

What about the risk-taking study (of Kinsbourne's chapter)? Do those results help clarify our choices? In that paradigm, subjects were required to press the level of a marble-dispensing machine in order to obtain pennies. There were two conditions. In one they were threatened by a painful shock if they continued pushing beyond a particular "magic number," while in the other they were threatened with the loss of all of the pennies they had won up until that time. In the threat of shock condition, the favorable responders on placebo took a relatively large number of risks, while on medication their risk-taking was considerably reduced. Equally significant, in the condition in which continued lever-pressing could result in losing all their money, there were no significant differences between subject groups, or between drug and placebo states.

First, we must ask ourselves why the favorable responders on placebo took more risks than controls in the "shock threat" condition. Were they relatively unresponsive to the threatened shock? Were they unable to inhibit themselves? Were they so pulled by the immediate gratification of winning pennies that they did not consider the painful consequences? And why, in the threat of monetary loss condition, was their behavior so "normal"? Apparently, here, they were as responsive to the threat of losing their pennies and/or they were as able to exert inhibitory control as the adverse responders. There is another point that intrigues me about these findings that has not been discussed. If we look at all subjects, in all drug states, it is evident that both groups of children were willing to take many more risks in the "money threat" condition than in the "shock threat" condition—roughly three times as many. Apparently money evokes strong approach tendencies in young children and the threat of losing one's winnings doesn't bring inhibitory processes into play until the winnings reach a certain size. However, the vision of Dr. Kinsbourne's research assistant going through the agonies of being shocked seems to have rather effectively dampened enthusiasm for the "game."

What conclusions can be drawn from this complex pattern of results? As Dr. Kinsbourne mentioned, both risk-taking behavior and the Lykken Maze have been studied in research with psychopaths. Perhaps some parallels between findings from the two subject populations will help us. As in the literature on hyperactivity, a number of investigators have been attracted by the possibility that the "avoidance learning deficit" that has been reported in psychopaths may be due to a failure to develop anticipatory anxiety in response to punishment. Although there is conflicting evidence on this issue, Schmauk (1970) found that a group of primary psychopaths scored significantly below normal control subjects "in anticipatory arousal, subjective anxiety and avoidance learning" (p. 325) when shock or negative feedback were used to punish designated errors on the Lykken Maze. Under a condition in which the wrong choices were punished by taking away quarters from a starting pile of 40 quarters, however, the primary psychopaths "showed significant increases on these three measures and scored at approximately the same level as the normal control group" (p. 325).

Thus, although Schmauk's psychopaths showed an avoidance deficit in two of the punishment conditions, they successfully learned to avoid one kind of punishment, losing money. Again, if you prefer to think in terms of inhibitory control, the psychopaths demonstrated adequate control only when confronted with the loss of money. This behavior is somewhat similar to that of Freeman's favorable responders, who took higher risks in the threat of shock condition but did not differ from the adverse responders when threatened with loss of money. Obviously, these results do not answer all of our questions, but they do suggest that the threat of money loss acts as a powerful inhibitor in psychopaths. Also, its effect on ADD children in a risk-taking situation does not differ from its effect on controls.

Recently, Gorenstein and Newman (1980) used Schmauk's findings and an impressive body of results from the "disinhibitory psychopathology" and animal septal lesion literature to argue that we may have to "change the theoretical emphasis in human disinhibition from deficient avoidance to heightened sensitivity to reward" (p. 312). If we put the research from our own laboratory and the other findings that I have reviewed together, I believe that we must consider the proposition that hyperactive children have an unusually strong inclination to seek immediate gratification and/or stimulation. However, response costs, involving the immediate removal of highly prized reinforcers, may be effective in keeping this inclination in check. Furthermore, contingency managers must take special care in controlling the valence of reinforcers and the consistency and contiguity of reinforcement schedules.

Interestingly, my stress on the importance of rapid administration of reinforcers and consistency of schedules agrees with advice Wender (1971) gave in his early treatment of this subject. However, I would modify his advice that we should use strong reinforcers: I see a very real danger that they will distract the ADD child from the task at hand and that their presence will "trigger" arousal to a supraoptimal level. Let me hasten to add that, at least in our early dealings with an ADD child, fairly immediate rewards must outweigh unpleasant consequences if we hope to capture and hold his attention.

This emphasis on immediate rewards also is in agreement with Dr. Kinsbourne's suggestion that a reward system involving "internalized standards or expectations of long-term reward is underactive in ADD children." In a similar vein, I have pointed to the children's apparent lack of "intrinsic motivation" (see Figure 1) and their failure to consider long-term consequences (Douglas and Peters, 1979; Douglas, in press, a). I have suggested that, along with carefully administered contingency management programs, a special effort must be made through cognitive training to help ADD children mediate between their own current behavior and long-term consequences. The need for this approach is strengthened by Gorenstein's and Newman's (1980) review that I mentioned earlier. These authors suggest that psychopaths may have a "general deficit in perceiving the connection between even neutral events that are related remotely in time" (p. 305).

Would it be impulsive of us, then, to conclude that ADD children's most fundamental deficit involves a defective reinforcement mechanism of the kind that I have suggested? Although I find the evidence that response to reinforcement plays a major role in the disorder, I would return to my original position that we are dealing with a complex, interacting system. Consequently, I advise that we let ourselves be guided by the information-processing model that Dr. Kinsbourne presents in Chapter 7 and continue to process more information before attempting to arrive at a final formulation.

REFERENCES

Ain, M. The effects of stimulus novelty on viewing time and processing efficiency in hyperactive children. Doctoral dissertation, McGill University, 1980.

Barkley, R. A., and Jackson, R. L., Jr. Hyperkinesis, autonomic nervous system activity, and stimulant drug effects. *Journal of Child Psychology and Psychiatry*, 1977, *18*, 347–357.

Benezra, E. Verbal and nonverbal memory in hyperactive, reading disabled and normal children. Unpublished doctoral dissertation, McGill University, 1980.

Douglas, V. I. Effects of medication on learning efficiency—Research findings: Review and Synthesis. In R. P. Anderson and C. G. Halcomb (Eds.), *Learning disability/minimal brain dysfunction syndrome*. Springfield, Ill.: Charles C. Thomas, 1976a, pp. 139–148.

Douglas, V. I. Perceptual and cognitive factors as determinants of learning disabilities: A review chapter with special emphasis on attentional factors. In R. M. Knights and D. J. Bakker (Eds.), *The neuropsychology of learning disorders: theoretical approaches*. Baltimore: University Park Press, 1976b, pp. 413–421.

Douglas, V. I. Treatment approaches: Establishing inner or outer control? In C. K. Whalen and B. Henker (Eds.), *Hyperactive children: The social ecology of identification and treatment*. New York: Academic Press, 1980a.

Douglas, V. I. Higher mental processes in hyperactive children: Implications for training. In R. M. Knights and D. J. Bakker (Eds.), *Rehabilitation, treatment, and management of learning disorders.* Baltimore: University Park Press, 1980.

Douglas, V. I. Attentional and cognitive problems. In M. Rutter (Ed.), *Developmental neuropsychiatry.* New York: The Guilford Press, in press, a.

Douglas, V. I. Attention deficit disorder in children: Are we any further ahead? *Canadian psychology/Psychologie canadienne,* in press, b.

Douglas, V. I. Attentional deficits in hyperactive children: The continuing debate. In F. J. Morrison (Ed.), *Advances in applied developmental psychology,* Vol. 2. New York: Academic Press, in preparation.

Douglas, V. I., and Peters, K. G. Toward a clearer definition of the attentional deficit of hyperactive children. In G. A. Hale and M. Lewis (Eds.), *Attention and the development of cognitive skills.* New York: Plenum Press, 1979.

Freeman, R. J. The effects of methylphenidate on avoidance learning and risk-taking by hyperkinetic children. Doctoral dissertation, University of Waterloo, Waterloo, Ontario, 1978.

Freibergs, V. Concept learning in hyperactive and normal children. Unpublished doctoral dissertation, McGill University, 1965.

Freibergs, V., and Douglas, V. I. Concept learning in hyperactive and normal children. *Journal of Abnormal Psychology,* 1969, *74,* 388–395.

Gordon, M. The assessment of impulsivity and mediating behaviors in hyperactive and nonhyperactive boys. *Journal of Abnormal Child Psychology,* 1979, 7:3, 317–326.

Gorenstein, E. E., and Newman, J. P. Disinhibitory psychopathology: A new perspective and a model for research. *Psychological Review,* 1980, *87:*3, 301–315.

Schmauk, F. J. Punishment, arousal, and avoidance learning in sociopaths. *Journal of Abnormal Psychology,* 1970, *76:*325–335.

Sykes, D. H., Douglas, V. I., Weiss, G., and Mide, K. K. Attention in hyperactive children and the effect of methylphenidate (Ritalin). *Journal of Child Psychology and Psychiatry,* 1971, *12:*129–139.

Tant, J. L. Problem solving in hyperactive and reading disabled boys. Unpublished doctoral dissertation, McGill University, 1978.

Tant, J. L., and Douglas, V. I. Problem solving in hyperactive, normal and reading disabled boys. *Journal of Abnormal Child Psychology,* 1982.

Weingartner, H., Rapoport, J. L., Buchsbaum, M. S., Bunney, W. E., Jr., Ebert, M. H., Mikkelsen, E. J., and Caine, E. D. Cognitive processes in normal and hyperactive children and their response to amphetamine treatment. *Journal of Abnormal Psychology,* 1980, *89:*1, 25–37.

Wender, P. *Minimal brain dysfunction in children.* New York: John Wiley, 1971.

Wender, P. H. Some speculations concerning a possible biochemical basis of minimal brain dysfunction. *Annals of the New York Academy of Sciences,* 1973, *205:*18–28.

9

Neuroendocrine and Cognitive Responses to Amphetamine in Adolescents with a History of ADD

BARRY D. GARFINKEL

EDITOR'S COMMENTS

Dr. Garfinkel presents a study in which behavioral and neuroendocrine variables in adolescents were measured. A residual ADD cohort was matched with a control group having no significant differences in age, height, weight, social class, or intelligence test scores.

A heparinized cannula was inserted into a dorsal hand vein and a baseline blood sample drawn. Samples were drawn every 20 minutes for four hours after the oral administration of 10 mg of d-amphetamine or placebo. The samples were analyzed for growth hormone and prolactin levels.

A Continuous Performance Task was administered prior to medication and every hour subsequently.

The data were analyzed statistically and indicated a trend that psychometric test results differentiated adolescents with a history of ADD from controls. This is consistent with the description of attention deficit persisting into late adolescence. Dr. Garfinkel concludes that the growth hormone responses to sympathomimetic drugs may reflect catecholamine differences between Residual ADD subjects and controls.

In his discussion, Paul Wender points out that the method used in the experiment by Barry Garfinkel presented a nice method of distinguishing dopaminergic from noradrenergic activity in the brain.

*　　*　　*

A variation of this paper has been submitted for publication to the *J. Am. Acad. Child Psychiatry* with co-authors Walter A. Brown, M.D., Steven H. Klee, Ph.D., William Braden, M.D. and Steven K. Shapiro, B.A.

Longitudinal studies suggest an association between childhood ADD and adult psychopathology (Hechtman, Weiss, and Perlman, 1980). Mendelson, Johnson, and Stewart (1971) and Weiss, Hechtman, Perlman, et al. (1979) observed that a significantly greater than normal proportion of ADD children became delinquent or exhibited signs of antisocial behavior as adolescents. Huessy, Metoyer, and Townsend (1974), in a follow-up study, observed twenty times the rate of delinquent behavior in former ADD children compared to the general population. Mendelson (1971) also noted that antisocial adolescents still had difficulty concentrating and were overly active and impulsive. Weiss, Kruger, Danielson, and Elman (1975) reported that adolescents who had been treated with methylphenidate (MPD) for ADD as children showed no significant differences in emotional adjustment, delinquency, and school performance when compared with those who were untreated, demonstrating permanency and stability of the clinical symptoms.

Outcome and family research in ADD has addressed two issues—namely, the association of ADD with specific adult psychopathology and transmission of ADD across generations. This research has sought the answers to whether family environment or genetic control over neurotransmission is most significant in determining the symptoms of ADD. Family studies by Morrison and Stewart (1971) and Cantwell (1972) indicate that biological fathers of ADD children have a much higher prevalence of alcoholism and sociopathy than fathers of controls and that biological mothers have an increased rate of diagnosis of Briquet's Syndrome. Cantwell (1976) showed that ten percent of the biological parents of ADD children had previously been regarded as ADD, and of this ten percent, all were currently diagnosed as suffering from either alcoholism sociopathy, or Briquet's Syndrome. Morrison and Stewart (1971, 1973) found a higher prevalence, with 19 out of 59 fathers of ADD children reporting ADD in their own childhood. These studies suggest that ADD itself persists in some individuals. These adult syndromes are also the same conditions genetically associated with depressive spectrum disease described by Winokur (1974).

Adoption studies show that nonbiological adopting parents of ADD children are significantly less likely to have a history of ADD, alcoholism, sociopathy, and Briquet's Syndrome compared to the biological parents, who have a high prevalence of these disorders (Safer, 1973). Safer also found that full siblings of ADD children, (i.e., having the same biological parents) were more likely to be diagnosed as exhibiting ADD than half-siblings. This research, therefore, suggests that the behavioral manifestations of ADD in children may be transmitted genetically.

Mann and Greenspan (1976); Shelley and Reister (1972); Wood, Reimherr, and Wender (1976); and Wender, Reimherr, and Wood (1981) showed that one outcome of childhood ADD is an adult or residual form of ADD. Adults with this condition were characterized by the following attributes: motor hyperactivity and attentional deficits persisting from childhood; affective lability; explosive temper; impulsivity; failure to complete tasks; impaired interpersonal relationships, and stress intolerance. Maletsky (1974), MacKay, Beck, and Taylor (1973); Safer and Allen (1975); Wood, Reimherr, Wender, and Johnson (1976), and Wender, Reimherr, and Wood (1981) have documented the efficacy of sympathomimetic medication in the ADD adolescent and young adult. The empirical evidence, therefore, suggests that ADD is a childhood disorder that has a high morbidity during adolescence and the early adult years, with indications for pharmacological management similar to that used for children.

Outcome studies have helped refine the criteria and transmission of the ADD syndrome. Research with animals and human neurotransmitter metabolites suggests the existence of an underlying neurochemical substrate in ADD (Shaywitz, Cohen, and Bowers, 1977). Selective destruction of dopaminergic pathways by 6-OHDA in immature rat pups resulted in behaviors analogous to those seen in children with ADD (Alpert, Cohen, Shaywitz, Piccirillo, et al., 1978), including learning difficulties and increased motor activity, which decreased with maturation. The motor activity diminished following amphetamine administration. Bareggi, Becker, Ginsburg, and Genovese (1979) demonstrated, in a genetically stable hybrid beagle, hyperactivity, impulsivity, impaired learning, and a positive response to amphetamine. Lower neuronal and CSF levels of norepinephrine, dopamine, and HVA were found, providing support for the concept of a monoamine basis to the behavior and pharmacological observations associated with ADD.

Human studies provide only limited support for dopaminergic and noradrenergic hypotheses underlying ADD. Shetty and Chase (1976) found no baseline differences in CSF HVA between ADD children and controls but, with amphetamine administration, there was a significant lowering of CSF HVA in index children alone, suggesting a dopamine hypersensitivity. Shaywitz, Cohen, and Bowers (1977) showed lower levels of HVA following probenecid loading in unmedicated ADD children when compared to controls. This finding provided tentative evidence of reduced central dopamine in these children.

There is suggestive but certainly not definitive evidence that monoamines, and the dopamine system in particular, are involved in the pathophysiology of ADD. One indirect way to study central monoamine activity is through peripheral neuroendocrine measures. Dopamine is involved in the regulation of both growth hormone (GH) and prolactin (PRL), probably sharing excitatory control over GH release with other neurotransmitters and having powerful inhibiting control over PRL (Meltzer, Fessler, Simonovic, Doherty, et al., 1979). In fact, there is good evidence to suggest that the Prolactin Inhibiting Factor may be dopamine itself (Takahara, Arimura, and Schally, 1974). Other factors such as stress, TRH (thyrotropin releasing hormone), and diet may also influence prolactin secretion (Panerai, Salerno, Manreschi, et al., 1977). These pituitary hormones have been studied primarily as a function of growth reduction in ADD children chronically treated with sympathomimetic medication (Greenhill, Puig-Antich, Chambers, Rubenstein, et al., 1981). They have not been studied in children as peripheral markers of the central monoamines that mediate their release.

Dopamine receptor blockers increase serum prolactin, whereas agonists, such as L-dopa, apomorphine and sympathomimetics decrease prolactin (MacLeod, 1976). D-amphetamine by blocking reuptake of monoamines at the presynaptic neuron, increasing MAO inhibition and direct receptor stimulation (Snyder, 1972), is a potent agonist of dopamine, norepinephrine, and serotonin.* GH elevation and prolactin inhibition have been observed following d-amphetamine administration (Meltzer, Goode, and Fang, 1978). However, Meltzer, et al. (1979) demonstrated that d-amphetamine increased dopaminergic activity and hence decreased plasma prolactin level under various experimental conditions including reserpine-induced catecholamine depletion. They were, however, unable to demonstrate any decrease in plasma prolactin in normal male rats following d-amphetamine alone.

The present study measured behavioral and neuroendocrine variables in adolescents with and without a history of ADD. If the dopamine or norepinephrine systems are implicated in ADD and these neurochemical features persist beyond childhood, growth hormone and prolactin responses to amphetamine in adolescents with a history of ADD should be different from those in adolescents without an ADD history.

METHOD

Subjects

Two groups of twelve male subjects, with a mean age of 17.4 years, agreed to participate in the study and provided informed written consent. Twelve were healthy subjects without a psychiatric history and free of ADD symptoms, recruited from local public schools and universities, and twelve had been treated at Bradley Hospital for ADD an average of 8 years prior to this study. All subjects with an ADD history had documented in their childhood records at least four of the following six symptoms: attentional deficit, increased hyperactivity,

---

*More recent experiments indicate that d-amphetamine increases DA at the synaptic cleft by enhancing release of cytoplasmic DA in the axonal bulb through its membrane (Fischer, J. F., and Cho, A. K.: Chemical release of dopamine from striatal homogenates: Evidence for an exchange diffusion model. *J. Pharm. and Experimental Therapeutics, 208*:203–209, 1979)–Editor.

impulsivity, aggression, learning disability, and motor incoordination. All index subjects had been treated for ADD but half had received medication. None was treated with stimulants during the 3 years preceding this study. All subjects were of normal intelligence and none had a DSM-III diagnosis of schizophrenia or major affective disorder. They were free of physical illness. There were not significant differences between the index and control subjects in: height (68 cm vs. 70 cm), weight (70 kg vs. 74 kg), age (207.5 months vs. 205.9 months), social class, or subtest scores on intelligence test.

Procedure

Subjects arrived at the hospital at 7:45 a.m. They had been instructed not to eat or drink anything after 10 p.m. the previous night. After a standard low-monoamine breakfast, an indwelling heparinized cannula was inserted into a dorsal hand vein and blood sample drawn. After the oral administration of either 10 mg of d-amphetamine or lactose placebo, blood was drawn every twenty minutes over the next four hours for a total of thirteen samples. Blood was analyzed for growth hormone and prolactin by radioimmunoassay. Half of the twelve index and control subjects were randomly chosen to receive placebo. This was a single-blind study with each subject knowing that he had a fifty percent chance of receiving amphetamine, and the investigators knowing who received the pharmacologically active drug.

Behavioral Measures

At baseline and every hour thereafter, the subjects performed a computerized Continuous Performance Test (CPT). The CPT was completed in a separate room, which contained an Apple II computer and video screen. Different letters were individually presented, each for 130 milliseconds, on a video monitor that was timed and controlled by computer. Letters were presented every 400 milliseconds at a rate of 2.5 per second. A total of 700 letters were presented in each test session, which lasted just over five minutes. Subjects were asked to press a bar whenever they saw a "T" preceded by an "S." This occurred seventy times in the series. Subjects, therefore, had to maintain a high level of attention. Two categories of errors were recorded: errors of omission when the target was neglected, and errors of commission when the bar was pressed although the target letter sequence was not actually presented. A higher error rate indicates a short attention span (errors of omission) and greater impulsivity (errors of commission); these are commonly observed among ADD patients. A total of five CPT sessions were administered over the four hours. Subjects completed the test using the dominant hand to press the bar, as the nondominant hand contained the heparinized cannula.

Neuroendocrine Measures

Every twenty minutes for four hours, 8 ml of blood were drawn. Heparinized saline kept the cannula patent. The samples were centrifuged and the serum was stored and frozen at -20°C until assays were performed for prolactin and growth hormone. GH was analyzed by double antibody radioimmunoassay (Boden and Soeldner, 1967). Prolactin was measured using the radioimmunoassay technique of Kennes, Gevart, and Franchimot (1976). The average within and between assay coefficients of variation were 11.8% and 14.0% for GH and 6.7% and 11.2% for prolactin.

RESULTS

Figure 1 graphically presents the continuous performance total error rate in the four groups of subjects at five equally spaced points across four hours. These graphs show that the index group's error rate started off and continued at a

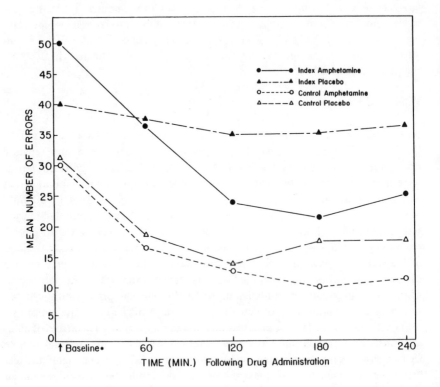

Figure 1. CPT total errors. (*) Placebo or amphetamine administered immediately after baseline, Time 0.

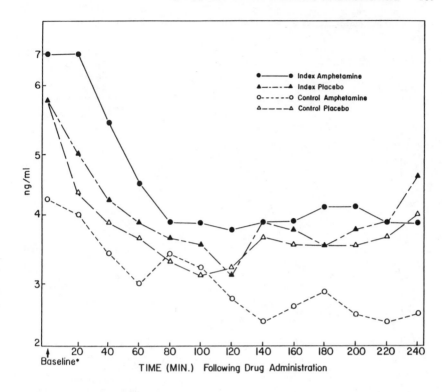

Figure 2. Prolactin levels. (*) Placebo or amphetamine administered immediately after baseline, Time 0.

higher level throughout the experiment. Only the index amphetamine group approached the control placebo performance, at 180 and 240 minutes following drug administration. All four groups showed improvement with practice. We used a three-factor analysis of variance with repeated measures (Winer, 1972). (This statistic was preceded by an Fmax test for homogeneity of variance; the Fmax value was not significant.) Main effects were obtained comparing groups' total error rate [F (1,20) = 11.80, $p < 0.005$) and time (F 4,80) = 14.39, $p < 0.001$]. Although index and control responses differed, they did not show a differential improvement over time.

There were no differences in serum prolactin between index and controls, or between subjects who received amphetamine and placebo (Figure 2). There was, however, a significant decrease in prolactin levels across time [F (12,240) = 13.84, $p < 0.001$]. These results suggest that the decrease in prolactin was not specific to either group or drug administration.

The two amphetamine groups show a clear elevation in growth hormone, with the two placebo groups showing only minor fluctuations (see Figure 3).

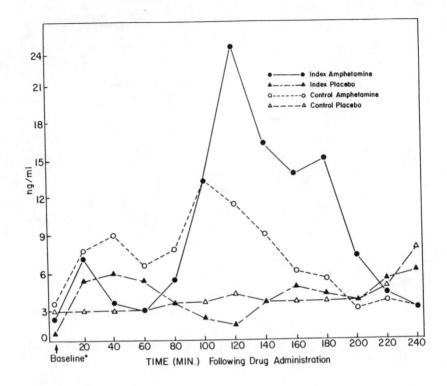

Figure 3. Growth hormone levels. (*) Placebo or amphetamine administered immediately after baseline, Time 0.

There also appear to be two times when growth hormone peaks, both early (100 and 120 minutes post drug administration) and later (180 minutes post drug administration) in the experiment. The significant differences were found by the three-factor analysis of variance with repeated measures (Fmax was not significant) for growth hormone following amphetamine administration [F (12,240) = 2.58, p <0.01]. The specific times that growth hormone differed in the amphetamine group compared to the placebo group were at 100 and 120 minutes (Neuman-Keuls test).

DISCUSSION

These preliminary findings indicate a trend that has not been reported before—namely, psychometric test results differentiating adolescents with a history of ADD from controls. The data are consistent with a previously documented suggestion of ongoing attention deficit that persists into late adolescence. Performance on a computerized CPT illustrates that the adolescent formerly diagnosed as ADD showed a higher CPT total error rate. This error rate did not improve with the administration of 10 mg of amphetamine, nor did the control group show an improvement in performance on this dosage of amphetamine (approximately 0.14 mg/kg). This negative finding is in contrast to clinical reports that document sympathomimetic clinical improvement continuing into the adult years. Thus, unlike findings reported by Rapoport, Buchsbaum, Weingartner, Zahn, et al. (1980), neither group in this experiment showed a continuous performance response to amphetamine.

There are a number of possible explanations for these results. First, the test itself may only distinguish ADD subjects from controls and may not be sensitive to drug effects at this dosage. This specific cognitive task (CPT) may not demonstrate improvement from the small dose administered. The very powerful practice effect may also obscure a subtle drug effect. This is further supported by the relative inability to identify clearly a "peak" performance on the CPT at the established maximum absorptive phase of amphetamine (Brown, Hunt, Ebert, Bunney, and Kopin, 1979). These preliminary findings indicate that, at this dosage, there is no discernible difference in the index's and control's amphetamine response as measured by a behavioral test. There was a trend, however, suggesting that CPT response of index subjects while on amphetamine approached the performance of controls on placebo (Figure 1). Similarly, the index group receiving amphetamine also seemed to show the largest improvement within the initial two hours of the experiment. Dose-response investigations might help delineate the underlying mechanism of this trend.

The preliminary neuroendocrine results indicate that prolactin inhibition is not observed following amphetamine administration. Other than the response observed in reserpenized laboratory animals, amphetamine alone does not consistently inhibit prolactin in humans. Though amphetamine is a powerful monoamine agonist, it does not appear to influence this system in vivo in adolescents. There was, however, a strong stress-inhibiting effect over the experimental period.

Baseline blood levels were taken at approximately 9:00 a.m., after breakfast, and the subject was oriented to the testing protocol. Prolactin secretion is a consequence of both circadian rhythm and sleep, although not to specific sleep phases (see Sassin, Frantz, Wiertzman, et al., 1972). Secretion appears to be self-regulated via the inhibiting control of the hypothalamus on the anterior pituitary and can be increased by a number of endogenous and exogenous factors including psychological stress, exercise, hypoglycemia, and sleep (de la Fuente and Rosenbaum, 1981). Prolactin suppression observed in the twenty-four subjects may be explained by the other factors. Since the baseline blood sample was taken at approximately the time when prolactin is at its lowest point

(Martin, Reichlin, and Brown, 1977), any suppression via sympathomimetic medication might be difficult to identify because of an already naturally occurring "bottoming out." Conversely, one can suggest that the baseline prolactin level is elevated in reaction to stress from the insertion of the cannula and/or the novel experimental circumstances. The significant decrease in prolactin over time, but not in response to the drug, may then simply be an expression of this stress.

The trend is for growth hormone in ADD adolescents to be much larger than for the controls. Though the tuberoinfundibular system is not the neurotransmitter system involved in ADD, this increased growth hormone response might reflect a generalized catecholamine hypersensitivity. The results show growth hormone to have a marked increase at 100 to 120 minutes following drug administration, corresponding to the peak of the absorption phase, and that is the period of time when amphetamine exerts its strongest behavioral effect (Brown, et al., 1979). There also appears to be a specific time/drug interaction, which indicates that the drug, not environmental or dietary factors, specifically produces the increase in growth hormone.

CONCLUSIONS

This study documents a continued cognitive deficit in adolescents who were diagnosed as ADD in childhood, compared to normal adolescents. These deficits reflect inattention and impulsivity persisting beyond childhood. Secondly, neuroendocrine response, specifically growth hormone, to sympathomimetic medication may reflect catecholamine differences between ADD subjects and controls. As growth hormone is controlled by both dopamine and norepineprine, abnormal elevation in growth hormone in response to d-amphetamine may reflect generalized CNS catecholamine hypersensitivity. It is important to determine whether these trends can be substantiated by enlarging the size of the samples and to see if other endocrine markers, such as cortisol, reflect a catecholamine difference between groups. Other cognitive, psychophysiological, and behavioral measures may aid in delineating this neuroendocrine substrate. Further studies in the laboratory should explore the clinical relevance of drug responders to nonresponders. Pharmacokinetic studies working with serum amphetamine levels would differentiate drug responders from nonresponders. Pharmacodynamic factors may be related to more fundamental differences in the brain, such as: different receptor sites; different clusters and types of receptors; and different levels of endogenous agonists and antagonists—namely, norepinephrine, dopamine, and serotonin (Forsman, 1976). Ongoing research is addressing these issues.

DISCUSSIONS

Paul H. Wender

It is a pleasure to discuss this chapter because of its aesthetic as well as its cognitive qualities. Barry Garfinkel has an attribute, rare in our field, of being creative; he employed a technique that has been utilized only sparingly in adult psychiatry—that of using neuroendocrinological response as a measure of brain functioning.

It's a clean experiment and I am assured he will replicate it. One of the fascinating things it suggests is that, in addition to decreased dopamine turnover as found by our and Bennett Shaywitz's homovanillic acid (HVA) studies, there may be decreased receptor sensitivity. Usually what seems to occur in the CNS is that, when neurotransmitter turnover decreases, the receptor becomes supersensitive. Similarly, if the receptor is blocked, supersensitivity generally occurs. So an additional interesting suggestion of Barry's experiment may be that, in addition to decreased turnover, there may be decreased sensitivity to dopamine in residual ADD.

C. Keith Conners

Dr. Garfinkel's study is important because it firmly establishes some biological differences between diagnosed MBD young adults and carefully matched controls. One presumes that the findings reflect central, rather than peripheral differences, but we might ask what peripheral mechanisms could account for his findings. Ronald Prinz and colleagues (Prinz, Roberts, and Hantman, 1980) recently reported high correlations among dietary intake of carbohydrates, carbohydrate/protein ratio, and several behavioral measures in both hyperactive and normal children. Both groups showed significant behavioral relationships with carbohydrate intake, but the hyperactives showed increases in activity level, measured by grid crossings. The findings suggest that sugar acts to disinhibit the hyperactive patients.

However, the direction of causality is not clear from this correlational study and it makes as much sense, physiologically, to assume that increased activity level leads to increased carbohydrate utilization, rather than the other way around.

We know that rats raised on a high sucrose diet can actually show lower fasting blood levels of glucose, thus appearing hypoglycemic (Kanarek and Marks-Kaufman, 1979). It has been suggested that lowering blood sugar levels from a high level back to normal actually leads to diminished brain glucose (Gjedde and Crone, 1981), as well as changes in osmolality of the blood–brain barrier, which leads to influx of fluids to the brain and consequent brain edema (Hudspeth, Peterson, Soli, and Trimble, 1981). Moreover, increased peripheral carbohydrate load will raise brain tryptophan and serotonin, depending upon circulating amino acids that compete for entry into the brain (Fernstrom and Wurtman, 1971).

Thus, there may be more than one mechanism by which peripheral dietary factors can cause changes in central nervous system function. The various factors that are related to gluconeogenesis—e.g., insulin release, glycogen, cortisol, fatty acids, epinephrine—cause changes in the measures Dr. Garfinkel has obtained for his groups. It would be of interest to compare their weights, dietary habits and, most of all, their blood glucose levels prior to and after the drug challenge.

General Discussion

Dr. Garfinkel: Keith Conners' comments are important, because clinically in interviewing and doing this follow-up of former ADD patients, three of them were subsequently diagnosed in late adolescence as being hypoglycemic by their family physicians. They have been on hypoglycemic diets, i.e., eating 6 to 8 very small meals a day. This type of diet may even out these swings. It will be of interest to look at glucose metabolism differences.

What was interesting was there was not only a latency difference and peak difference for GH, but all the subjects that we have run (we have run many who are not included in this report) show a very great difference in breakaway phenomena as well (in the final hour of sample collection). The different peaks and breakaway phenomena are in keeping with Keith's comments. It could be, keeping in mind that they actually fast during this period, that the fast itself influences growth hormone production. A very interesting observation is that the index group, at the tail end of the fast, showed a very different growth hormone pattern. It's highly elevated, where the controls are continuing on a lower level. There are three factors to investigate: (1) glucose and fasting, (2) chronic control, and (3) acute state control. The chronic control of GH is primarily under adrenergic mediation, whereas the acute state may be dopaminergically controlled. This will need to be investigated.

Dr. Shaffer: If there were dietary or peripheral differences between the groups, would you expect them to affect the latent period, the breakaway phenomenon, or the peak?

Dr. Garfinkel: Primarily, we observe the dietary influences in terms of the breakaway phase. In the acute phase, we are looking at a dopaminergic system. If we are looking at the latency period, I think we are primarily looking at noradrenergic and serotonergic phenomena. In general, it's three different systems interacting.

Dr. Cantwell: I think Barry has the opportunity with large numbers to do some subdivision of the ex-ADD population, because there will be ex-ADDs (people identified in childhood) who will have definable psychopathology at follow-up and there will be those who will not.* It will be interesting to see if there are differences both on their task performance and also in the growth hormone and prolactin levels. If there is, that would suggest another area where there is a persistent defect in those who have taken a deviant outcome. The other point is: if you take omission and commission, as indicated, as the more impulsivity, more inattentiveness (again with larger numbers you may be able to subdivide into those who have more problems with impulsivity than they do with attention and vice-versa) you can look to see over time what that's associated with, either differences in the neuroendocrine response or differences in other types of clinical outcome. It is interesting that it looked, from the graph, as if the amphetamine in the ex-ADD had a much greater effect on the measure of impulsivity than it did on the inattention, considering the difference between placebo and amphetamine response in the ex-ADD group. This is kind of counter to what people say. It raises some questions about the centricity of "attention" in this particular problem.

Dr. Garfinkel: With regard to these ex-ADD's, what we have done so far is call back 55 of Dr. Laufer's former patients; of those, we have applied the Utah criteria and had them self-rate themselves on the Conners' rating scale for adults, which Reimherr and Wender modified. So we had two ratings; clinical interview as well as self-rating, identifying whether they had ADD, residual type. We selected those who met best both the Utah criteria and self-rated scale for ADD. Those who scored highest on residual ADD, by combining these two criteria, were used in this study.

Dr. Bellak: I support Hans Huessy's finding that imipramine may be extremely helpful to a good number of patients (in my case, in adults) and remains helpful over a long stretch of time. This is important for those who actually treat such people because of the social difficulties in prescribing amphetamine-like drugs, in and outside of the hospital, where there is usually a great deal of resistance.

There is one other point, especially for laboratory scientists who don't see people very much. Whatever ails persons with ADD is tremendously increased in premenstrual women: that should lend itself to some endocrinological hypothesis!

---

*Dr. Garfinkel has addressed this question in a paper to appear in the second volume of this series—Editor.

REFERENCES

Alpert, J. E., Cohen, D. J., Shaywitz, B. A., Piccirillo, M., and Shaywitz, S. E. Animal models and childhood behavioral disturbances: Dopamine depletion in the newborn rat pup. *J. Amer. Acad. Child Psychiat.*, 1978, *17*: 239–251.

Bareggi, S. R., Becker, R. E., Ginsburg, B. E., and Genovese, E. Neurochemical investigation of an endogenous model of the "hyperkinetic syndrome" in a hybrid dog. *Life Sciences,* 1979, *24*:451–488.

Boden, G., and Soeldner, J. S. A sensitive double antibody radioimmunoassay for human growth hormone (HGH): Levels of HGH following rapid tolbutamide infusion. *Diabetologia,* 1967, *8*:413–421.

Brown, G. L., Hunt, R. D., Ebert, M. H., Bunney, W. E., and Kopin, I. J. Plasma levels of D-amphetamine in hyperactive children. *Psychopharmacology,* 1979, *62*:133–140.

Cantwell, D. P. Psychiatric illness in families of hyperactive children. *Arch. Gen. Psychiat.,* 1972, *27*:414–417.

Cantwell, D. P. Genetic factors in the hyperkinetic syndrome. *J. Amer. Acad. Child Psychiat.,* 1976, *15*:214–223.

de la Fuente, J. R., and Rosenbaum, A. H. Prolactin in psychiatry. *Amer. J. Psychiat.,* 1981, *138*:1154–1160.

Fernstrom, J. D., and Wurtman, R. J. Brain serotonin content: Increase following ingestion of carbohydrate diet. *Science,* 1971, *174*:1023–1025.

Forsman, A. D. Individual variability in response to haloperidol. *Proc. Roy Soc. Med.,* 1976, *69* (Suppl. 1):9–13.

Gjedde, A., and Crone, C. Blood-brain glucose transfer: repression in chronic hypoglycemia. *Science,* 1981, *214*:456–457.

Greenhill, L. L., Puig-Antich, J., Chambers, W., Rubinstein, B., Halpern, F., and Sachar, E. J. Growth hormone, prolactin, and growth responses in hyperkinetic males treated with d-amphetamine. *J. Amer. Acad. Child Psychiat.,* 1981, *20*:84–103.

Hechtman, L., Weiss, G., and Perlman, T. Hyperactives as young adults: Self-esteem and social skills. *Canad. J. Psychiat.,* 1980, *25*:478–483.

Hudspeth, W. J., Peterson, L. W., Soli, D. E., and Trimble, B. A. Neurobiology of the hypoglycemia syndrome. *J. of Holistic Medicine,* 1981, *3*:60–71.

Huessy, H. R., Metoyer, M., and Townsend, M. Eight to ten-year follow-up of 84 children treated for behavioral disturbance in rural Vermont. *Acta Paedopsychiat.,* 1974, *40*:230–235.

Kanarek, R. B., and Marks-Kaufman, R. Developmental aspects of sucrose-induced obesity in rats. *Physiol. Behav.,* 1979, *23*:881–885.

Kennes, F., Gevaert, Y., and Franchimont, P. Homologous radioimmunoassay for human prolactin. *Int. J. Nucl. Med. Biol.,* 1976, *3*(1):21–28.

MacKay, M. C., Beck, L., and Taylor, R. Methylphenidate for adolescents with minimal brain dysfunction. *N Y State J. Med.,* 1973, *73*:551–554.

MacLeod, R. M. Regulation of prolactin secretion. *Frontiers of Neuroendocrinology,* 1976, *4*:169–194.

Maletsky, B. M. D-amphetamine and delinquency. *Dis. Nerv. Sys.,* 1974, *35*: 543–547.

Mann, H. B., and Greenspan, S. I. The identification and treatment of adult brain dysfunction. *Amer. J. Psychiat.,* 1976, *133*:1013–1017.

Martin, J. B., Reichlin, S., and Brown, G. M. *Clinical neuroendocrinology.* Philadelphia: F. A. Davis Co., 1977, pp. 129–145.

Meltzer, H. Y., Fessler, R. G., Simonovic, M., Doherty, J., and Fang, V. S. Effect of d- and l-amphetamine on rat plasma prolactin levels. *Psychopharmacology,* 1979, *61*:63–69.

Meltzer, H. Y., Goode, D. J., and Fang, V. S. The effect of psychotropic drugs on endocrine function. I. Neuroleptics, precursors, and agonists. In M. A. Lipton, A. DiMascio, and K. F. Killam (Eds.), *Psychopharmacology: a generation of progress.* New York: Raven Press, 1978, pp. 509–530.

Mendelson, W., Johnson, N., and Stewart, M. A. Hyperactive children as adolescents: A follow-up study. *J. Nerv. Ment. Dis.,* 1971, *153*:273–279.

Morrison, J. R., and Stewart, M. A. A family study of the hyperactive child syndrome. *Biol. Psychiat.,* 1971, *3*:189–195.

Morrison, J. R., and Stewart, M. A. The psychiatric status of the legal families of adopted hyperactive children. *Arch. Gen. Psychiat.,* 1973, *28*:888–891.

Panerai, A. E., Salerno, F., Manneschi, M., et al. Growth hormone and prolactin responses to thyrotropin-releasing hormone in patients with severe liver disease. *J. Clin. Endocrinol. Metab.,* 1977, *45*(1):134–140.

Prinz, R. J., Roberts, W. A., and Hantman, E. Dietary correlates of hyperactive behavior in children. *Journal of Consulting and Clinical Psychology,* 1980, *48*:760–769.

Rapoport, J. L., Buchsbaum, M. S., Weingartner, H., Zahn, T. P., Ludlow, C., and Mikkelsen, E. J. Dextroamphetamine: its cognitive and behavioral effects in normal and hyperactive boys and men. *Arch. Gen. Psychiat.,* 1980, *37*:933–943.

Safer, D. J. A familial factor in minimal brain dysfunction. *Behav. Genet.,* 1973, *3*:175–183.

Safer, D. J., and Allen, R. P. Stimulant drug treatment of hyperactive adolescents. *Dis. Nerv. Sys.,* 1975, *36*:454–457.

Sassin, J. F., Frantz, A. G., Weirtzman, E. D., et al. Human prolactin 24 hour pattern with increased release during sleep. *Science,* 1972, *177*:1205–1207.

Shaywitz, B. A., Cohen, D. J., and Bowers, M. B. CSF monoamine metabolites in children with minimal brain dysfunction: evidence of alteration of brain dopamine. *J. Pediat.,* 1977, *90*:67–71.

Shelley, E. M., and Reister, A. Syndrome of MBD in young adults. *Dis. Nerv. Sys.,* 1972, *33*:335–339.

Shetty, T., and Chase, T. N. Central monoamines and hyperkinesis of childhood. *Neurology,* 1976, *26*:1000–1002.

Snyder, S. H. Catecholamines in the brain as mediators of amphetamine psychosis. *Arch. Gen. Psychiat.,* 1972, *27*:169–179.

Takahara, J., Arimura, A., and Schally, A. U. Suppression of prolactin release by a purified porcine PIF preparation and catecholamines infused into a rat hypophysial portal vessel. *Endocrinology,* 1974, *96*:462–465.

Weiss, G., Hechtman, L., Perlman, T. et al. Hyperactives as young adults: A controlled prospective ten-year follow-up of 75 children. *Arch. Gen. Psychiat.,* 1979, *36*:675–681.

Weiss, G., Kruger, E., Danielson, U., and Elman, M. Effect of long-term treatment of hyperactive children with methylphenidate. *Canad. Med. Assn. J.,* 1975, *112*:159–165.

Wender, P. H., Reimherr, F. W., and Wood, D. R. Attention deficit disorder ('MBD') in adults. *Arch. Gen. Psychiat.,* 1981, *38*:449–456.

Winer, B. J. *Statistical principles in experimental design.* New York: McGraw-Hill, 1972, pp. 559–567.

Winokur, G. The division of depressive illness into depression spectrum disease and pure depressive disease. *Int. Pharmacopsychiatry,* 1974, *9*:5–13.

Wood, D. R., Reimherr, F. W., Wender, P. H., and Johnson, G. E. Diagnosis and treatment of minimal brain dysfunction in adults. *Arch. Gen. Psychiat.,* 1976, *33*:1453–1460.

Pharmacokinetic, Neuroendocrine, and Behavioral Substrates of ADD

BENNETT A. SHAYWITZ

EDITOR'S COMMENTS

In this chapter, Dr. Shaywitz presents basic pharmacological information that will permit a physician to prescribe methylphenidate (MPD) in a more precise and rational manner. He focuses upon the relationship between blood levels of MPD and a variety of neurochemical and behavioral parameters. Tests used were the Children's Personal Data Inventory, the Woodcock-Johnson Achievement Test, and the WISC.

Children were studied at two different doses of methylphenidate, approximately 0.3 mg/kg and 0.6 mg/kg. The plasma concentration was observed 2.5 hours after administration of the lower dose and 1.9 hours after administration of the higher dose. Terminal half-lives averaged about 2.5 hours at both doses. The mean maximum concentration of the lower dose was 11 mg/ml and of the higher, 20 mg/ml. The area under the curve, which the author feels is a better measure for total drug availability, was twice that of the lower dose for the higher dose.

Growth hormone and prolactin were measured in response to MPD. A significant decline in prolactin was observed with an increase in growth hormone, both peaking at the time of peak plasma MPD concentration.

This is a summary of a paper by: Sally E. Shaywitz, M.D., Robert J. Hunt, M.D., Peter Jatlow, M.D., Donald J. Cohen, M.D., J. Gerald Young, M.D., George M. Anderson, Ph.D. and Bennett A. Shaywitz, M.D., from the Departments of Pediatrics, Neurology, Laboratory of Medicine in the Yale Child Study Center: Acute and Chronic Effects of Methylphenidate in Children with Attention Deficit Disorder: Neurochemical, Pharmacologic and Behavioral Response (*Pediatrics,* 69:688–694, June 1982).

Results of an acute study with drug-naive patients was compared with chronic administration of MPD for both doses of the drug.

Percentage of change in the Conners' Parent Teacher Rating Scale was plotted against MPD concentration, with a significant correlation coefficient. A number of attentional tasks were also used in Bennett Shaywitz's experiments as well as the paired-associate learning task.

*   *   *

This chapter addresses all of the conflicting issues about the use of pharmacotherapy in children with Attention Deficit Disorder, but more realistically, focuses upon just one aspect of the role of stimulants and the use of stimulants, in particular, methylphenidate (MPD), in children with Attention Deficit Disorders. I hope to give you a sense of the way we have approached the use of MPD and how we have attempted to determine basic pharmacologic information, which we hope will be able to permit the physician who prescribes the medicine to use the drug in a more thoughtful, more precise and more rational manner.

Our studies focus upon the relationship between blood levels of MPD and a variety of neurochemical and behavioral parameters. We began these studies with the realization that, while there have been real advances in the diagnosis and delineation of the group of children with ADD (the recent application of DSM-III criteria to ADD), the current practice of using MPD in such children is, really, at a primitive level compared with, for example, the use of anticonvulsants in seizure disorders. Non-neurologists should be aware that when we prescribe anticonvulsants to a child with a seizure disorder, we routinely give the drug first at a certain mg/kg level, but then follow the medication with frequent blood levels. This is something that has been done since plasma levels have been readily available for most of the anticonvulsants in the last 20 years. As you know, phenobarbital has been available since the early part of the 20th century. Dilantin (phenytoin) has been available since 1938 and blood levels on both these common anticonvulsants have been clinically available since the 1960s. We are able to use blood levels because there has been a great deal of information obtained on the rate of absorption of all the anticonvulsants I mention here, not only phenytoin and phenobarbital, but newer agents, such as valproic acid and carbamazepine.

Contrast this, if you will, with the usual approach to the administration of MPD in children with ADD. Here, we most usually decide that we will give MPD at a certain mg/kg dose and if the child has no response at that level, we can increase the medication. We tend to use our clinical judgment as to what is a response and what is not. We tend to use anywhere from 0.3 mg/kg to 1.0 mg/kg as the optimal dose. The precise dose of MPD yields, as far as the blood levels are concerned, I would characterize as at a primitive level compared to the way we would use anticonvulsants. All this has changed in the last several years, mainly because of the introduction of a gas chromatographic assay for MPD. This assay has really facilitated the determination of blood levels and allowed us to perform a series of experiments that we designed to examine a number of clinically relevant issues relating to MPD.

Let us describe both the initial series of studies as well as some more recent investigations that were performed in a more sophisticated, double-blind study. Our first thought was to look at MPD after acute administration. That is, to see what concentrations of MPD were attained after a single dose of the drug. We elected to do this on what we considered a fairly homogeneous group of youngsters, at least clinically. We studied a group of 14 boys, all between 7–12 years of age, who had been referred to our Learning Disorder Unit. All of these children were diagnosed as ADD to DSM-III criteria. They all were of normal intelligence as measured on Wechsler scales. In fact, the mean of their verbal I.Q.s was 98, the mean of their performance, 104; and their full-scale mean was 100. We also tended to use a relatively high SES (socio-economic scale) group of youngsters and all had scores of 203, using the Hollingshead index, representing the predominantly middle-class population at our clinic. All of the boys were studied in a drug-naive state; that is, if they had been on medications, we made sure they were off medications for at least a month prior to the time of investigation.

We used a number of different diagnostic instruments. The principal instrument was the Childrens' Personal Data Inventory, developed by Dr. Sally Shaywitz (1982). This is a fairly detailed, 846-item questionnaire that has been factored into approximately 10 different scales. In addition to this fairly comprehensive historical instrument, we also used the usual clinical interview, a very detailed neuromaturational examination focusing upon soft signs, as well as the more routine neurologic and pediatric examinations. We used a standardized achievement test, the Woodcock-Johnson, and we, of course, used the WISC, as mentioned before. Any child who was chosen for the study was admitted to our Childrens' Clinical Research Center; the child was generally admitted very early in the morning, between 7–7:30. At that point, an I.V. was placed in an antecubital vein and at 9:00 we administered MPD. Blood samples were collected prior to administration of MPD, to obtain stable baseline values for our neurochemical parameter. Samples were taken at 30-minute intervals for several hours and then at hourly intervals, up to periods of 5–10 hours after drug administration. We first looked at two different dosages: a low dose, which was approximately 0.3 mg/kg, and a higher dose, which was double that, 0.6 mg/kg. The children were not fed breakfast, although they did get a snack, but they all received a standard lunch.

Figure 1 shows a drug profile in one of these youngsters. One little boy was 10 years old. We gave him 0.3 mg/kg of MPD. The concentration increases so that, finally, after 3 hours, MPD peaks at around 8 ng/ml. Over the next

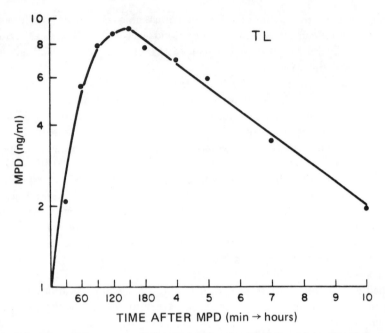

Figure 1. Dose-time curve of plasma levels of methylphenidate after 0.3 mg/kg of methylphenidate intravenously in 10-year-old boy. From Shaywitz et al. (1982). Copyright American Academy of Pediatrics. Reprinted by permission.

7 hours, it declines in a linear relationship during the elimination phase. The ordinate is plotted on a logarithmic scale. For comparison, Figure 2 shows the elimination after we gave a dose of 0.6 mg/kg, this time to an 11-year-old boy. The concentration of MPD peaked at about 1½ hours and then declined in a nice linear fashion over the next few hours. The last 7 points all lie along a straight line. Peak concentration here, at this higher dose, is around 16 ng/ml or 17 ng/ml, considerably higher than the concentration at the lower dose, approximately double.

Peak plasma concentration of MPD was observed 2.5 hours after administration of the lower dose and 1.9 hours after administration of the higher dose (these numbers are not really significant). Terminal half-lives averaged about 2.5 hours at both the low and the high dose. As you would imagine, there was a marked difference in the maximal plasma concentrations, depending on the dose administered, and we saw a maximum concentration mean of about 11 ng/ml after the low dose and of 20 ng/ml after the higher dose. The area under the curve, which is probably a better measure of total drug available in the body, for the higher dose is double that for the lower dose.

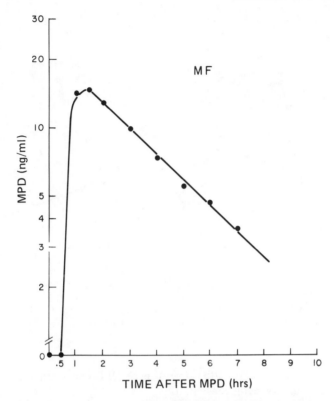

Figure 2. Dose-time curve of plasma levels of methylphenidate after 0.6 mg/kg of methylphenidate intravenously in 11-year-old boy. From Shaywitz et al. (1982). Copyright American Academy of Pediatrics. Reprinted by permission.

We also were interested in measuring growth hormone and prolactin responses after MPD. Prolactin is believed to be influenced by dopaminergic mechanisms and MPD is believed to exert its effects via central catecholaminergic, probably primarily dopaminergic, systems and we would, of course, expect alterations in prolactin after MPD. In Figure 3, following the administration of MPD, are the mean concentrations for all patients taking the low dose (because we had more patients taking the low dose). As the concentration of MPD starts increasing, concentration of prolactin has declined, and stays down for several hours and then starts coming back up again. This is a significant decline that I think indicates that MPD certainly influences serum prolactin. These data on prolactin are a little more consistent than has been observed in older patients receiving MPD. Growth hormone has the opposite response than prolactin—that is, as MPD increases, growth hormone tends to

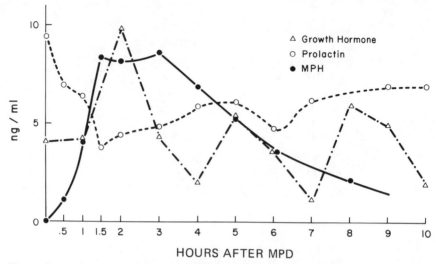

Figure 3. Dose-time curves of methylphenidate, prolactin, and growth hormone for low-dose (0.3 mg/kg) patients. From Shaywitz et al. (1982). Copyright American Academy of Pediatrics. Reprinted by permission.

increase and, in fact, peaks at the time of peak MPD concentration, as was the case for minimum prolactin concentration.

I think that the findings of the acute study are really very important because they indicate that in a large sample of children with ADD, the time until peak concentration of MPD is about 2.5 hours and the elimination half-life is about 2.5 hours. While there is a previous report in the literature indicating that these pharmacokinetic parameters are the ones to use, that previous report was based on a very small number of children of a variety of different ages and it wasn't really clear what their diagnoses were (Hungund, Perel, Hurwic, et al., 1979). I think our study is really the first time that anybody has looked at MPD concentration in a fairly large group of children who have been chosen so as to be as homogeneous as possible.

Let me move on now to the study of how a physician might want to use MPD concentrations in a clinical way, that is, not in the hospital sampling I.V.s with an I.V. heparin-lock, but in the clinical situation. We have designated the next phase of the study as the so-called *chronic study*. The children in this portion of the study were also part of our Learning Disorders Unit and here we used children from ages 5-16. Again, any child designated as ADD had to have a normal I.Q. The mean verbal I.Q. was 104; performance, 97; and full-scale, 100. The way we did this study was to bring the children into the clinic in the

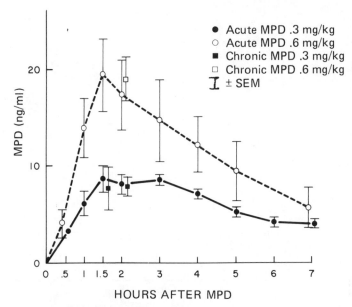

Figure 4. Plasma levels of methylphenidate under two dosages and two conditions of drug administration. From Shaywitz et al. (1982). Copyright American Academy of Pediatrics. Reprinted by permission.

morning, after their parents had administered MPD at home; or, in some cases, we decided to give them MPD in the clinic. In any case, we knew exactly when the children had received the MPD and we sampled at either 1.5 hours, or at 2 hours, and again tried to use a low dose, about 0.3 mg/kg, and a higher dose, essentially double (0.6 mg/kg). In this particular study, we also used several behavior rating scales in the hopes of gaining some sense of the relationship between MPD levels and clinical response. The clinical instruments used were our own behavior rating scale that was developed by Sally Shaywitz, as well as the Conners' abbreviated 10-item Parent-Teacher Rating Scale, and other local impression scales.

It is difficult to know how to show our results here, and in Figure 4, what I have tried to do is compare the results of children who are taking MPD essentially in this chronic fashion, that is, every day, and try to compare them to the results that we obtained in the acute study. Basically, what is shown is MPD levels after a low dose and after a high dose. Obviously, the lower levels are obtained after the low dose and the high levels were after the high dose. What is intriguing here is that the children who are in the chronic portion of this study have concentrations at 1.5 hours and at 2 hours that are very comparable

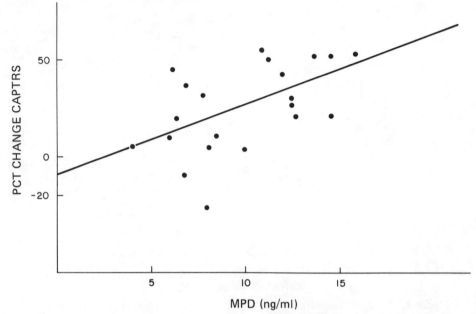

Figure 5. Relationship between plasma methylphenidate concentration in ng/ml and percentage of change on Conners Abbreviated Parent-Teacher Rating Scale. From Shaywitz et al. (1982). Copyright American Academy of Pediatrics. Reprinted by permission.

to those observed in the acute study. Basically, children who received 0.3 mg/kg have an average concentration of MPD of about 8 ng/ml at 2 hours. Those receiving double that dose have an average concentration of MPD, at 2 hours, of close to 19 ng/ml.

One of the intriguing findings of this study was just what the relationship was between the MPD concentration and clinical improvement. It is very difficult to know how to assess clinical improvement, because just about everybody in our study, with a couple of exceptions, tended to have a good response to MPD.

In Figure 5, we have plotted the percentage of change in the Conners' Parent-Teacher Rating Scale against the MPD concentration in ng/ml. There is a positive relationship, with a significant correlation between the two. The reason for showing this is to give you a sense of how you might want to apply an MPD concentration in clinical practice, and I think Figure 5 shows that there is a relationship between MPD concentration and clinical response.

An interesting finding, I think, was obtained when we looked at two patients in our study who did not respond. There are actually three children who did not respond. Two of the children were receiving a low dose—that is, 0.3 mg/kg—and in each of these children MPD concentration at 2 hours was at the lower limit of detectability, that is 1-2 ng/ml. The average concentrations obtained after 0.3 mg/kg for our subjects was about 8 ng/ml after 2 hours, so the two children who did not respond really had very markedly reduced concentrations. They didn't absorb the medication and just had no detectable concentrations in their blood. A third child was receiving the higher dose of MPD, that is 0.6 mg/kg. She had not responded either, and her MPD concentration in 2 hours was about 7 ng/ml while the usual concentration at this time is about 18-20 ng/ml. While we really can't say for sure what a therapeutic concentration of MPD is, we can say, at least that after 0.3 mg/kg, those children who failed to respond had levels of MPD that were below 7 ng/ml. It is a little difficult to talk about a therapeutic level. Although I initially stated, "Wouldn't it be interesting if we could use MPD concentrations in the same way we use anticonvulsant concentrations," you have to remember that you are giving MPD once a day or twice a day, and you are essentially achieving a peak level and then the concentration is declining, whereas anticonvulsants are maintained at a steady-state level. The only other drug that is used the way MPD is used, at least a commonly administered drug, is something like theophylline, where you try to obtain a peak level.

I indicated that it's really quite interesting to correlate the clinical response with MPD concentration and to try to place administration of MPD on a more rational footing than we had been able to achieve before. I think we've accomplished our goal. Clearly, we know a great deal about MPD pharmacokinetics now and we know, within reasonable limits, what levels to expect 2 hours after administration of dosages of 0.3 mg/kg and 0.6 mg/kg. We also know the elimination half-lives are about 2.5 hours and we can essentially estimate what concentrations are after administration. I think this will prove to be very useful in defining a number of different clinical responses. I also think it indicates that we really should be looking at MPD concentrations any time we are doing a drug study using MPD. For example, Marcel Kinsbourne has recently published a study showing the paired-associate learning test in relationship to MPD (Swanson, Kinsbourne, Roberts, et al., 1978). Increasingly, in that study, his peak effect on the paired-associate learning test was approximately 2-4 hours after MPD which, as you know, is about the time we see a peak blood level of MPD. That is quite interesting.

We just finished a large double-blind study looking at two different doses of MPD (0.3 mg/kg and 0.6 mg/kg), measuring behavioral parameters. We measured a number of attentional tasks. We also used the paired associate learning task and I don't have data to show you at this point, but I will tell you that a preliminary run through the data indicates that the higher doses of MPD and the higher plasma levels achieved in these higher doses seem to be the most effective. This suggests that the notion that was first espoused by Sprague and Sleator several years ago (1977), that there is a U-shaped response to MPD—that is, lower doses might produce a better response than higher doses, at least for attention—is probably not going to bear up under closer scrutiny.

DISCUSSION

Marcel Kinsbourne

One won't see many adverse responders if one uses Conners' criterion of a score above 15 on both his questionnaires to generate the study samples. But, if one does include them, one gains additional information, as we have shown. An adverse time-response curve, which we have seen many a time, occurs when the child's performance deteriorates as the drug takes effect and improves when the drug wears off. One may also see the same child who on a low dose has a favorable response have an adverse response on a high dose. The adverse response enables one to deconfound those changes attending stimulant medication that are relative to its effects on learning from those that are not. As I have already mentioned, heart rate is one. Heart rate goes up with stimulants, whether the child will do well or badly on the cognitive task. As for the dose-time response, we have found nesting curves with dose by time response.

Let us consider the published work of my colleagues at Children's Hospital, Chan, Sullivan, and Swanson (1980). They developed a microassay of methylphenidate and produced half-life data for intravenous methylphenidate in hyperactive children. They measured both methylphenidate and its metabolite, Ritalinic acid. For methylphenidate, they found a half-life from 2 hours upwards as one increased the dose. Ritalinic acid had a substantial longer half-life, about 3½ hours more. The more important question was: do some children need much higher doses to achieve a favorable response than others do? There are two possibilities. One is that the so-called high-dose responders, as we called them, have inefficient gastrointestinal absorption and therefore need a higher dose to be effective. They still respond within the same serum-level range as do the low-dose responders. The other possibility is that, at a given serum level, some children will respond, some won't. Since the target mechanisms are in the brain, for some children higher levels of the drug are needed to generate a response than are needed for others.

The results demonstrated clearly that the second is the case. As one increases oral dose, one sees a corresponding increase in the serum level of both the drug and its metabolite in children, whether they are high- or low-dose responders. In other words, the high-dose responders begin to respond at higher serum levels of the agent than do the low-dose responders. The individual difference in drug dose for optimal response should be pursued at the level of the *target* areas in the brain.

REFERENCES

Chan, Y. M., Sullivan, S. J., Swanson, J. M., Deber, C. M., Thiessen, J. J., and MacLeod, S. Gas chromatographic/mass spectrometric analysis of methylphenidate (Ritalin) in serum. *Clin. Biochem.*, 1980, *13*:266–272.

Hungund, B. L., Perel, J. M., Hurwic, M. J., et al. Pharmacokinetics of methylphenidate in hyperkinetic children. *Br. J. Clin. Pharmcol.* 1979, *8*:571.

Shaywitz, S. E. Classification of attention deficit disorder: Newer diagnostic schema and assessment scales. *Schizophr. Bull,* 1982, *8*:360–424.

Shaywitz,, S. E., Hunt, R. J., Jatlow, P., Cohen, D. J., Young, J. G., Anderson, G. M., and Shaywitz, B. A. Acute and chronic effects of methylphenidate in children with attention deficit disorder: neurochemical, pharmacologic, and behavioral response. *Pediatrics,* 1982, *60*(6):688–694.

Sprague, R. L., and Sleator, E. K. Methylphenidate in hyperkinetic children: Differences in dose effects on learning and social behavior. *Science,* 1977, *198*:1274.

Swanson, J., Kinsbourne, M., Roberts, W., et al. Time-response analysis of the effect of stimulant medication on the learning ability of children referred for hyperactivty. *Pediatrics,* 1978, *61*:21.

11

The Psychophysiology of Stimulant Drug Response in Hyperkinetic Children

C. KEITH CONNORS AND MARY V. SOLANTO

EDITOR'S COMMENTS

Keith Conners and Mary Solanto, a doctoral student at the time, performed a study to measure cognitive, motor, and physiological response systems at the same time as they obtained dose-time-action curves. The questions they addressed in this study were: Are dose-response curves the same for cognitive and motor behaviors, or different, as Sprague and Sleator (1977) found? Is there basically one time-action curve for methylphenidate (MPD), or are there different mechanisms that lead to different time-action curves? Finally, they investigated whether peripheral autonomic changes were related to the dose-time of MPD. In addressing the last question, the authors attempted to see if there was any difference between the sympathetic and the parasympathetic autonomic nervous system responses to MPD.

Three dosages of MPD were used: 0.3 mg/kg, 0.6 mg/kg, and 1.0 mg/kg, administered p.o.

One diagram shows errors of commission during the reaction-time test; their reduction was strongly dose-related. There was also found a notable difference in reaction-time after the lunch break, and the authors postulate a postprandial effect. According to the authors, seat and feet activity are reduced at the 1.0 mg/kg dose over a much more sustained period than with the smaller doses.

Portions of this chapter appeared in Solanto, M. V., and Conners, C. K.: The psychophysiology of stimulant drug response in hyperkinetic children. *Psychophysiology,* in press.

The authors suggest that serotonin may have been overlooked in the regulating, sustained inhibitory action over behavior. The authors derive from their data that possibly the two dimensions of ADD most responsive to stimulant drug effects are: attention and conduct disorder. The analysis of their data also implies that there is no single dosage level (such as 0.3 mg/kg of MPD) that is optimal for *all* cognitive functions. The authors suggest that higher levels of task complexity may draw upon both the phasic alertness needed for accurate performance as well as a greater degree of behavioral inhibition.

*   *   *

There have been three phases of research on the effects of stimulant drugs on children's behavior. The first phase, following Bradley's initial observations (Bradley, 1937), was a series of basic efficacy studies. Bradley's own studies were based on a somewhat heterogeneous group of children hospitalized for severe behavior disorders, many of whom had demonstrable organic dysfunction, such as epilepsy or postencephalitic behavior disorder. Subsequent controlled, double-blind studies showed that about 70%–80% of the children improved in behavior, as judged by clinicians, teachers and parents. About 20%–30% of the children in placebo groups also showed improvement. These studies have been meticulously reviewed by Barkley (1977). Since measures of improvement were primarily judgments by teachers, parents, and clinicians, it was primarily overt, disturbing behavior among these children that was being measured as a response to stimulant therapy.

The second phase of research was the study of dose-response relationships. This work, largely initiated by Robert Sprague, John Werry, and colleagues (Sprague and Sleator, 1977), showed that dosage requirements for optimal cognitive and social behaviors were different. In their now-classic paper—a model for its rigorous design and measurement technique—they purported to show that whereas the optimal dosage for immediate memory was about 0.3 mg/kg of methylphenidate, the optimal dosage for motor behavior and social behavior improved in linear fashion, with increasing doses up to 1.0 mg/kg.

The third phase of investigation was the study of time-response effects. Swanson, Kinsbourne, and colleagues (1978), used a paired-associate learning test to demonstrate that the peak performance occurs about 2 hours after drug ingestion.* Their data are shown in Figure 1. Questions of how generalizable such findings are across subjects and tests and how they relate to social behaviors await further investigation.

Such findings, while important from a clinical therapeutic point of view, did not address the question of the mechanism whereby the stimulants achieve their effects. Without such knowledge we can gain little understanding of the

---

*Cf. paper by Shaywitz, "Pharmacokinetic, Neuroendocrine and Behavioral Substrate of ADD, this volume—Editor.

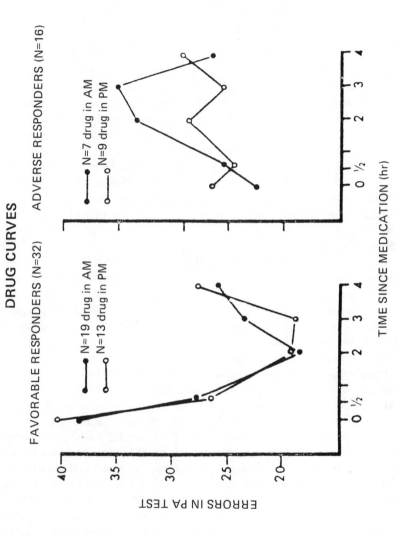

Figure 1. Effect of MPD on errors in paired-association test, responders and nonresponders.

brain functions being altered by the drugs. The three phases of empirical study have really contributed very little to our understanding of what is wrong with the brains of these children, whom we so facilely referred to as having "MBD." To achieve such understanding requires a different question from that of the efficacy or the dose-response and dose-time studies accomplished so far.

One approach to the study of brain mechanisms is to combine several of the features of previous studies: That is, to measure cognitive, motor, and physiological response systems *at the same time* as one obtains dose-time-action curves. We have completed such a study (Solanto and Conners, 1982). This study poses the following questions: Are dose-response curves the same for cognitive and motor behaviors, or different, as Sprague, et al., have claimed? Is there basically one   time-action curve for methylphenidate (as implied by Kinsbourne's and Swanson's use of paired-associate learning as representative of drug response) or are different mechanisms at work, which lead to different time-action curves? Finally, how are the behavioral effects of methylphenidate related to changes at the physiological level? In particular, are peripheral autonomic changes related to the dose-time-action effects of the drug, and if so, how do they relate to the changes at the behavioral level? This latter question requires some elaboration.

Change in digital temperature of the fingers primarily reflects arterial blood flow that is regulated by the sympathetic nervous system. Sympathetic activation leads to peripheral digital vasoconstriction, causing colder finger temperature. Vasodilatation, on the other hand, is accomplished by a passive enlargement of the vascular bed and thus reflects sympathetic inhibition. Finger blood-flow and temperature have proven to be sensitive indicators of the adrenergic effect of stimulant drugs.

Heart rate, on the other hand, is dually innervated by both adrenergic and cholinergic systems, with sympathetic activation causing heart rate acceleration. Reciprocal parasympathetic control, through vagal influences on the heart, regulates deceleration. Porges (1976; Porges, Walter, Korb, and Sprague, 1975) has argued that the cholinergic effects of stimulants parallel a *central* cholinergic inhibitory influence that accounts for behavioral inhibition and improved performance. By measuring this dually innervated system, heart rate, as well as the sympathetically controlled digital vasoconstriction system, it should be possible to discern whether one or both systems are at work in response to stimulants. By also simultaneously recording both cognitive and motor behavior, one should be able to see how the autonomic effects of stimulants correlate with these two behavioral response systems. This was the strategy of the present study. (We also simultaneously observed electromyographic and electrodermal responses, but these will not be discussed here.)

Subjects for this study were 10 carefully selected children who had participated in our food additive studies. Ages ranged from 6 to 12 years. All were deemed appropriate for stimulant drug therapy, both by virtue of diagnosis and failure to respond to other treatments. Details of diagnostic criteria are presented elsewhere (Solanto and Conners, in press).

Each subject acted as his own control under these dosages of methylphenidate: 0.3 mg/kg, 0.6 mg/kg, and 1.0 mg/kg administered orally at 9 a.m. on three different test days. Matching placebo was given on two other test days distributed randomly among the drug days. Each session included a baseline measure of task and physiological responses followed one hour later by drug administration. Additional sessions were carried out approximately each hour thereafter over the next four hours. Each test session on a given day consisted of four phases: A resting baseline ("pre-rest"), a five-minute period of adaptation ("rest"), passive listening to a repeated tone, and a serial warned reaction-time test with a fixed foreperiod warning interval (a measure of attention). Errors of

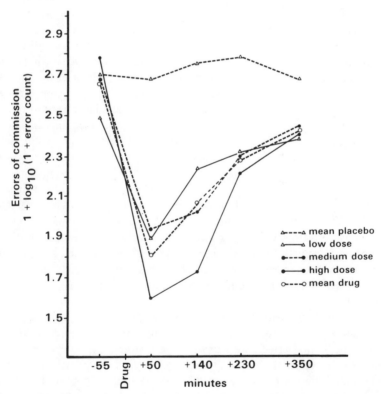

Figure 2. Errors of commission during the reaction-time test on methylphenidate and on placebo.

commission were recorded, as were the number of the seat and feet movements in a specially wired activity chair.

Let us first consider the stimulant drug effect on the behavioral measures. Figure 2 shows the errors of commission during the reaction-time test. These responses represent excess responses by the subject during the warning period or after his initial response, often being what would generally be regarded as "fiddling" behavior.

These responses show a constant level during the placebo days but a prompt reduction about one hour following drug. This reduction is strongly dose-related: higher doses lead to less fiddling. The behavior shows a distinctly time-limited U-shaped course, with most of the effect being lost two hours after drug. (It is of interest that the peak effects are one hour earlier than reported in the Swanson and Kinsbourne paired-associates work).

Figure 3 shows the results for reaction time. There is a notable difference from the previous curve: In addition to the decrease in reaction time one to two hours after drug, there is a temporary increase at 230 minutes post-drug. The increase of reaction time at 230 minutes post-drug coincides with the session immediately after the lunch break, and it is our opinion that the slower reaction time reflects a postprandial effect. Interestingly, there appears to be a drug interaction with this postprandial effect. It looks as though performance on placebo days gets progressively slower with each session later in the day, until *after* the lunch break, when performance actually improves compared with baseline. On drug days, the combined effect of drug and lunch is to worsen performance; i.e., to slow reaction time. On nondrug days, lunch appears to offset a decline in performance, probably occurring as a result of boredom and/or fatigue. Further work on blood glucose levels and stimulant drugs seems indicated.

Figure 4 presents the data for seat and feet movements. Here there is a unique interaction with dosage: under the low and medium doses of methylphenidate, the function is U-shaped and exactly like the performance curves for other measures. However, under the *high dose*, activity level (adjusted for placebo trend) actually shows a continued decline through the period of observation. Whereas on placebo days the children get progressively more restless during the day, restlessness continues to decline on the higher dose of 1.0 mg/kg throughout the observation period.

Thus, at a behavioral level one might argue that our data suggest two mechanisms being affected by the drug. For the attentional responses there is a sharply time-limited effect, with higher doses causing a greater degree of performance improvement, but not altering the U-shaped time course. Postprandial effects complicate the picture, acting like fatigue and boredom to slow reaction time. In contrast, seat and feet activity are reduced at the higher dose over a sustained period of time, never returning to the baseline.

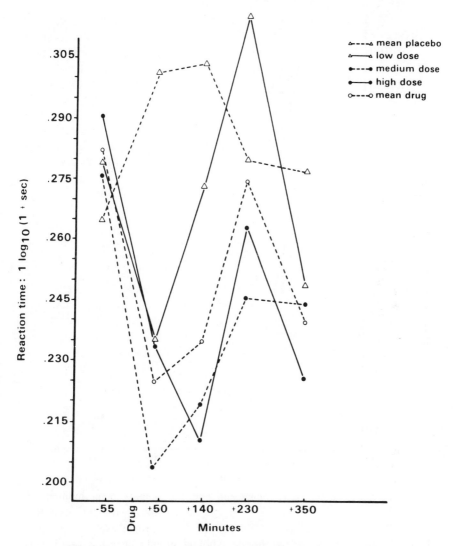

Figure 3.   Reaction time on methylphenidate and on placebo.

How are these effects related to the autonomic changes occurring at the same time? Figure 5 presents the finger temperature data. As with the behavioral measures of attention, one sees a complete return to baseline levels 2 hours after drug, even with the highest dose. The continued increase in temperature beyond baseline after 3 hours may reflect a postprandial effect, the effect of relaxation

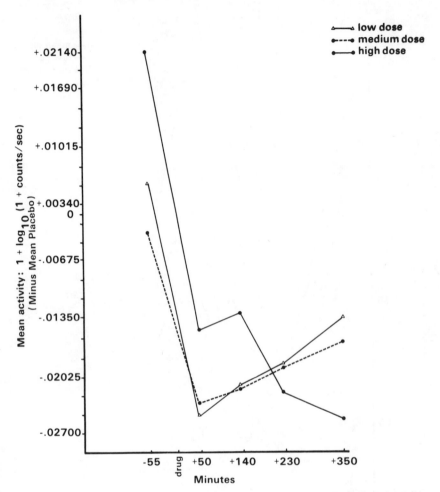

Figure 4. Seat and feet movements under several dosages of methylphenidate.

during the session, or an autonomic rebound effect. In any case, there is a striking resemblance of these curves to those of the attentional measures, suggesting a close link between the autonomic and behavioral drug effects.

Figure 6 presents the heart rate data. Here we see that the low dose again produces a small effect, which returns to baseline within two hours and remains essentially identical to placebo (including the presumed postprandial effect). The high and medium doses, which produce a much more dramatic effect at 50 minutes (most of which dissipates by two hours post-drug), show a strong postprandial effect and then return close to the placebo level. There is relatively little

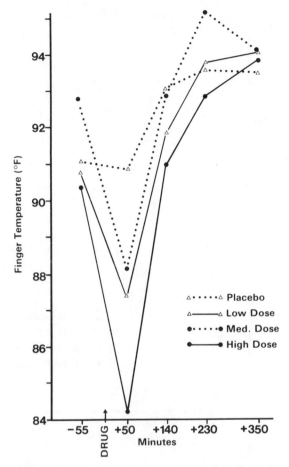

Figure 5. Finger temperature data on several dosages of methylphenidate and on placebo.

indication that this dually-innervated system differs in character from the finger-temperature response system. The return of the medium- and high-dose curves to placebo levels is somewhat slower and less complete in the heart rate data, but basically parallels the changes in finger temperature and attentional measures. In contrast, gross motor activity shows a sustained decrease at higher dose levels.

Thus, the behavioral and autonomic drug effects are consistent with the existence of two separate physiologic systems having different dose-time-action characteristics. Others have also hypothesized dual mechanisms in hyperkinetic behavior, based upon dual catecholamine pathways (Wender, 1975), frontal lobe

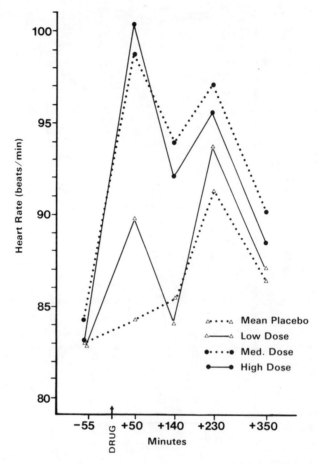

Figure 6. Heart rate on several dosages of methylphenidate.

and reticular functions (Rosenthal and Allen, 1978), frontal-temporal information processing (Dykman and Ackerman, 1976), and attentional vs. impulse
control (Douglas, 1972).

One can only speculate at this point what these two mechanisms are at a
biochemical or neural organization level. Direct tests have not been encouraging.
One possibility that may have been prematurely overlooked is the role of serotonin in regulating sustained inhibitory action over behavior. The serotonin
hypothesis has not received support from investigation of peripheral platelet
serotonin in hyperactive children (Ferguson, Pappas, Trites, et al., 1981). However, studies of this problem have used relatively small samples and have not

paid attention to the possibility of a dual basis for "hyperactivity"; i.e., patients have generally been assumed to represent a homogeneous group. The possibility that patients might improve in response to stimulant therapy for quite different reasons, in different target behaviors, seems not to have occurred to anyone. In a recent study, Irwin, Belenduk, McCloskey, and Freedman (1981) identified a subgroup of attention-deficit disorder children who were hyperserotonemic and who had significantly lower levels of plasma total and protein-bound tryptophan, as well as a higher percentage of free tryptophan, than those children with normal serotonin levels. Animal studies indicate that stimulants increase free tryptophan and thus make it more available for brain uptake (Brase and Loh, 1975).

Reduction of brain serotonin by drugs or lesions aggravates shock-induced fighting and predatory killing in mice (Breese and Cooper, 1975; Sheard and Davis, 1976). Dietary supplementation with tryptophan reverses this effect. Serotonin is known to inhibit locomotor activity and aggressive behavior in animals, and also has widespread brain inhibitory functions (Fuxe and Ungerstedt, 1970). Serotonergic effects are potent inhibitors of experimentally induced hyperactivity in animals and have a well-known role in tonic inhibitory effects on sleep and activity cycles. There are also important mutual inhibitory functions between cholinergic and serotonergic actions in the brain (Pradhan and Bose, 1978).

Supposing, for the moment, that the behavioral and physiological response to stimulants represents a dual rather than unitary effect, and that two separate mechanisms are operative, what are the implications for diagnosis and treatment? If it is the case that the respective brain mechanisms (whatever they might be) are orthogonal, it follows that there are at least four different patterns of dysfunction that could be identified if each dimension is dichotomized (poor attention, poor impulse control; good attention, poor impulse control . . . etc.). There could also be "mixed types." In fact, it seems likely that mixed types are more frequent in the usual convenience samples studied in clinical settings, with pure impulse disorders or attention disorders being somewhat rare. Factor analysis of our parent and teacher scales and cluster analysis have consistently supported the existence of an aggressive (conduct disorder?) factor and an inattention factor (Conners, 1973; Conners and Blouin, 1980). It seems likely that attentional and impulse-control functions are only two dimensions along which brain activity is organized, but perhaps the two dimensions most relevant to drug effects. From a diagnostic point of view, then, global categories such as "attentional-deficit disorder" and "conduct disorder," as defined in DSM-III, represent only convenient abstractions from a more complex admixture of intersecting dimensions that occur in nature. If individual children have varying degrees of dysfunction of attentional and impulse control dimensions, and these dimensions reflect the operation of specific brain mechanisms responsive to drugs (but with differing dosage and time-action characteristics), proper measurement (*not* diagnosis) is the sine qua non of understanding when and how to use the drugs.

One implication of this analysis is that there is no single dosage level (such as 0.3 mg/kg of methylphenidate) that is optimal for *all* cognitive functions. Insofar as a specific test (such as the Sernberg short-term memory test or paired-associates test) relies upon both phasic alerting as well as more tonic inhibitory functions, it will require dose adjustments accordingly. Few tests are factorially pure enough neatly to sample only one dimension of brain function. Moreover, the particular loading of an individual on the dimensions of impulsive and attentional symptomatology will have a lot to do with the impact of a given dose on that child. It would seem to be wishful thinking to hope that one cognitive test will satisfactorily represent the brain's response to stimulants; or that a drug effect on a cognitive test will be generalizable to impulsive behavior (or motor overflow), which probably represents an entirely different underlying dimension of brain function.

How, then, does one reconcile these considerations with the observations of Sprague that higher doses of methylphenidate actually impair cognitive function on the Sternberg task relative to the more modest dose of 0.3 mg/kg? In that experiment it was only performance on the more difficult levels of the task that showed the decline at higher dosage levels. Our serial reaction-time task, as in other types of simple vigilance or continuous performance tasks, is relatively nondemanding of the subjects' effort. All one must do is remain relatively alert and attentive, but there is little requirement to screen out other stimuli or inhibit competing responses. We suggest that higher levels of task complexity draw upon both the phasic alertness needed for accurate performance *as well as a greater degree of behavioral inhibition.* This latter requirement engages an additional brain control mechanism or biochemical substrate. This hypothesis obviously requires more direct test.

Harry Harlow once remarked: "If it's a dichotomy, it's wrong." Nevertheless, I am fearlessly proposing that the "simple and sovereign theory" (to paraphrase Gordon Allport) of a single optimum dose level for stimulants and a single time-action course is inconsistent with the complexity of the empirical data at hand. Undoubtedly such dichotomies as tonic-phasic, adrenergic-cholinergic, frontal-reticular, or adrenergic-serotoninergic are also too simplistic, but at least they appear to be one step in the right direction. The provocative interactions of dietary tryptophan with stimulant drugs, and the potential consequences of sugar-induced alterations of tryptophan/serotonin for "the" hyperkinetic child provide us with a challenging research program for this mysterious entity we call MBD/ADD—or should it be MBD/ADDs?

DISCUSSION

Robert L. Sprague

I am delighted to see time-dose studies being conducted, and I think such studies will help us understand what happens to children taking psychotropic medication. Ultimately, information is needed on the 24-hour time course and 6-hour (typical school day) time course.

I am curious as to why the different time-response curves are obtained. I really do not have any insights, other than to note some similarity to time-response curves seen with other psychotropic drugs. With neuroleptic drugs, it is common to observe Parkinsonian symptoms early (matter of days) in the course of treatment and major therapeutic effects later.

REFERENCES

Barkley, R. A. A review of stimulant drug research with hyperactive children. *Journal of Child Psychology and Psychiatry*, 1977, *18*:137–165.

Bradley, C. The behavior of children receiving benzedrine. *Am. J. Psychiatry*, 1937, *94*:577–585.

Brase, D. A., and Loh, H. H. Possible role of 5-hydroxytryptamine in minimal brain dysfunction. *Life Science*, 1975, *16*:1005–1015.

Breese, G. R., and Cooper, B. R. Behavioral and biochemical interactions of 5, 7-dihydroxytryptamine with various drugs when administered intracisternally to adult and developing rats. *Brain Research*, 1975, *98*:517–527.

Conners, C. K. Psychological assessment of children with Minimal Brain Dysfunction. *Annals of the New York Academy of Sciences*, 1973, *205*:283–302.

Conners, C. K., and Blouin, A. G. Hyperkinetic syndrome and psychopathology in children. In B. B. Lahey (Chair), Is there an independent syndrome of hyperactivity in children? Symposium presented at the meeting of the American Psychological Association, Montreal, September 1980.

Douglas, V. I. Stop, look and listen: The problem of sustained attention and impulse control in hyperactive and normal children. *Canadian Journal of Behavioral Science*, 1972, *4*:259–282.

Dykman, R. A., and Ackerman, P. T. The MBD problem: Attention, intention and information processing. In R. P. Anderson and C. G. Halcomb (Eds.), *Learning disability/minimal brain dysfunction syndrome: research perspectives and applications.* 1976, Springfield, Ill. Charles C Thomas.

Ferguson, H. B., Pappas, B. A., Trites, R. L., Peters, D. A. V., and Taub, H. Plasma free and total tryptophan, blood serotonin and the hyperactivity syndrome: No evidence for the serotonin deficiency hypothesis. *Biological Psychiatry*, 1981, *16*:231–238.

Fuxe, K., and Ungerstedt, U. Histochemical and functional studies on central monoamine neurons after acute and chronic amphetamine administration. In E. Costa and S. Garattini (Eds.), *International symposium on amphetamines and related compounds.* New York: Raven Press, 1970.

Irwin, M., Belendiuk, K., McCloskey, K., and Freedman, D. X. Tryptophan metabolism in children with attentional deficit disorders. *J. Psychiat.,* 1981, *138*:1082–1085.

Porges, S. W. Peripheral and neurochemical parallels of psychopathology: A psychophysiological model relating autonomic imbalance to hyperactivity, psychopathy and autism. In H. W. Reese (Ed.), *Advances in child development and behavior.* Vol. II. New York: Academic Press, 1976.

Porges, S. W., Walter, G. F., Korb, R. J., and Sprague, R. L. The influence of methylphenidate on heart rate and behavioral measures of attention in hyperactive children. *Child Development,* 1975, *46*:727–733.

Pradhan, S. N., and Bose, S. Interactions among central neurotransmitters. In M. A. Lipton, A. DiMascio, and K. F. Killam (Eds.), *Psychopharmacology: A generation of progress.* New York: Raven Press, 1978, pp. 271–282.

Rosenthal, R. H., and Allen, T. W. An examination of attention, arousal and learning dysfunction of hyperkinetic children. *Psychological Bulletin,* 1978, *85*:689–715.

Sheard, M. H., and Davis, M. Shock-elicited fighting in rats: Importance of intershock interval upon the effect of P-chlorophenylalanin (PCPA). *Brain Research,* 1976, *111*:433–437.

Solanto, M. V., and Conners, C. K. A dose-response and time-action analysis of autonomic and behavioral effects of methylphenidate in attention deficit disorder with hyperactivity. *Psychophysiology,* 1982, *19*(6) in press.

Sprague, R. L., and Sleator, E. K. Methylphenidate in hyperkinetic children: Difference in dose effects on learning and social behavior. *Science,* 1977, *198*:1274–1276.

Swanson, J. M., Kinsbourne, M., Roberts, W., and Zucker, K. Time-response analysis of the effect of stimulant medication on the learning ability of children referred for hyperactivity. *Pediatrics,* 1978, *61*:21–29.

Wender, P. H. The minimal brain dysfunction syndrome. *Annual Review of Medicine,* 1975, *26*:45–62.

Appendices

Remarks on the Diagnosis of Various Entities Comprising MBD/ADD in France, Belgium, and Central Europe

GUY WILLEMS AND LEWIS M. BLOOMINGDALE

In Belgium, because of ethical problems concerning medical diagnosis versus psychological diagnosis, only children having attentional, hyperkinetic, and learning dysfunction problems are considered to have the diagnosis MBD/ADD. A child who is hyperkinetic without having learning dysfunction is not treated with psychostimulants for MBD/ADD, but is referred for psychotherapy to a professional psychotherapist—either a psychologist or psychiatrist. MBD/ADD is considered a neuropsychological entity. The major neuropsychological symptom is attention deficit, but other neuropsychological problems exist, such as: memory deficit, either short-term or long-term; acalculia; and dyslexia. All children considered to have MBD/ADD have learning dysfunction, with or without hyperkinesis.

In France there are considered to be a number of different entities, such as: "Instrumental Trouble" (*Trouble Instrumenteaux*). A child with this syndrome has to have more than one of the following symptoms: (no specific cut-off number is agreed upon) problems of hand laterality; problems of body image; problems of spatial orientation; problems of temporal orientation; psychomotor disturbance; neuromotor soft signs; problems of rhythm (as with the Stanbak Test); or problems of Gestalt recognition (as with the Rey or Bender Gestalt figures). Usually these children have a performance IQ that is less than their verbal IQ by approximately 10–20 points. These children with instrumental problems (as described above) are sent to special schools with a special department for *Trouble Instrumenteaux*. There they receive psychomotor training for whatever of the above symptoms requires therapy. Children with the above syndrome are considered to have learning dysfunction. They may, in addition, be described in the category of either "clumsy" and/or hyperkinetic children.

A child with hyperkinesis may be treated in the special schools in the department of *Trouble Instrumenteaux*, or he may be placed in the department for *Trouble Caracteriel*. *Trouble Caracteriel* includes character disorders that would be considered in the United States to be borderline or psychopathic/sociopathic personality disorders. Such children receive psychotherapy—either institutional, family, or individual outpatient—as treatment.

"Clumsy children" are described in France as having the *Syndrome Debilité du Dupré*. These children are deficient in their neuromotor development and receive psychomotor training.

In addition, there is a psychoanalytic entity described as *Dysharmonie Cognitive*, or cognitive dysharmony. Gibello (1976) describes cognitive dysharmony as having the following characteristics: depression, dysgnosia, dyschronia (hyperkinesis), dyspraxia (clumsiness). Cognitive dysharmony actually refers to the heterogeneity, or specific lags, of the phases of learning described by Piaget. Gibello, and also Malarrivé, Bourgeois, and Fonta (1977) consider the mood disturbance in this entity to be due to depression, or the manic defense against depression, as described by Melanie Klein. Childhood depression, as currently described in DSM-III, is not recognized in France. The "depression" mentioned by Gibello in his description of cognitive dysharmony is defined as: insomnia, hypokinesis, difficulty in initiation of movement or activity, and/or enuresis. According to the psychoanalytic theory held by many French psychoanalysts, hyperkinesis and the Kleinian manic defense have to do with early separation anxiety. According to this theory, the mother interferes with the normal tentative exploratory movements of the child away from her and with the reestablishment of contact as the child may wish. In France, MBD is considered to refer to problems in the relationship between mother and infant.*

In German-speaking countries, e.g., Germany and parts of Switzerland, MBD/ADD is considered to be a psycho-organic syndrome always caused by prenatal, perinatal, or immediately postnatal brain damage, even though it may not be possible to establish that such brain traumata actually occurred. These differences in classification should be kept in mind in regard to the papers by Dr. Robert Corboz and Dr. Guy Willems (Chapter 4 and 12, respectively).

---

*It is interesting that Shaywitz's rat model of hyperkinetic children bears out this theory (Pearson et al., 1980).

REFERENCES

Gibello, B. Disharmonie cognitive. *Revue de Neuropsychiatrie Infantile*, 1976, *24*:439–452.

Malarrivé, J., Bourgeois, M., and Fonta, D. Notre experience de l'enfant hyperkinetique, Congrés Organisé par la Société de Neurologie Infantile, Marseille, France, December 1977.

Pearson, D. E., Teicher, M. H., Shaywitz, B. A., Cohen, D. J., Young, J. G. and Anderson G. M.: Environmental influences on body weight and behavior in developing rats after neonatal 6-hydroxydopamine. *Science*, 1980, *209*:715–717.

Preliminary Report of Cross-Cultural Study and Cognitive Strategies of ADD Children

ROBERT L. SPRAGUE

EDITOR'S COMMENTS

The foregoing chapters are discussed further by Dr. Sprague, and he brings a brief overview of the topics to bear thereon.

A preview of Robert Sprague's cross-cultural investigations, not hitherto published, involving the administration of the Conners' Teacher Rating Scale by a number of teachers in six countries, is presented next. These are extremely valuable data for anyone who is interested in the question of whether or not, correcting for cultural differences and size of school classes, the incidence of ADD is approximately the same worldwide, or shows significant variance not accounted for by other factors. If the answer is the former, we are apparently dealing with a distribution similar to that of schizophrenia, which appears to show very little variation cross-culturally.

In 1971, Paul Wender published, in his classic monograph, distribution curves wherein giantism and dwarfism are indicated to have independent causes, so that there is an upward deflection at both ends of the normal distribution curve (Figure 1). If we assume that the Conners' 39-point Teachers' Rating Scale operationally defines a syndrome that approximates ADD, an assumption that is currently made by most researchers in selecting index vs. control groups, scrutiny of Figure 1 in Dr. Sprague's contribution shows that it does not appear to be an expectable negative exponential curve. Rather, there appear to be troughs for all countries between Conners' Scores 1 and 2 for the four countries plotted. There is certainly a suggestion that ADD is a syndrome and not just the lower end of the Gaussian curve, arbitrarily designated. Robert Sprague has not yet analyzed his data and the significance of this observation is still unclear.

It should also be noted that the transcultural colleagues of Dr. Sprague used dozens of teachers to obtain their data. Ronald Trites (1979) studied the

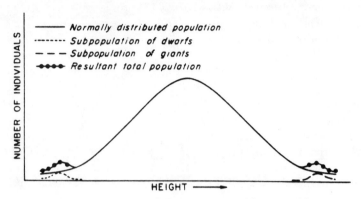

Figure 1. Height frequency distribution curves: normal, diseased, and resultant. From P. H. Wender, *Minimal Brain Dysfunction in Children.* New York: John Wiley and Sons, 1971, pp. 45.

geographical distribution of hyperactivity in Ottawa. His findings indicated that a number of different schools need to be included in determining the incidence or prevalence of ADD for a city (or, presumably, country), covering the geographical limits as much as possible. Since Robert Sprague discussed Trites' paper, it may be assumed that the teachers who cooperated with his colleagues were from different schools and it would be useful for him to include this issue in his future publication.

Dr. Sprague also introduces the problem of investigating the cognitive strategies used by ADD children vs. controls in solving problems (cf. Chapters 7 and 8).

*   *   *

Authors of a new book, *The Brain,* a collection of papers published by *Scientific American*, make insightful remarks about integration of neurochemical, neurophysiological, and neuropsychological theories. Crick, the Nobel Laureate, states, "It is sobering to note that the major breakthroughs in molecular biology also have to do with mechanisms that originated very long ago," (Crick, 1979, p. 137). For us to try to understand the astronomically complex central nervous system of man with our present inadequate technology is problematical; perhaps we need a new systems technology to aid us in obtaining this understanding. I do not mean that we should not seriously try to understand the workings of man's brain, but perhaps we do not yet have the analytic tools to assess the complexities of the human central nervous system.

Bloomingdale mentioned that brain functioning should be related to Attention Deficit Disorder. Attention, at least from a psychological theory point of view, is extremely complex; there are at least four, maybe five factors that have been theoretically identified and subsequently supported by empirical research (Krupski, 1981). First is an arousal factor. Another is selective attention. A third factor is allocation of effort by the individual into the attention process. A fourth factor is sustaining attention over a period of time, a factor that is probably measured by the CPT (Continuous Performance Task). Finally, the fifth factor is emotional connotation; that greatly influences attention.

Chapter 5 involved a population of children from a different country; thus, it raises problems of interpreting data from different populations, whether from a different country or different populations within this country.

Dr. Barbara Keogh, a special educator at UCLA, has examined hundreds of studies from the learning disabilities literature in an attempt to identify the most useful markers to describe populations of such children. There are obvious markers such as age, sex, age on onset, and measures (specified in an operational sense) taken. I simply suggest that the area of Attention Deficit Disorders needs a thorough review by Keogh, or someone like her, to identify pertinent population markers. Then, perhaps, it would be possible to compare studies conducted in the United States with studies from different countries.

In the context of cross-national comparisons, I present data from my laboratory for several reasons. First, this is an opportunity to present this cross-cultural research. There are only two or three published studies of this kind, and another study with a sample size of almost 15,000 subjects should add useful information. Second, it is exceptionally difficult to prepare cross-cultural research for publication. In our series of studies, there are eight investigators in six different countries and, for various reasons, we have not published an overall analysis, in contrast to country-by-country analyses in national journals of the respective nations. This is one discouraging aspect of cross-cultural projects. One measure, Dr. C. Keith Conners' Teacher Rating Scale, was completed by dozens of teachers in each of the six countries. Our colleagues and the total number of children for whom they collected teacher ratings are as follows: Dr. Roslyn Glow, Adelaide, Australia, 2,475; Dr. Walter Eichlseder, Munich, Germany, 5,307; Dr. Farideh Salili, Hong Kong, 4,426; Dr. G. Hoosein Azan-Tarrahian, Mashad, Iran, 473; Dr. John S. Werry, Auckland, New Zealand, 415; Dr. Elena Granell de Aldaz, Caracas, Venezuela, 612; and Drs. Martin Maehr and Jack Fyans from the United States, 291 in 1974 and 732 in 1979, for a total of 14,731. Table 1 shows the number of children by age, sex, and country. Figure 1 presents the distribution of percents of children obtaining a given total score for four nations on the shortened 10-item version of the scale. As you know, on the Conners Scale the best score is zero, which indicates a minimum of "bad" behavior, as reported by the teacher. The higher the score, the worse the child's behavior. It is obvious from Figure 1 that the spread of total scores is a "J" distribution with the largest percentage of the scores accumulating at zero, although the pattern for all countries is not exactly the same, e.g., United States teachers assigned a greater percentage of zeros than did teachers in New Zealand.

Table 1. Total Number of Children by Country, Sex, and Age

Country	Total	3–4 Yrs.		5 Yrs.		6 Yrs.		7 Yrs.		8 Yrs.	
		M	F	M	F	M	F	M	F	M	F
Australia	2,475	11	13	145	110	151	145	169	158	160	161
Germany	5,307					110	127	227	232	314	297
Hong Kong	4,426	227	156	147	130	190	184	272	175	243	186
Iran	473				1	57	11	49	22	55	33
New Zealand	415					15	19	28	30	37	43
United States (74)	291			4	10	22	18	14	22	24	27
United States (79)	732							96	98	175	163
Venezuela	612	6	1	30	33	75	44	26	30	27	41
Total by sex		244	170	326	284	620	548	881	767	1035	951
Total by age		414		610		1168		1648		1986	
Total males	7,953										
Total females	6,778										
Grand total	14,731										

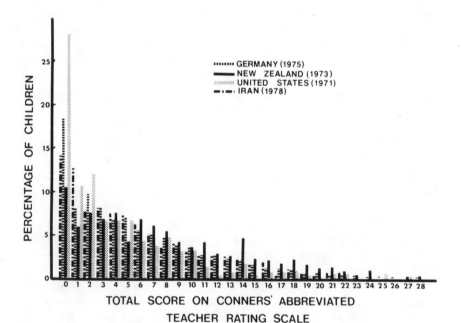

Figure 1. Total scores on Conners' Abbreviated Teacher Rating Scale for children in four countries.

Table 1 (continued)

9 Yrs.		10 Yrs.		11 Yrs.		12 Yrs.		13 Yrs.		14 Yrs.		15 Yrs.		16 Yrs.		17 Yrs.		18 Yrs.	
M	F	M	F	M	F	M	F	M	F	M	F	M	F	M	F	M	F	M	F
177	166	222	171	180	190	64	73	1	7	1									
307	261	323	370	395	332	380	313	355	248	277	156	146	65	43	14	15			
215	172	195	181	204	171	223	180	236	227	170	165	78	59	20	12	3	2	2	1
22	27	23	42	45	25	31	10	10	5	1	2	2							
35	34	37	35	37	31	18	10												
21	18	18	24	30	26	10	2	1											
89	93	12	6																
46	38	54	36	30	10	29	30	17	7	3	2								
912	809	884	865	921	785	755	624	616	495	452	325	224	126	63	26	18	2	2	1
1712		1749		1706		1379		111		777		350		89		20		3	

It is very interesting that in this large sample of ratings, a maximum score of 30 has not been assigned as yet. This may mean that teachers are exceedingly reluctant to assign the maximum "bad" score no matter how disturbed the child is.

These are children in public school classes in the various countries. One of the obvious factors that may influence the ratings is the size of the class, which differs greatly from country to country. The data from prerevolutionary Iran were obtained from a city named Mashad, where schools usually contain classes of 45 students each, a number considerably larger than the average class size in the United States. Such factors should be considered when interpreting cross-cultural data.

It must be remembered that it is much easier to lump after the data is collected, with adequate information about background variables, than to split data that are not so adequately identified when collected. Thus, it seems to be methodologically better to collect data that may be partitioned readily than prematurely to aggregate the data.

Chapter 9 is an excellent example of an attempt to interrelate neuropsychological, neurophysiological, and neurochemical variables. Conceptually tying together such diverse variables is very difficult to do but, as Dr. Wender said, "It is a nifty experiment." The task(s) used in such experiments should be carefully considered, because the importance of the task demand placed on the child is coming under closer scrutiny (Krupski, 1981). The Continuous

Performance Task is simple and boring. Typically, hyperactive children encounter problems in school not because of simple tasks that they are requested to do, but because of complicated tasks, which tax their ability more than their boredom.

Considering this dimension of complexity, I discuss a task that we developed to measure the cognitive strategies a child uses to solve this relatively complicated visual match-to-sample task. Rather than bore you with a lengthy background and rationale for the match-to-sample task, let it be sufficient to say the task has been used extensively in animal psychopharmacological studies that provide a useful empirical foundation. Further, clinical tests, such as the Kagan Matching Familiar Figures Test, which has been used repeatedly to assess hyperactive children, is really a match-to-sample task, using relatively crude measures to total time and total errors.

In a match-to-sample task that was automated using relatively cumbersome electromechanical relay equipment, 24 hyperactive children participated in a study that involved the children's coming to the laboratory on four days under conditions of baseline and randomized (across sessions) conditions of placebo or 0.3 mg/kg and 0.7 mg/kg of a stimulant, methylphenidate. The match-to-sample equipment was designed to record each response (inspection of a visual stimulus) and the length of time of each inspection in tenths of a second. This was done in an attempt to assess the strategy the child was using to solve the match-to-sample problem by studying his pattern of inspection responses rather than, for example, monitoring eye scanning movements, which is technologically very difficult (Flintoff, Barron, Swanson, Ledlow, and Kinsbourne, in press).

Figure 2 is a representation of how one trial on the match-to-sample would appear if all the apertures were open at once. Never were the seven apertures simultaneously open to display the stimuli, as shown in Figure 2, during the course of the experiment. To inspect any of the seven apertures (only one aperture at a time would open for inspection), the child had to press a button immediately below the aperture and hold the button down for as long as he wished to inspect that particular stimulus. (Inspection time equalled time from sample display to correct button contact to match sample.)

The child was instructed to start with the lower center aperture on each trial to see the "sample," for which he was to find the exact "match" in the top row of six apertures. He was also instructed to remember the sample, since it disappeared from view when he released the button. He was encouraged to start his inspections to find the match in the upper left-hand aperture, because English readers typically scan written material left-to-right. There were no restrictions on his strategy of inspections; he could inspect any aperture, in any sequence, for as long as he wished, and he could return to the sample as often as he wanted. After the child satisfied himself (set his own internal criteria for "sameness"), he pressed the test button to indicate that he was ready to be

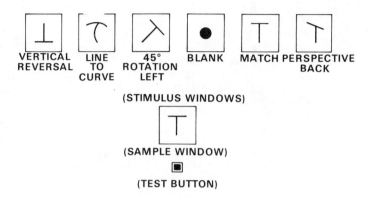

VERTICAL | LINE | 45° | BLANK | MATCH | PERSPECTIVE
REVERSAL | TO | ROTATION | | | BACK
| CURVE | LEFT

(STIMULUS WINDOWS)

(SAMPLE WINDOW)

(TEST BUTTON)

Figure 2. Match-to-sample stimulus array.

tested and then he pushed his choice for the match in the row of six apertures. If he was correct on the first test try, a counter, easily visible to him, recorded five points; if he was wrong, he had to correct his answer with another choice, but he received only four points on the second test response, three on the third, and so on, in descending order to one point. After the experimental session, the points he earned could be exchanged for desirable toys at a "store" he had seen before the session started.

The stimuli were modifications of letter-like forms, which were selected because there are normative data on the relative difficulty of the various transformations (Gibson, 1965). For control purposes, on each trial one to five blanks, which carried no information, were included. (A blank was a single dot.) There were 36 slides, containing 216 stimuli, presented in counterbalanced conditions according to the categories listed in Table 2. These categories of stimuli were randomized across the six aperture locations in the 36 trials.

Remember that each response of the child and also the inspection time were recorded. This extensive recording produced about 20 pages of printout per child per session for a total of 1,920 pages. The data have not been completely analyzed, but the addition of an Apple microcomputer in 1982 has greatly speeded the process.

From these voluminous printouts, an attempt was made to assess the child's cognitive strategy. For example, inspection of the sample is crucial, for the child must hold an "accurate representation" of it in his memory, if he is correctly to select the match and earn the maximum points on the test. Remember, each stimulus disappears from view when its button is released. An effective strategy is for the child repeatedly to inspect the sample. This strategy can be

Table 2. Description of Match-to-Sample Task

36 Trials of 6 apertures each = 216	
Match	36
Blank	90
Rotation transformation	20
Reversal transformation	20
Perspective side transformation (15)	30
Perspective back transformation (15)	
Line to curve transformation (10)	20
Curve to line transformation (10)	
	216

Each of above stimuli appeared the same number of times in each aperture portion during a testing session.

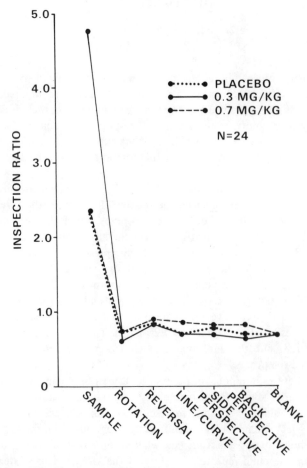

Figure 3. Inspection ratios for all the classes of stimuli.

measured by the inspection ratio for a particular stimulus, such as the sample, that is, the number of sample responses per 36 trials. If there were 72 sample responses, the inspection ratio would be 2; if there were 144, the ratio would be 4, etc. It should be obvious that the sample ratio cannot be lower than 1.0, since the child must inspect the sample at least once per trial: $36/36=1.0$.

Figure 3 presents the inspection ratios for all the classes of stimuli but the sample inspection ratio is the only ratio of interest here. On placebo and 0.7 mg/kg of methylphenidate, the children produced an inspection ratio of about 2.3. But on the low dose, which we think is the best dose for cognitive tasks (Sprague and Sleator, 1977), the inspection ratio was dramatically increased to 4.7. This is, I believe, strong evidence that different doses of stimulant can alter the ways a hyperactive child attempts to solve (strategy) a complex problem. At this point, the oft-used sentence, "More research is needed," can aptly be applied.

Studies are now underway to obtain match-to-sample data from normal children, unreferred children with poor attention scores as rated by their teacher, and referred attention-deficit-disordered children. Again, preliminary analyses indicate clear differences in patterns of responding, which imply different strategies used by normal and attention disordered children.

REFERENCES

Crick, F. H. C. Thinking about the brain. In A Scientific American Book. Scientific American (Eds.), *Brain*. San Francisco, Freeman, 1979.

Flintoff, M. M., Barron, R. W., Swanson, J. M., Ledlow, A., and Kinsbourne, M. Methylphenidate increases selectivity of visual scanning in children referred for hyperactivity. *Journal of Abnormal Child Psychology*, in press.

Gibson, E. J. Learning to read. *Science*, 1965, *148*:1066-1072.

Krupski, A. An interactional approach to the study of attention problems in children with learning handicaps. *Exceptional Education Quarterly*, November 1981, *1*:1-11.

Sprague, R. L., and Sleator, E. K. Methylphenidate in hyperkinetic children: Differences in dose effects on learning and social behavior. *Science*, 1977, *198*:1274-1276.

Trites, R. L. Prevalence of hyperactivity in Ottawa, Canada. In R. L. Trites (Ed.), *Hyperactivity in children*. Baltimore: University Park Press, 1979, pp. 29-56.

Wender, P. H. *Minimal brain dysfunction in children*. New York: John Wiley, 1971, pp. 44, 45.

Werry, J. S., Sprague, R. L., and Cohen, M. N. (1975). Conners' Teacher Rating Scale for use in drug studies with children—an empirical study. *J. Abnorm. Child Psychol.*, 1975, *3*:217-229.

Index